KU-278-336

Montenegro

Northern
Mountains
p110

Central
Montenegro
p90

Dubrovnik
(Croatia) ◉
p126

Bay of
Kotor
p34

Adriatic
Coast
p63

04475111

Contents

PLAN YOUR TRIP

ON THE ROAD

JAZ BEACH P71

TOWN WALLS, KOTOR P45

Contents

PERAST P42

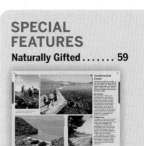

Welcome to Montenegro

Bursting at the seams with majestic mountains, breathtaking beaches and larger-than-life locals, Montenegro proves once and for all that good things do indeed come in small packages.

A Warm Welcome

It's nigh on impossible to come across a travel section without someone trumpeting Montenegro as the new 'it' destination. And though the country is rightfully revelling in the spotlight, the people remain as they've always been: candid, convivial and charming. Unlike in many other emerging destinations, hassling and scamming visitors isn't big on Montenegrins' agenda; for the most part, you're more likely to encounter a spontaneous bear hug than a bothersome tout. Whether you're chasing highland hospitality or coastal comradery, expect gregarious greetings, the shirt off your host's back and the addition of at least 5kg; these folks love to feed.

Where Land & Sea Embrace

It's not even 300km from tip to toe, but Montenegro's coastline crams in some of Europe's most spectacular seaside scenery. Mountains jut sharply from crystal-clear waters in such a way that the word 'looming' is unavoidable. Ancient walled towns cling to the rocks and dip their feet in the water like they're the ones on holiday. In summer, the whole scene is bathed in the scent of wild herbs, conifers and Mediterranean blossoms. All of this – and much, much more – is wrapped up into an area two-thirds of the size of Wales.

Go Wild

When the beaches fill up with Eastern European sunseekers, intrepid travellers can easily sidestep the hordes by getting off the beaten track in the rugged mountains of Durmitor and Prokletije, the primeval forest of Biogradska Gora, or in the many towns and villages where ordinary Montenegrins go about their daily lives. Hike, horse ride, mountain bike or kayak yourself to somewhere obscure and chances are you'll have it all to yourself. This is, after all, a country where wolves and bears still lurk in forgotten corners.

Living on the Edge

Ever since the Roman Empire split in two 1600 years ago, Montenegro has sat on the borderline between east and west. The richness of its cultural history can be seen in the mosaic floors of Roman villas, flamboyantly painted Orthodox monasteries, ornate Catholic churches, elegant minarets of mosques, and the sturdy fortresses built by the numerous powers that have fought over these lands. Then there's the legacy of 50 years as a non-aligned communist state, independent of both the Eastern Bloc and the West. For those with even a passing interest in European history, it's a fascinating place.

Why I Love Montenegro

By Tamara Sheward, Writer

If all the world's a stage, then Montenegro struts upon it, continuously playing out the most dramatic act. There's not an iota of the insipid to be found here; from its backdrop of soul-stirring mountains and captivating coastline to its passionate populace and lively, living history, this is a country with charisma. I've been knocked off my feet here more times than I can count – by the staggeringly spectacular scenery, the heartfelt backslaps walloped into me by highland giants, and the frightfully strong *rakija*. No matter how often I visit, Montenegro floors me every time.

For more about our writers, see p192

Montenegro

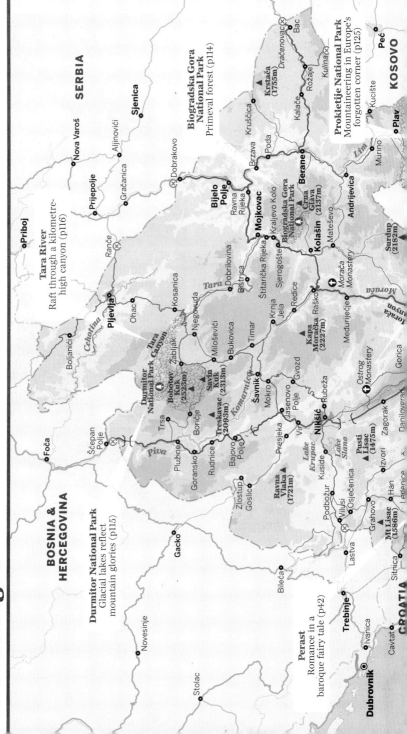

Durmitor National Park
Glacial lakes reflect
mountain glories (p115)

Tara River
Raft through a kilometre-
high canyon (p116)

**Biogradska Gora
National Park**
Primeval forest (p114)

Prokletije National Park
Mountaineering in Europe's
forgotten corner (p125)

Perast
Romance in a
baroque fairy tale (p42)

BOSNIA &
HERCEGOVINA

SERBIA

KOSOVO

CROATIA

0   25 miles
0   50 km

Novesinje

Stolac

Gacko

Bileca

Trebinje

Dubrovnik

Ivanica

Cavtat

Sitnica

Lastva

Grahovo

Mt Lisac
(1586m)

Han

Ledenice

Vilusi

Osječenica

Podbožur

Kuside

Lake
Krupac

Lake
Slano

Pusti
Lisac
(1475m)

Izvori

Zagorak

Danilovgrad

Gorica

Ostrog
Monastery

Rubeža

Nikšić

Vir

Jasenovo
Polje

Mokro

Gvozd

Presjeka

Ravna
Vlaka
(1721m)

Zlostup
Goslice

Plužine

Goransko

Rudnice

Bajovo
Polje

Boričje

Trsa

Treskavac
(2093m)

Savin
Kuk
(2313m)

Bobotov
Kuk
(2523m)

Šavnik

Komarnica

Durmitor National Park

Tara Canyon

Žabljak

Trsa

Šćepan
Polje

Foča

Piva

Bojanići

Pljevlja

Ohac

Njegovuda

Kosanica

Miloševići

Bukovica

Timar

Dobrilovina

Bistrica

Tara

Cehotina

Rance

Priboj

Prijepolje

Gračanica

Aljinovići

Nova Varoš

Sjenica

Dobrakovo

Ravna
Rijeka

Bijelo
Polje

Mojkovac

Kraljevo Kolo

Štitarička Rijeka

Sjerogošte

Raško

Redice

Krnja

Jela

Kapa
Moračka
(2227m)

Biogradska Gora
National Park

Bjela
Glava
(2137m)

Kolašin

Mateševo

Međuriječje

Morača
Monastery

Morača

Morača
kanjon

Brzava

Poda

Kruščica

Krstača
(1755m)

Berane

Andrijevica

Rožaje

Kalače

Kulina

Dračenovac

Bać

Murino

Lim

Plav

Kucište

Peć

Surdup
(2182m)

Gorica

Herceg Novi
Relax on sunny squares (p36)

Kotor
Living history within ancient walls (p45)

Njegoš Mausoleum
A tomb with a view (p92)

Budva
A miniature, less-frantic Dubrovnik (p65)

Sveti Stefan
Inviting sands and island views (p74)

Cetinje
Treasure troves in the old Royal Capital (p93)

Ulcinj
A vibrant slice of Albanian culture (p84)

Stari Bar
Enigmatic ruins to explore (p82)

Lake Skadar National Park
Floating meadows of water lilies (p97)

Ostrog Monastery
Cliff's-edge serenity and spirituality (p107)

ALBANIA

PODGORICA

Adriatic Sea

ELEVATION

2000m
1500m
1000m
750m
500m
250m
0

Montenegro's
Top 16

1

Kotor

1 Time-travel back to a Europe of moated walled towns with shadowy lanes and stone churches on every square. It may not be as impressive as Dubrovnik's or as shiny as Budva's, but Kotor's (p45) Old Town feels much more lived-in and ever so dramatic. The way it seems to grow out of the sheer grey mountains surrounding it adds a thrill of foreboding to the experience – as if they could at any point chose to squeeze the little town in a rocky embrace.

Njegoš Mausoleum

2 Once upon a time there was a Black Mountain. And on top of that mountain there was a tomb guarded by two granite giantesses. And inside the tomb, under a canopy of gold, there rested a great hero, lying in the arms of a giant eagle. This fairy-tale location is the final resting place (p92) for the very real 19th-century *vladika* (bishop-prince) Petar II Petrović Njegoš. The simple but affecting structure and monumental statuary do little to distract from the remarkable views over all of Old Montenegro.

GILMANSHIN / SHUTTERSTOCK ©

OPIS ZAGREB / SHUTTERSTOCK ©

Lake Skadar National Park

3 Shared between Montenegro and Albania, the Balkans' largest lake is home to an extraordinary array of birdlife. On the Montenegrin side, a national park (p97) encompasses island monasteries, old stone villages famous for their wine, and the serpentine loops of the Crnojević River. Descending from the mountains, the river winds sluggishly through the water lilies on its journey to the lake and the conical pair of mountains that the locals affectionately call 'Sofia Loren'. No Italian actress ever looked so sublime.

Sveti Stefan

4 The postcard-perfect fortified island village of Sveti Stefan (p74) is a wonder to behold. It's a little slice of Mediterranean heaven, with oleanders, pines and olive trees peeking between the terracotta roofs of pink stone dwellings. You may have to content yourself with the views; access to the island is limited to guests of the exclusive resort that owns it. Instead, laze on the beach, take a stroll through the woods to Pržno, and go crazy taking photographs – it's hard to get a bad shot.

Mountain Eyes, Durmitor National Park

5 Reflecting the beauty of the Durmitor range's imposing grey peaks are 18 glacial lakes, known as *gorske oči* (mountain eyes). The largest and most beautiful is Black Lake (p116); its inky appearance is caused by the surrounding black pines and the peak known as the Bear (Medjed) rearing above it. Black Lake is a breeze to get to and a delight to walk around, but other, more remote lakes await discovery further up along the park's hiking trails. Top left: Black Lake

Perast

6 An oversized village comprised almost entirely of elegant baroque palaces and churches, romantic Perast (p42) forms a worthy centrepiece to the entire Bay of Kotor. The positioning is perfect, sitting at the apex of the inner bay, looking straight down the narrow channel leading to the outer section. Catch a boat to Gospa od Škrpelja (Our-Lady-of-the-Rock Island), one of two tiny islands sitting just offshore, where a sky-blue dome covers a church filled with votive offerings left by grateful sailors. Top right: Hotel Conte (p43), Perast

Stari Grad, Budva

7 Budva's walled Old Town (p65) rises from the Adriatic like a miniature, less frantic Dubrovnik. There's an atmosphere of romance and a typically Mediterranean love of life palpable around every corner. While away the hours exploring the labyrinth of narrow cobbled streets, visiting tiny churches and charming galleries, drinking in al fresco cafe-bars, snacking on pizza and being inspired by the gorgeous sea views from the Citadela. When it's time to relax, there's a beach on either side.

Rafting the Tara River

8 It's hard to get a decent view of the beautiful Tara Canyon (p116) – its sheer tree-lined walls, up to 1300m high, tend to get in the way. The effect is most impressive from the water, which goes some way to explaining why rafting is one of the country's most popular tourist activities. You'll hit a few rapids, but outside of April and May it's a relatively gentle experience, gliding over crystalline waters through a landscape untouched by human hands.

Ulcinj

9 There's a special buzz to Ulcinj (p84), Montenegro's southernmost town – an indefinable excitement that's particularly apparent on summer nights, when the beachfront thrums with Eastern-tinged pop and a constant parade of holidaymakers. Look up: minarets compete with oversized socialist sculpture, and the imposing walls of the Old Town perch high on the cliff. Continuing along the coast, rocky coves give way to the long sandy expanses of Velika Plaža (Big Beach) and the clothing-optional island, Ada Bojana. Bottom: Mala Plaža (p84)

Ostrog Monastery

10 No photo can do justice to the wonder that is Ostrog Monastery (p107). Set in a seemingly sheer mountain wall, it's impossible to frame a picture that reveals its height without reducing the luminous white monastery to little more than a speck. Orthodox Christians consider this Montenegro's holiest site; whether you're a believer or not, it's an affecting place. The complex includes several stone churches, but none is more atmospheric than the cave chapels of the Upper Monastery, their rock walls covered in centuries-old frescoes.

Hiking the Prokletije Mountains

11 They're the 'Accursed Mountains', but for hikers and climbers this rugged range (p125) in the east is more divine than damned. Snaking across Montenegro, Albania and Kosovo, Prokletije makes up the highest part of the Dinaric Alps. The Peaks of the Balkans trail winds 192km through the range, crossing between all three countries with tracks that veer from easy to extreme. Whether you tackle the entire trail or take a brief amble, a Prokletije pilgrimage leaves you feeling on top of the world.

MILA ATKOVSKA / SHUTTERSTOCK ©

ISTANKOV / GETTY IMAGES ©

JTB PHOTOS / GETTY IMAGES ©

Stari Bar

12 While there's not much to recommend the modern industrial town of Bar, there's a real gem hidden in the hinterland. The ancient city of Stari Bar (p82) lies in enigmatic ruins atop a bluff surrounded by gnarled olive trees, many of which are more than a thousand years old. The city itself has been here for around 2800 years but its current state of dilapidation dates from a bombardment in 1878. The whole place is laid bare for you to explore.

Biogradska Gora National Park

13 Nestled within the folds of the Bjelasica mountains, Biogradska Gora (p114) has such a peaceful, solitary, untouched-by-the-world feel to it that you might not want to leave. The national park's showcase is pretty Lake Biograd (pictured), but further enchantments await on the hiking tracks through one of Europe's most significant remaining tracts of virgin forest. This green world is quite unlike the rocky terrain that characterises most of the country's mountains, and in autumn it kicks up its heels and turns on a colourful show. Top right: Lake Biograd

The Museums of Cetinje

14 Cetinje may have been stripped of its capital status by Podgorica, but Montenegro's erstwhile royal city still boasts the country's richest and most important museums (p93). Spanning centuries of history, the four museums – collectively known as the National Museum of Montenegro – include everything from palaces to bullet-riddled relics to Montenegro's first billiard table (owned by Petar II Petrović Njegoš, of course). Two galleries, a monastery and a host of handsome historic buildings amp up Cetinje's cultural cachet. Above right: Biljarda (p93)

The Kotor–Lovćen Road

15 One of the most memorable highlights of Montenegro is the simple joy of travelling along its many scenic routes and taking in the beauty and power of the landscape. The back road (p48) connecting Kotor with Cetinje is one of the very best – looping up and up, providing jaw-dropping views of the Bay of Kotor and the Adriatic beyond. Any white-knuckle moments caused by the narrowness of the road and its sheer drops are compensated for by vistas of lavender-grey mountains and glassy green water. Below: Bay of Kotor (p34)

Herceg Novi

16 Between the bustling waterfront promenade and the busy highway lies an unassuming Old Town; it's here that the very essence of Herceg Novi (p36) hides. Catholic and Orthodox churches abound in equal profusion, cafe-bars set up their tables on sunny squares, and hulking fortresses huddle in silent menace. Order a glass of wine and soak it all in. The town beaches may not be great, but some of Montenegro's very best are only a short boat ride away.

KSHAVRATSKAYA / GETTY IMAGES ©

OLLIRG / SHUTTERSTOCK ©

Need to Know

For more information, see Survival Guide (p163)

Currency
Euro (€)

Language
Montenegrin (extremely similar to Bosnian, Croatian and Serbian)

Visas
Many nationalities are entitled to a stay of up to 90 days without a visa.

Money
ATMs widely available. Credit cards are accepted in larger hotels but aren't widely accepted elsewhere.

Mobile Phones
Local SIM cards are a good idea if you're planning a longer stay and can be used in most unlocked handsets. Mobile calls are expensive in Montenegro but the main providers offer heavily discounted rates to calls within their network; it's not uncommon for businesses to advertise three different mobile numbers on different networks.

Time
Central European Time (GMT plus one hour)

When to Go

Žabljak
GO Jan–Sep

Kolašin
GO Jan–Oct

Kotor
GO May–Oct

Podgorica
GO Apr–Jun & Sep

Budva
GO May–Oct

Warm to hot summers, mild winters

High Season (Jul–Aug)
➡ The warmest, driest, busiest and most expensive time to visit.

➡ Accommodation should be booked well in advance; some places enforce three-day minimum stays.

Shoulder (May–Jun & Sep–Oct)
➡ The best time to come, with plenty of sunshine and average water temperatures over 20°C.

➡ Some beach bars and restaurants are closed and activities can be harder to arrange.

Low Season (Nov–Apr)
➡ The ski season kicks in, with peak prices in Kolašin and Žabljak.

➡ Many hotels, restaurants and bars on the coast close their doors and prices plummet.

Useful Websites

Montenegrin National Tourist Organisation (www. montenegro.travel) Packed full of information, photos and some downloadable resources.

National Parks of Montenegro (www.nparkovi.me) All five national parks are covered, with information about activities and park fees.

Explore Montenegro (www. montenegroholidays.com) Specialises in apartment rentals, especially at the top end, as well as flights and tours.

Visit Montenegro (www. visit-montenegro.com) One of the most informative of the commercial sites.

Lonely Planet (www.lonelyplan et.com/montenegro) Destination information, hotel bookings, traveller forum and more.

Important Numbers

International access code	☏00
Country code	☏382
Police	☏122
Ambulance	☏124
Roadside assistance	☏9807

Exchange Rates

Australia	A$1	€0.68
Canada	C$1	€0.69
Croatia	1KN	€0.13
Japan	¥100	€0.88
New Zealand	NZ$1	€0.64
Serbia	100DIN	€0.81
UK	£1	€1.15
US	US$1	€0.68

For current exchange rates see www.xe.com

Daily Costs

Budget: Less than €85

➡ Dorms or shared room in private accommodation €11-18

➡ Pizza slice €2.50

Midrange: €85–185

➡ Double room in midrange hotel €50-100

➡ Apartment rental €50-150

➡ Sit-down meal in a traditional restaurant €8-30

Top End: More than €185

➡ Double room in an upmarket hotel €120-500

➡ Fish meals that stare back at you while they're served €25-55

Opening Hours

Montenegrins have a flexible approach to opening times. Even if hours are posted on the door of an establishment, don't be surprised if they're not heeded. Many tourist-orientated businesses close between November and March.

Post offices 7am to 8pm Monday to Friday, sometimes Saturday. In smaller towns they may close mid-afternoon, or close at noon and reopen at 5pm.

Banks Generally from 8am to 5pm Monday to Friday, 8am to noon Saturday.

Shops 9am to 8pm. Sometimes they'll close for a few hours in the late afternoon.

Restaurants, cafes & bars 8am to midnight. If the joint is jumping, cafe-bars may stay open until 2am or 3am.

Arriving in Montenegro

Podgorica Airport Taxis charge an average €10 fare for the 9km to central Podgorica. There are no buses.

Tivat Airport Taxis charge €5 to €7 for the 3km to Tivat, €15 for Kotor and €20 for Budva. There are no buses.

Dubrovnik Airport (Croatia) There are no buses directly to Montenegro, but buses to Dubrovnik Bus Station (24km in the wrong direction) are timed around flights (35KN). From Dubrovnik there are seven buses a day to Herceg Novi (€12) and Kotor (€15.50), two of which continue to Podgorica (€19). Herceg Novi travel agencies and accommodation providers can usually pre-arrange a transfer for €45.

Getting Around

Bus Buses link all major towns and are affordable, reliable and reasonably comfortable.

Car While you can get to many places by bus, hiring a car will give you freedom to explore some of Montenegro's scenic back roads. Some of these are extremely narrow and cling to the sides of canyons, so it may not suit the inexperienced or faint-hearted.

Train Trains are cheap but the network is limited and many carriages are old and can get hot. The main line links Bar, Virpazar, Podgorica, Kolašin, Mojkovac and Bijelo Polje, and there's a second line from Podgorica to Danilovgrad and Nikšić.

For much more on **getting around**, see p172

PLAN YOUR TRIP NEED TO KNOW

What's New

Peaks of the Balkans Hiking Trail

The 192km trail winds through Montenegro, Albania and Kosovo, offering superb hiking in the mighty Prokletije Mountains. You'll discover highland hospitality, jaw-dropping panoramas and remnants of the bad-blood days between the countries. (p124)

Podgorica Accommodation

Previously the domain of corporate hotels and dreary digs, Podgorica has lifted its game, with some excellent new apartments, hostels, boutique hotels and B&Bs dotting the lay-your-hat landscape. (p103)

Lipa Cave

Montenegro is riddled with caverns and underground coves, but the huge Lipa Cave – 4km out of Cetinje – is the only one open for organised visits. New daily tours cater to everyone from sprogs to speleologists. (p95)

Direct Flights to Tivat

Many visitors to the Bay of Kotor traditionally flew into Dubrovnik and hit the road from there. No longer; as of 2016, Tivat Airport welcomes direct budget flights from Gatwick, Manchester, Moscow, Belgrade and other European cities. (p172)

Via Dinarica Hiking Trail

This 1930km trail links Slovenia, Serbia, Croatia, Bosnia and Herzegovina (BiH), Montenegro, Albania, Kosovo and Macedonia. It enters Montenegro from BiH and crosses Durmitor National Park. (p117)

Tara Canyon Ziplining

Steel your nerves for a rip-roaring ride on this award-winning zipline that whizzes above Europe's deepest river canyon and parallel to the Tara Bridge. The bird's-eye views are tremendous...if you're brave enough to open your eyes. (p118)

Glamping

Given Montenegro's reputation for attracting the well heeled, it's no surprise the glamping craze has finally hit the country. Enjoy the Great Outdoors sans grubbiness (or all that setting-up bother) in luxury tents at Camp Full Monte and Olive Tree Glamping. (p40, p85)

Budva Waterpark

What's a tourist town without a water park? Montenegro's most visited destination now boasts one of its own, thanks to the opening of the €13m Aqua Park Budva. It's one of the largest of its kind on the Adriatic. (p67)

Underground Wine Tours

Combine history with a drop (or three) of Montenegrin wine, and you get the Šipčanik wine cellar tours. They're held deep underground – in a former secret Yugoslav Army aircraft hangar – right beneath the vineyard in which the grapes are grown. (p106)

Nikšić Arts Scene

One of Montenegro's most industrial cities is usually passed over by travellers, but a revival of its art scene by the renegade PUNKT collective has made it a worthy stop for those keen on cutting-edge culture. (p108)

Alternative Adventures

As tourism blossoms in Montenegro, so does the creativity of operators. Take a submarine ride beneath the Bay of Kotor, explore Skadar by horseback, quad-bike up Mt Lovćen or stand-up paddleboard (SUP) around remote Lake Šas. (p48, p98, p92, p88)

For more recommendations and reviews, see lonelyplanet.com/Montenegro

If You Like...

Historic Towns

Kotor Frozen in time behind its walls, Kotor may look like a movie set but it's still very much a living town. (p45)

Perast Baroque buildings line the water's edge in Montenegro's prettiest little town. (p42)

Budva's Stari Grad Like a mini-Dubrovnik, Budva's walled Old Town juts out over the blue Adriatic waters. (p65)

Ulcinj's Stari Grad Set high on a bluff above the beach, the uneven cobbled lanes within Ulcinj's walls ooze antiquity. (p84)

Herceg Novi's Stari Grad It doesn't have all its walls, but the marbled heart of Herceg Novi has plenty of sunny squares. (p36)

Cetinje The dinky old royal capital is crammed full of 19th-century buildings and interesting churches. (p93)

Stari Bar Clamber your way through the gorgeous ruins of Bar's original cliffside settlement; there's enough enigmatic rubble left to imagine how it was in its glory days. (p83)

Beaches

Kraljičina Plaža Near Čanj, this pretty stretch of pink sand can only be reached by boat. (p77)

Drobni Pijesak Green hills and turquoise waters frame this secluded cove, hidden from view below the coastal road. (p76)

Žanjic & Mirišta These neighbouring beaches gaze out to sea from their remote perch near the end of the Luštica Peninsula. (p57)

Lučice Lined with cypress trees and oleanders, and with picturesque church-topped islets offshore, Lučice is a Mediterranean dream. (p76)

Jaz Can't choose between socialising and sunbathing? Do both! This broad, pebbly and eminently swimmable beach is lined with bars, abuzz with water sports, and masquerades as a stage during one of Montenegro's craziest music festivals. (p71)

Sveti Stefan The island view from the pink sands is sublime; neighbouring Miločer Beach is even better, but the day-use fee is exorbitant. (p74)

Amazing Views

Njegoš Mausoleum Perched on one of the Black Mountain's peaks, this dramatic tomb offers views over all of Old Montenegro. (p92)

Kotor–Lovćen road The entire Bay of Kotor is laid out before you as you negotiate the old Austrian road to Lovćen. (p45)

Sveti Stefan Pull into the viewing bays on the highway to enjoy spectacular views over the walled island village turned resort. (p74)

Kotor's Town Walls Sublime views are the reward for the gruelling 1350-step climb up Kotor's ancient fortifications. (p45)

Kolašin–Andrijevica road This minor road through the mountains opens up to breathtaking views of the Komovi and Prokletije mountains and the Lim valley. (p112)

Plužine–Šćepan Polje road Incredible riverside road that twists and turns through 56 narrow carved-stone tunnels. Pull over to admire the frothing, peacock-blue waters below and the wormhole-like tunnels behind you. (p123)

Local Cuisine

Njeguši Producing the country's best *pršut* (prosciutto) and cheese, this village is synonymous with traditional Montenegrin cooking. (p92)

Konoba Ćatovića Mlini Adriatic coastal cuisine is well represented by this atmospheric family-run restaurant, hidden in a fold of the Bay of Kotor. (p41)

Kolašin Montenegrin mountain food is at its best in Kolašin's traditional restaurants. (p113)

PLAN YOUR TRIP IF YOU LIKE...

Mon Ami Wine House Producing varietals you've almost certainly never heard of before, Montenegro's smaller winemakers are under-represented in the nation's restaurants. Taste some at this cute little shop in Kotor. (p50)

Šipčanik Wine Cellar Take a tour beneath the very vineyard where some of Montenegro's most popular wines are grown; the cellar itself is a rehabilitated, erstwhile-abandoned secret aircraft hangar. (p106)

Religious Art & Architecture

Ostrog Monastery Set on a mountainside and visible for many miles, this gleaming white monastery is Montenegro's most significant Orthodox site. (p107)

Morača Monastery The country's most beautiful monastery, filled with highly acclaimed frescoes and icons. (p112)

St Tryphon's Cathedral Kotor's Catholic cathedral is a masterpiece of Romanesque architecture and is home to many lovingly crafted religious objects. (p45)

Hussein Pasha Mosque A soaring minaret, elegant domes and elaborate frescoes, inside and out, make this Montenegro's most impressive mosque. (p120)

Gospa od Škrpjela The gorgeous blue-domed Catholic church on Our-Lady-of-the-Rock Island is filled with devotional treasures. (p42)

Piva Monastery Originally built in the 16th century, this mountain monastery was painstakingly moved from its lakeside location to higher ground in the late 1960s to make way for a hydro-electric dam. (p123)

Top: Ostrog Monastery (p107)
Bottom: Local market, Cetinje (p93)

Month by Month

January

The ski season kicks off, heralding peak prices in Kolašin and Žabljak; it's low season everywhere else.

✦ Orthodox Christmas

Held on 7 January, the traditional Orthodox Christmas is marked by church services and unbridled feasting; the night before, oak branches (*badnjak*) are burned and prayers are offered for good luck and happiness in the coming year.

February

The ski season is in full swing in the north. Despite chilly temperatures in the Bay of Kotor (average highs of around 12°C), residents find reasons to celebrate.

✦ Mimosa Festival

Herceg Novi gets a jump on spring with this festival, which has been held, perhaps coincidentally, since the flower-power era of the late 1960s. Expect concerts, sports events, majorettes and lots of yellow blooms. (p38)

✦ Carnival

The traditional pre-Lent festivities continue to be held in the once predominantly Catholic towns of Kotor and Tivat. Expect Venetian-style masked balls (for adults and for children), concerts, theatre performances and parades. (p49, p53)

March

The ski season continues up north but spring arrives elsewhere, with average highs jumping above 10°C in Podgorica and hitting around 15°C on the coast.

✦ Camellia Day

Not to be outdone by mimosa, the camellia gets its moment in the springtime sun with this festival held in both Kotor and Stoliv in mid-March. (p48)

April

You might get a few skiing days at the beginning of the month before the rising temperature melts the snow and speeds up the flow of the Tara River – leading to the start of the rafting season.

✦ Carnival of Budva

Bucking tradition in favour of warmer weather, Budva gets into the Venetian swing of things in late April, with parades, folk music, concerts and DJs. (p67)

May

Late spring is a great time to visit Montenegro, with average high temperatures in the 20s everywhere except the mountains. Rafting is at its most thrilling and accommodation prices move into the shoulder-season bracket.

✦ Spring Break Festival

The otherwise calm sands of little Kamenovo Beach

get all stirred up during this two-day electronic music festival that attracts big-name DJs from across Europe. (p73)

June

Summer brings with it warm, dry days and rising accommodation prices on the coast, but not yet peak rates. Tourist-orientated businesses reopen, including beach bars and restaurants.

☆ Theatre City

Budva comes over all thespian for six weeks from mid-June, with performances held in such dramatic spots as the Citadela and in front of the Old Town's walls. (p67)

✯ Southern Soul Festival

The silly season kicks off in earnest at Velika Plaža's happening Copacabana Beach, with four full-on days (from late June to early July) of terpsichore and tunes. (p89)

July

The official start of 'The Season'. Peak rates kick in, temperatures soar, beach clubs crank into life and tourists flood the beaches. In the mountains, the weather is perfect for hiking.

✯ Sea Dance Festival

This fantastic, frenetic three-day electronic and alternative music festival on the sunny sands of Jaz

Top: Fašinada festival (p42), Perast
Bottom: Sea Dance Festival (p72), Jaz Beach

Beach (near Budva) attracts tens of thousands of merrymakers. (p72)

 Kotor Art

Continuing through to August, Kotor's summer arts umbrella shelters several well-established festivals, such as Don Branko's Music Days (classical music) and Perast's International Klapa Festival (traditional Dalmatian unaccompanied singing). International companies head to the Children's Theatre Festival in early July. (p48)

 Fašinada

On 22 July Perast men row decorated boats laden with stones to Gospa od Škrpjela in a centuries-old tradition, adding to the artificial island created by their ancestors. The event is now accompanied by the Perast to Tivat yacht regatta. (p42)

Summer in the Old Capital

Cetinje's summer-long celebration of all things cultural, edible and potable kicks off in the height of the season and runs until September. If you're looking for a reason to stop lazing around the beach, this is it. (p95)

August

August is the hottest and driest month, sometimes resulting in wildfires. The party continues on the coast and Lake Skadar is at its very best, but in Podgorica it gets unbearably hot.

Boka Night

Kotor goes crazy on its night of nights – celebrated since the 19th century (and possibly before) – with a parade of lavishly decorated boats, Old Town parties and seemingly never-ending fireworks. (p49)

September

Temperatures drop back to the 20s and 'The Season' comes to an abrupt halt, with prices dropping and some beach businesses disappearing – despite the weather remaining lovely. It's a great time to visit.

September Days

The surprisingly artsy town of Nikšić goes culture-crazy during this autumn festival: art, music, theatre, literature, food and traditional events fill the calendar all month long. (p108)

October

On the coast, sea and water temperatures remain in the 20s but rainfall increases. Rafting comes to an end. The autumn leaves put on a show in Biogradska Gora National Park.

Days of Pljevlja Cheese

If you dig dairy, this one's for you; three solid days of stuffing yourself with Pljevlja's famous salty cheese and other fantastically fattening foods. (p120)

November

Wrap up warm and bring a raincoat. November is the wettest month and temperatures drop to the low teens, with average lows falling below freezing level in the mountains.

December

Rainfall remains high. On the coast, many businesses remain completely closed. Towards the end of the month you might get some days on the ski slopes.

Festival of Wine & Bleak

Blast away the winter blues by heading to Lake Skadar's Virpazar village and consuming the two things the area is known for: locally produced wine and the lake fish called bleak. (p98)

Itineraries

A Taste of Montenegro

This 325km trip zigzags from the coast to Montenegro's heartland then back to the beaches again, taking in some of the country's most emblematic sights. It requires a car.

Start in **Herceg Novi** and slowly wind your way towards **Kotor**, allowing at least an hour in **Perast** en route. All three are ancient bayside towns filled with old churches and marbled squares. The next morning, take the dazzling drive to the historic Montenegrin capital **Cetinje** through Lovćen National Park, stopping to visit the **Njegoš Mausoleum** on the way. Explore Cetinje's museums and galleries by day, its lively cafe-bars by night.

Next day, head up to the dramatically positioned **Ostrog Monastery** before sweeping south to **Podgorica** to roam the small capital and sample its up-and-coming bar scene. On day four, continue to **Virpazar** for a chilled-out two-hour cruise on Lake Skadar. Carry on down to **Sveti Stefan**, check into somewhere with an island view and head to the beach. Spend your last day in **Budva**, splitting your time between exploring the Old Town and lazing on the sand.

The Full Monte

Most of Montenegro's big-hitting beauty spots are covered in this almost-800km itinerary.

Base yourself in **Herceg Novi** and take a boat or kayak trip to Rose, Mamula Island, the Blue Grotto and the beaches of the Luštica Peninsula. Stop at Morinj and Risan on your way to **Perast**, and don't miss the boat trip to Gospa od Škrpjela island. Continue to **Kotor** and use the walled town as a base to visit Dobrota, Prčanj and Stoliv. Then head through Lovćen National Park to **Cetinje**, making time for a quick tour of **Lipa Cave** before stopping in **Ostrog Monastery**. Carry on north though the Piva Canyon to **Šćepan Polje**, the main staging point for rafting trips down the Tara River. Stay the night at one of the rafting camps, and take on the river on a half-day trip. Hop back in the car and take the scenic road east from Plužine through Durmitor National Park to **Žabljak**. Allow some time to enjoy the park and, at a minimum, make sure you hike around the Black Lake.

Follow the road along the Tara River to the isolated Dobrilovina Monastery then continue on to **Biogradska Gora National Park** – you can stay in the cabins here or continue on to the upmarket hotels in **Kolašin**. Stop at the **Morača Monastery** on your way to **Podgorica**, then hang out in the capital for a day. Continue down to **Virpazar** for a morning's cruise on Lake Skadar. Skirt the Rumija Mountains until the road shies away from the Albanian border and hooks down to the buzzy beachside town of **Ulcinj**. Be sure to visit Velika Plaža before continuing back up the coast. Stop to check out the charming ruins of **Stari Bar** before you get to the beach town of **Petrovac**. Continue along the coast, stopping at the beaches of **Sveti Stefan** and **Pržno** before finishing up in **Budva**, with its walled Old Town and busy promenade.

If you're travelling by bus, you'll need to pare back the itinerary a little. From Kotor, the easiest way to Cetinje, Ostrog or rafting is on a day tour. Swap the Plužine–Žabljak road for a Nikšić–Žabljak bus. To get from Žabljak to Kolašin, you'll need to go via Pljevlja or Podgorica. From Virpazar, take a train to Bar followed by a bus to Ulcinj.

The Coast

Spend a day in **Herceg Novi** and consider a kayak tour or a boat trip to the beaches on the Luština Peninsula. The following day, make your way slowly to Kotor, stopping to view the Roman mosaics at **Risan** and the baroque beauty of **Perast**. Base yourself in **Kotor** on day three; climb the fortifications, hike the Vrmac Ridge, explore neighbouring coastal villages or just hang out in the fascinating Old Town.

If you've got a car, take the serpentine road up to **Lovćen National Park**, then spend the rest of the day exploring the museums and galleries of **Cetinje** before heading to **Budva** for the night. If you're travelling by bus, head straight to Budva and save Cetinje for another day.

For the following two days, base yourself anywhere on the stretch of coast between Budva and Petrovac. Budva is the easiest place to arrange a day tour to Ostrog Monastery and Lake Skadar, or a rafting trip on the Tara River, while **Petrovac** is more family-friendly, with a relaxed vibe and great beaches nearby. Close neighbours **Pržno** and **Sveti Stefan** also have excellent accommodation options, great restaurants and striking coastal views.

No matter where you put down roots, make sure you take the walk through the woods from Sveti Stefan to Pržno. A car or bike will get you to hidden bays such as Drobni Pijesak and Rijeka Reževići, and there are several monasteries to explore, including Podmaine and Podostrog, near Budva, and Reževići and Gradište, near Petrovac.

Continue south until you get to the Sozina tunnel near Sutomore, and drive through it to **Virpazar**, gateway to Lake Skadar, to take a boat cruise and enjoy a village-style meal in one of Montenegro's top restaurants. Retrace your steps back to the coast, and head southeast to visit the ruins of **Stari Bar** on your way to **Ulcinj**. The atmosphere of this largely Albanian town is quite different from anywhere else in Montenegro and there's a palpable buzz on the streets at night. The succession of rocky coves heading east from the crowded town beach are great for snorkelling. Nearby is the 12km continuous stretch of sand known as **Velika Plaža** and just across the Bojana River there's a further 3km of beach on the nudist island **Ada Bojana**.

The Hidden North

This mountainous 650km loop combines some of Europe's most beautiful drives with visits to isolated monasteries and ample opportunities for wilderness hiking. You won't be able to tackle this route in winter, as snows close the Plužine–Žabljak road.

Spend the morning exploring the nation's capital and biggest city, **Podgorica**, and then head through Danilovgrad to the extraordinary **Ostrog Monastery**. Continue on through Nikšić where the highway passes through farmland before reaching **Piva Monastery**, with its sumptuous frescoes, and the start of the Piva Canyon. From here the road passes through tunnels cut into the canyon walls until you reach the Bosnian border at **Šćepan Polje**, the main rafting base. Check yourself into one of the rafting camps for the night.

Start day two with a half-day's rafting on the Tara River and then jump in the car and double back through the canyon as far as Plužine. From here, take the scenic mountain road through Durmitor National Park to **Žabljak**. Spend the rest of this and the next day hitting the park's hiking tracks.

On day four, drive east to the Tara Bridge and head north to **Pljevlja** to visit Montenegro's most beautiful mosque and a picturesque Orthodox monastery. Double back to the Tara Bridge and continue southeast along the river road. Consider making Eko-Oaza Suza Evrope your pit stop for this leg; from here you can walk to the secluded **Dobrilovina Monastery** and to a swimming hole on the river.

Continue to **Mojkovac** and head north around the Bjelasica Massif and down through Berane to Plav. Base yourself nearby for a day's hiking in **Prokletije National Park**; make sure you fit in a visit to the Ottoman town of **Gusinje**. The next day, take the awe-inspiring back road through Andrijevica to **Kolašin**, Montenegro's best mountain resort. Spend the rest of the day tackling the tracks through **Biogradska Gora National Park**.

The road back to Podgorica follows the Morača Canyon and is just as extraordinary as any on this trip. At the start of the canyon, call in to admire the exquisite frescoes and icons at peaceful **Morača Monastery**. You might also like to offer a prayer for your safety on the scenic but treacherous road ahead.

Plan Your Trip

Outdoor Activities

Montenegro's diverse landscape lends itself to so much more than simply lazing on the country's beautiful beaches. Five national parks beckon, taunting nature buffs and adrenaline addicts with all the adventurous activities that such mighty mountains, rivers and lakes can inspire. And when nature calls, why resist?

Need to Know

When to Go

The best time for a well-rounded roster of adventures is May and early June, when the melting ice adds thrills to a rafting trip and the wildflowers are bursting into bloom.

Sea and air temperatures are highest in July and August, but you'll be battling the crowds on the beaches and there are sometimes wildfires during particularly hot summers. Otherwise, it's a good time to be in the mountains.

September and October are also good options, especially if you like your hikes accompanied by a blazing backdrop of autumn colour.

Ski buffs should head north between January and March.

What to Pack

You'll need a pair of sturdy hiking boots and you should consider packing a compass or GPS device, first-aid kit and a torch (flashlight).

If you're a serious rock climber or mountaineer, it's best to bring any specialist gear you might need with you.

On the Water

Rafting

This is Montenegro's premier active drawcard. Commercial rafting is well established on the Tara River and once you've experienced the spectacular canyon you'll understand why. The season runs between April and October.

Kayaking

The Bay of Kotor and Lake Skadar are both brilliant places for a paddle, and several operators specialise in day tours. Very experienced white-water kayakers can take on the rapids of some of Montenegro's rivers, but you're best to take local advice first as some stretches are dangerous.

Diving

Not all the landscape, wildlife and history is above ground. Montenegro's azure waters hide caves, shelves, springs and thousands of years' worth of shipwrecks – those Ulcinj pirates were busy chaps and WWII added to the collection. Visibility ranges from 10m to 25m but is usually around 15m. The main fauna you're likely to spot are swarms of young dentex, gilt-head bream and the occasional lobster or sea turtle.

Kolašin 1450 Ski Resort (p113)

The best times to dive are from the middle of May until September, when the surface water is up to 25°C, dropping to 16°C under 30m (you'll need a 7mm neoprene wetsuit). You'll find diving operators in Budva, Pržno and Ulcinj.

Kitesurfing

At the far south of the coast, the Velika Plaža and Ada Bojana area has taken off as one of the Mediterranean's kitesurfing hubs. It's a great place to learn the sport.

On Land

Hiking

Thanks to the enthusiastic members of mountain clubs all over the country, Montenegro has an excellent network of hiking tracks – although they're not all well maintained or well marked.

Whether you're armed with a tent or just planning a day walk, be well prepared for sudden changes in temperature and storms, and note that water supplies can be limited.

The main difficulty serious walkers and mountaineers will face is access to accommodation on longer expeditions. Mountain huts are available in some places but it can be difficult for the independent traveller to access them. Adventure-focused travel agencies can help with this, and can also arrange experienced guides from the local club. Montenegro's Mountaineering Association (www.pscg.me) can also help.

Some of the best short hikes include the easy circuits of Biogradska Gora's Lake Biograd and Durmitor's Black Lake (p116), and the Vrmac ridge in the Bay of Kotor. Hard-core hikers should consider tackling the Peaks of the Balkans trail (Prokletije Mountains) or the 180km Coastal Mountain Traversal (p92).

Canyoning

Montenegro is run through with countless canyons, and organised expeditions up, down and through them are becoming more popular. Nevidio (p118), just south of Durmitor National Park, is one of the most visited; active tours of Sopot (p40) near Herceg Novi, Škurda (p48) above

EXPERT HELP

Rafting, kayaking, canyoning and skiing can be easily organised when you get to Montenegro, but arranging mountain guides, access to huts, specialist equipment and logistical support for more difficult expeditions can be a nightmare. If you're planning an action-intensive holiday, it is well worth engaging the services of one of the agencies that specialise in such things. Options include the following:

Black Mountain (p38)

Montenegro Adventures (p103)

Undiscovered Montenegro (p171)

Montenegro Adventure Centre (p67)

Explorer Tourist Agency (p113)

Anitra Travel Agency (p108)

Summit Travel Agency (p118)

Active Travels Montenegro (p38)

Montenegro+ (p53)

Kotor and Rikavac and Medjurečje (p79) near Bar are also available. Of these, only Rikavac is suitable for kids; for the rest, a modicum of physical fitness is required, as are strong swimming skills.

If you're an experienced canyoner looking to choose your own adventure, get in touch with the crew at Extreme Canyoning (www.extremecanyoning.com); the website also has a full list of canyons in Montenegro and neighbouring Serbia.

Cycling

With so many mountains in Montenegro, it's no surprise that mountain biking is on the agenda. The National Tourist Office (www.montenegro.travel) has developed five 'top trails', outlined in a Wilderness Biking pamphlet (available from tourist offices). Montenegro Biking (www.pedalaj. me) is an independent affiliation of bike enthusiasts; their website has a wealth of information of Montenegrin trails and tours.

Montenegro Bed and Bike (www. bedandbike.me) is an accommodation network of cyclist-orientated hotels, hostels and eco-villages.

For a single day's cycling, consider the Vrmac ridge (starting near Kotor), the loop track from Cetinje through Lovćen

National Park or the loop from Virpazar through Crmnica field.

Skiing

Montenegro's ski season lasts from roughly January to March, with the peak time being around New Year. The best-equipped ski resort is near Kolašin, but the most reliable skiing is in Durmitor National Park, where there are slopes close to Žabljak with options for beginners or serious skiers. There are also small ski centres near Nikšić and Rožaje in the east. Cross-country skiing can be undertaken in Lovćen and Durmitor National Parks.

In the Air
Paragliding & Parasailing

Montenegro has plenty of precipices from which you can hurl yourself and while hang-gliding is yet to take off, paragliding is starting to soar. If you want the feeling of flying without having to jump off anything, you might like to try the less vertigo-inducing option of parasailing. Both activities are offered from near Bečići.

Regions at a Glance

Bay of Kotor

Views
Architecture
Food

Vistas of the Bay

Whether gazing at it from water level or from high above on the Lovćen road, the bay's mountain ramparts and inky waters will take your breath away.

Echoes of Venice

Built to last out of gleaming stone, the Bay of Kotor's numerous palaces and churches owe much to the influence of its one-time taskmaster to the north. Nowhere is this more apparent than in Perast, a little town bathed in the baroque.

Coastal Cuisine

The seafood dishes of the coast represent the best of the country's traditional cuisines. Try specialities such as grilled squid, fish soup, squid-ink risotto or simply grilled fish, drizzled with olive oil, parsley and garlic.

p34

Adriatic Coast

Beaches
History
Entertainment

Beach Life

Clear waters, mountain backdrops and a sunny summer conspire to bring the Mediterranean fantasy into reality. Rows of umbrellas and recliners blanket the busier beaches, but you can escape the tourist hordes in secluded spots such as Kraljičina Plaža and Drobni Pijesak.

Walled Towns

From the marbled streets of Budva's Old Town, to the cobbled lanes of Ulcinj's, to the ruins of Stari Bar, the coast's walled towns will transport you through time.

Party Central

Come summer, Budva becomes Montenegro's party capital. Up to 5000 people regularly dance the night away at the open-air Top Hill nightclub, while down by the water, a string of al fresco bars and clubs pulls punters day and night.

p63

Central Montenegro

Nature
History
Monasteries

National Parks

From the depths of Lake Skadar to the heights of Lovćen, Central Montenegro's national parks protect a broad range of habitats. Birdwatchers will find plenty to twitch about, especially around Skadar, which is categorised as a wetland of international importance.

The Royal Capital

Much of Montenegro's history, culture and national identity is tied to Cetinje, its former capital. That story is told through the town's historic buildings and an array of museums.

Spiritual Outposts

The monastic life is integral to the Serbian Orthodox faith, and this region is blessed with the country's most significant shrine, Ostrog Monastery. Almost as affecting are the tiny island monasteries scattered around Lake Skadar.

p90

Northern Mountains

Nature
Activities
Monasteries

Mountain Majesty

Large areas of rugged wilderness blanket this region, from Durmitor in the northwest to Prokletije in the southeast and Bjelasica in between. It's an extraordinary landscape that never fails to astound.

Outdoor Adventures

Durmitor is the activity capital of Montenegro. The big three are rafting, hiking and skiing, but there's also the potential for rock climbing, canyoning and mountaineering.

Frescoes & Icons

Not only does Morača Monastery have an exquisite setting, it contains an extraordinary wealth of religious art. Morača may be the most beautiful of Montenegro's monasteries, but Piva, Dobrilovina and Pljevlja's Holy Trinity are no slackers either.

p110

Dubrovnik (Croatia)

Views
Architecture
History

The City & the Sea

Gazing down upon the spectacularly beautiful Old Town provides such a thrill that the town's most popular attractions provide opportunities to do just that. Circle the city walls for an intimate perspective or take the cable car up Mt Srd for the bird's-eye view.

Stone & Marble

Wandering amid the honey-coloured stone buildings of the Old Town is like walking through a textbook on the history of European architecture. Everywhere you look there are impressive Romanesque, Gothic, baroque and Renaissance structures – still standing and still in use, despite the wartime battering.

Museums

Learn about the Republic of Ragusa in the Rector's Palace or brush up on more recent events at the Homeland War Museum and War Photo Limited.

p126

On the Road

Dubrovnik (Croatia) ⊙
p126

Northern Mountains
p110

Central Montenegro
p90

Bay of Kotor
p34

Adriatic Coast
p63

Bay of Kotor

Best Places to Eat

➡ Ribarsko Selo (p58)

➡ Byblos (p55)

➡ Konoba Ćatovića Mlini (p41)

➡ Galion (p50)

➡ Konoba Školji (p43)

Best Places to Sleep

➡ Hotel Aurora (p38)

➡ Hotel Hippocampus (p49)

➡ Klinci Village Resort (p58)

➡ Regent Porto Montenegro (p53)

➡ Old Town Hostel (p49)

Why Go?

Gorgeous, breathtaking, majestic, divine; however hefty your thesaurus, the brain-blowing beauty of the Bay of Kotor will leave you struggling for superlatives. Hemmed in by commanding cliffs and shape-shifting between rippling gulfs and sparkling straits, the cobalt cove even manages to defy geographic description: is it a fjord? A submerged canyon? It seems there's only one way to define *Boka Kotorska*: unmissable.

Scattered with photogenic medieval towns admiring their reflections in peacock-blue inlets, the compact bay – or simply 'Boka', as it's known in local parlance – is stitched together by a series of scenic, serpentine roads, making it easy to explore. As if determined to prove the 'good things come in small packages' adage, the region crams in everything from island monasteries and show-stopping citadels to adventure sports and extraordinary eateries, where waterfront views induce as much drooling as the fresh seafood. Whatever your bliss, you'll find it at Boka.

When to Go

➡ May is dry, with mild temperatures and fragrant Mediterranean foliage in bloom.

➡ June is the best month, with temperatures in the high 20s, low rainfall and off-peak prices.

➡ July and August are the hottest and driest months – but also the busiest and most expensive.

Climate

The weather in the outer section of the bay isn't markedly different from the pleasant Mediterranean climate of the coast. Southwest-facing Tivat has a reputation for being one of the sunniest spots. Cloud often drapes the high cliffs of the inner bay.

Crkvice in the Orjen massif above Risan is said to have the highest rainfall in Europe, averaging 5300mL per annum. The record was in 1937 when it hit 8065mL. Luckily, the karstic nature of the terrain causes the water to disappear into the limestone rather than flooding the towns below.

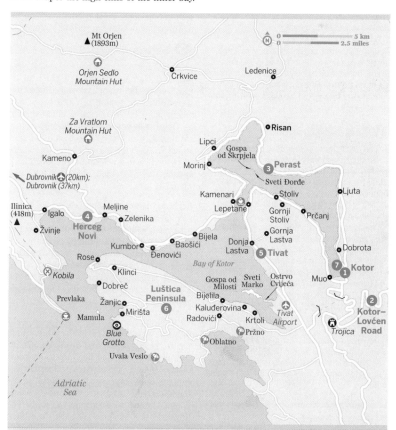

Bay of Kotor

1 Kotor's Old Town (p45) Randomly roaming the atmospheric laneways until you're at least a little lost.

2 Back road to Mt Lovćen (p48) Winding your way to dizzying views on the snaking back road from Kotor to Lovćen National Park.

3 Perast (p42) Admiring the baroque beauty of historic palazzos and churches.

4 Herceg Novi (p36) Cooling off in the shade with a drink on Trg Herceg Stejpana.

5 Tivat (p52) Seeing how the other half lives

in glitzy, glamorous Porto Montenegro.

6 Luštica Peninsula (p56) Losing yourself within the olive groves in the remote byways.

7 Kayaking (p48) Paddling your way to island fortresses, remote beaches and sea caves on a day tour.

ⓘ Getting There & Away

Jadranski Put (Adriatic Hwy) connects the Bay of Kotor to Dubrovnik and to Budva. A highway leaves the bay at Lipci, near Risan, and connects to the main Trebinje–Nikšić highway. Kotor and Cetinje are linked by a narrow and precipitous – but extremely scenic – back road that dates back to the Austrian occupation. There's an ambitious plan – as yet unfulfilled – to connect the two by a 15km cable car.

There are frequent buses to Budva and Podgorica from all around the bay, with some services heading as far as Sarajevo and Belgrade. Buses head between Kotor and Dubrovnik six times a day, via Herceg Novi.

Tivat airport welcomes domestic and international flights.

ⓘ Getting Around

A road wends its way around the entire coast, narrowing considerably between Kotor and the car ferry and on the Luštica Peninsula. From Kotor the main road takes a tunnel and comes out near Tivat airport. A car ferry crosses back and forth between Kamenari and Lepetane at the bay's narrowest point.

There are three main bus routes in the Boka. Frequent services take the coastal road from Herceg Novi to Kotor, stopping at all the villages along the way. Buses also connect Herceg Novi to Tivat via the car ferry and Kotor to Tivat via the tunnel.

In summer, taxi boats are a useful form of transportation, particularly between Herceg Novi and the beaches on the Luštica Peninsula. They're easy enough to find in the busy marinas in July and August but more difficult at other times. **Montenegro Water Taxi** (☏ 069-973 737; www.watertaxi.info; ⊘7am-midnight Jun-Aug, 8am-8pm Apr, May & Sep-Nov) is a reliable option.

Herceg Novi

☏ 031 / POP 19,536

Standing at the entrance to the Bay of Kotor like an eager host, Herceg Novi (Херцег Нови) welcomes visitors with bright bouquets, sparkling seas and almost-constant sunshine. Can't find the party? Look down; it's all happening in Stari Grad (Old Town), a few dozen wonky steps below the main street. Though its shiny squares, elegant churches and formidable fortresses are centuries old, they're brought to life by the buzz of clattering cafes and the sound of pianos drifting from the windows of music schools. Further down, pebbly beaches and concrete terraces offer access to the bay's

best – and cleanest – swimming. Follow the pedestrian-only promenade and you'll hit Igalo, famed for its therapeutic mud.

'Novi' means 'new', and while this is indeed one of the newer towns on the bay, it's no spring chicken; the city was founded in 1382. 'Herceg' refers to Herceg (Duke) Stjepan Vukčić, who fortified the town in the 15th century; the most dramatic of the remaining fortifications are a little younger.

◉ Sights

Ulica Njegoševa AREA
(Map p37) Herceg Novi's Stari Grad is at its most impressive when approached from the pedestrian-only section of Ulica Njegoševa, which is paved in the same shiny marble as Dubrovnik and lined in elegant, mainly 19th-century buildings. The street terminates in cafe-ringed Trg Nikole Đurkovića, where steps lead up to an elegant crenulated clock tower (Map p37) (1667) that was once the main city gate.

Archangel Michael's Church CHURCH
(Crkva Sv Arhanđela Mihaila; Map p37; ⊘7am-midnight Jun-Aug, to 9pm Sep-May) Built between 1883 and 1905, this beautifully proportioned, domed Orthodox church sits flanked by palm trees at the centre of gleaming white Trg Herceg Stjepana (known as Belavista to the locals). The archangel is pictured in a mosaic above the door under an elegant rose window.

Kanli Kula FORTRESS
(Map p37; admission €2; ⊘9am-7pm) Kanli Kula means 'bloody tower', and this notorious former prison more than lived up to its name during Herceg Novi's years of Turkish rule (roughly 1482–1687); in the dungeon below the lower set of flagpoles, you can see where doomed inmates carved into the walls. The huge fort is a far more pleasant place these days, offering stupendous views over the town from its sturdy walls. During summer, it often hosts musical and theatrical performances.

Forte Mare FORTRESS
(Map p37) The bastion at the town's seaward edge was rebuilt by the Venetians during their 110-year stint as overlords (before the Austrians, French, Russians, Montenegrins, Austro-Hungarians, Serbs, Germans and Italians all had their turns). It's now used for film screenings on summer nights. In the sea below, you can see the ruins of the Citadela (Map p37), a victim of a major earthquake that hit the coast in 1979.

Herceg Novi

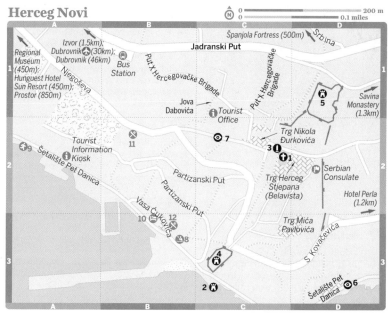

Herceg Novi

◉ **Sights**

1 Archangel Michael's
   Church.. C2
2 Citadela C3
3 Clock Tower...................................... C2
4 Forte Mare C3
5 Kanli Kula D1
6 Šetalište Pet Danica D3
7 Ulica Njegoševa.............................. C2

⊕ **Activities, Courses & Tours**

8 Kayak Herceg Novi........................... B3
9 Yachting Club 32 .... A2

🛏 **Sleeping**

10 Hotel Aurora...................................... B3

🍽 **Eating**

11 Gradska Kafana................................. B2
12 Konoba Feral...................................... B3

Šetalište Pet Danica   WATERFRONT
(Map p37) Named after five young women
named Danica who died during WWII, this
pedestrian promenade stretches along the
waterfront for more than 5km from Igalo to
Meljine. It's lined with summer bars, shops,
concrete swimming platforms and the odd
rocky cove; in places it ducks in and out of
tunnels carved through headlands. The strip
follows the route of a former train line that
once linked the coast to Sarajevo.

Regional Museum   MUSEUM
(Zavičajni muzej; www.rastko.rs/rastko-bo/muzej;
Mirka Komnenovića 9; admission €2; ⊙ 9am-5pm
Mon-Sat) Apart from the building itself (a
fabulous bougainvillea-shrouded baroque
palace with absolute sea views), the highlight of this little museum is its impressive
icon gallery.

Savina Monastery   CHRISTIAN MONASTERY
(Braće Grakalić bb; ⊙ 6am-8pm) From its hillside location on the town's eastern fringes,
this peaceful Orthodox monastery enjoys
wonderful coastal views. It's dominated by
the elegant 18th-century **Church of the Dormition** (Crkva Uspenja Bogorodice, literally
'the falling into sleep of the Mother of God'),
carved from Croatian pinkish stone. Inside
there's a beautiful gilded iconostasis, but
you'll need to be demurely dressed to enter.
The smaller church beside it has the same
name but is considerably older (possibly 14th
century) and houses the remains of frescoes.

ⓘ STEP BY STEP

Herceg Novi is extremely hilly and the fastest way from the highway to the beach is via one of the numerous sets of steps. Charming as the stairways *(stepenište)* are, they make Herceg Novi one of the most challenging towns in Montenegro for the mobility-impaired.

The monastery grounds also include a vineyard, part of the Savina Winery (www.castelsavina.me) located on the neighbouring estate.

Savina is well signposted from the large roundabout on the highway at Meljine.

🏃 Activities

Herceg Novi is arguably the country's best base for arranging active pursuits, with a diverse network of professional, customer-focused, environmentally aware businesses offering a huge variety of options.

Kayak Herceg Novi   KAYAKING

(Map p37; ☑ 067-531 366; www.kayak-hercegnovi.com; Zalo Beach; hire per 1/4/8hr from €5/15/25) Don't just admire the beautiful bay from the Old Town and along the promenade: hop aboard a kayak and explore it! In addition to rentals, this outfit also runs guided kayaking tours (half-/full day from €20/50) to Rose, Dobreč, Igalo and Mamula Island.

Yachting Club 32   BOATING

(Map p37; ☑ 069-263 888; Šetalište Pet Danica 32) Hires jet skis (€45 per 30 minutes), pedal boats (€7 per hour) and mountain bikes (€3/6/15 per one hour/three hours/day). If all that sunshine has tuckered you out, it's a top spot to kick back with a drink and do some water-watching.

Adriatic Blue   SCUBA

(☑ 069-524 442; www.divingmontenegro.com) This friendly group explores the wrecks, underwater caves and islands of Boka Bay. Intro dives (€50), two-tank dives (€70) and PADI courses (from €300) include all gear and boat transfers.

Active Travels Montenegro   ADVENTURE

(☑ 068-658 285; www.activetravelsmontenegro.com) Local guys with excellent English lead rafting, hiking and canyoning trips, vineyard visits and sightseeing tours.

Black Mountain   ADVENTURE

(www.montenegroholiday.com) 🖉 An excellent full-service agency that can arrange pretty much anything, anywhere in the country, including mountain biking, diving, rafting, hiking, paragliding, canyoning, boat trips and wine tasting. It can take care of the basics too, such as accommodation, car hire and transfers.

🎉 Festivals & Events

Mimosa Festival   PARADE, MUSIC

(www.hercegfest.co.me; ☉ Feb) A mash of yellow blooms, marching majorettes, concerts and sports events.

🛏 Sleeping

Private rooms start at about €15 to €20 per person. Many advertise online, or look for signs saying *'sobe'* (rooms).

★ Hotel Aurora   BOUTIQUE HOTEL €€

(Map p37; ☑ 067-552 319; www.aurorahotel.me; Šetalište 5 Danica 42; d/apt €70/100; P 🛜) Famous (and famously quirky) Serbian director Emir Kusturica is to thank for converting Herceg Novi's former train station into this gorgeous seaside inn. The vintage rooms and apartments are comfortable and characterful (ask for one with a sea view) and the Aurora's location – right on the rambling promenade – is the best in town. There's a good on-site bar and restaurant, and – of course – a small cinema.

Hunguest Hotel Sun Resort   RESORT €€

(☑ 031-355 022; www.hunguesthotels.hu; Sveta bubala bb; d €105-260; P ❄ 🛜 ☒) The beach it straddles may be concrete, but the incredible pools, gorgeous bay views and excellent location near town more than make up for the lack of sand. The Hunguest is a sprawling beast with seemingly thousands of (fairly generic but good) rooms, and is a favourite with kids: if you prefer something intimate, look elsewhere. There are three restaurants, tennis courts, and a tour desk on-site.

★ Hotel Perla   HOTEL €€€

(☑ 031-345 700; www.perla.me; Šetalište Pet Danica 98; s/d/apt from €65/130/210; P ❄ 🛜) It's a 15-minute stroll from the centre but if it's beach you're after, Perla's position is perfect. The helpful staff speak excellent English and the front rooms of this medium-sized modern block have private terraces and sea views. Bikes are available for hire and there's a great kids' playground by the beach.

✖ Eating & Drinking

★ **Konoba Feral** SEAFOOD €€

(Map p37; ☑ 069-560 232; Vasa Ćukovića 4; mains €8-22) A *feral* is a ship's lantern, so it's seafood, not wild cat, that takes pride of place on the menu. The grilled squid is excellent; all meals come with massive servings of vegetables and salads. The wine list includes vintages from the nearby Savina Monastery. This charming place is consistently ranked as the best in town; book ahead if you want to sit on the terrace.

Gradska Kafana MEDITERRANEAN €€

(Map p37; ☑ 031-324 067; www.gradskakafana.me; Njegoševa 31; mains €6.50-15; ⊗ 8am-midnight) It may have a humble name (Gradska Kafana translates to 'city tavern'), but sophisticated dishes such as almond-stuffed squid and grilled prawns soaked in honey and orange sauce give the game away: this is a classy joint. The building itself could never be mistaken for a mere 'tavern', either: the former villa has been elegantly restored to match the beauty of its sea views.

Prostor BAR

(Njegoševa 78; ⊗ 7am-1am Mon-Thu, 7am-2am Fri & Sat, 10am-1am Sun) The name means 'space', and while there's not much of it in this gorgeous old building, Prostor is wonderful fun. On busy nights (especially when there's live music), it gets cramped, wild and smoky; you can catch a breather on the sweet outside terrace.

ℹ Information

Tourist Information Kiosk (Map p37; Šetalište Pet Danica bb; ⊗ 9am-11pm May-Sep) There are further kiosks in Igalo (Sava Ilića bb), Kamenari (500m from the ferry) and near the big roundabout in Meljine.

Tourist Office (Map p37; ☑ 031-350 820; www.hercegnovi.travel; Jova Dabovića 12; ⊗ 9am-10pm daily Jul & Aug, 9am-4pm Mon-Fri & 9am-2pm Sat Sep-Jun)

ℹ Getting There & Around

BOAT

Taxi boats ply the coast during summer, charging about €15 for a trip to the beaches on the Luštica Peninsula. You'll sometimes get a better rate in Igalo where there's more competition.

BUS

Buses stop at the **station** (Map p37; ☑ 031-321 225; Jadranski Put) just above the Old Town. There are frequent buses to Kotor (€4,

one hour), which stop at all of the small towns around the bay. Buses to Budva (€5 to €6) go via Kotor or on the ferry through Tivat (usually quicker, depending on the queues). Frequent services head to Cetinje (€7, 2½ hours) and Podgorica (€9, three hours), with some continuing as far as Rožaje (€17.50, seven hours).

International destinations include Dubrovnik (€10, two hours depending on time at the border), Sarajevo (€24, seven hours, at least two daily) and Belgrade (€30, 13 hours).

CAR

A torturous, often gridlocked, one-way system runs through the town, so you're best to park in the car park opposite the bus station if you're day tripping. In the centre of town, street parks are divided into two zones charged at either 50c or 80c per hour, or €5 per day; purchase tickets from newsagents or kiosks, circle the time and date, and display them on your dashboard. You can also pay by SMS: follow the directions on the signs.

TAXI

Taxi More (☑ 19730; www.taximore.com; minimum fare €1.30, per km 90c) Advertises set fares to Dubrovnik Airport (€60), Tivat (€45), Kotor (€50), Budva (€60) and Podgorica Airport (€110). You'll pay extra if there are queues for the Kamenari car ferry.

Around Herceg Novi

Herceg Novi's coastal sprawl starts at Igalo to the west, where the muddy silt from the sea floor is said to have therapeutic qualities. Heading east along the bay, you'll pass beachside communities at Zelenika, Kumbor, Đenovići, Baošići and the industrial town of Bijela before reaching Kamenari, where a ferry plies the waters to and from Lepetane. The beachy Boka vibe along this stretch may be in for a makeover; there are plans to open a mega-resort near Kumbor in 2018.

◎ Sights

Mt Orjen MOUNTAIN

Hulking Mt Orjen (1893m) separates Herceg Novi from Hercegovina and is higher than the more famous Mt Lovćen. It's a popular spot for hiking and mountain biking (bring plenty of water). A hiking trail commences near the bus station at Herceg Novi (look for the red and white markings); heading towards Kotor, take the first road to the left, followed quickly by a right turn. This is the start of the mammoth Coastal Mountain Traversal (p92) hiking path, which goes on to Lovćen, the shores of Lake Skadar, Mt Rumija and Bar.

There are more than 60km of marked tracks on the mountain. A relatively easy 16km round-trip hike goes from Herceg Novi to the small Sv Ilija church; follow the coast to Igalo and take the signposted trail.

For six months of the year, there is snow on Mt Orjen; even on a summer's day you should be prepared for a storm.

Planinarski Klub Subra (www.pksubra.me; guide per day from €70), the local mountaineering club, operates two huts on the mountain and can arrange guides.

Activities

Sopot Canyon   ADVENTURE SPORTS

Not far from Herceg Novi, this little-visited canyon was opened up in 2016 for organised expeditions with Active Travels Montenegro (p38). Five-hour canyoning trips (€115) include hiking through water, swimming and abseiling down waterfalls (15m to 65m). For confident swimmers aged 16 and up.

Sleeping

Camp Full Monte   CAMPGROUND €

(067-899 208; www.full-monte.com; campsite per person €12, tent rental 3-night minimum €20-25; May-Sep) Hidden in the mountains near the Croatian border, this small campground offers solar-generated hot water, odourless composting toilets and a whole lot of seclusion. In case the name didn't give it away, clothing is optional. There's a fully equipped kitchen, but meals can also be arranged. Customised 'glamping' holidays (week/fortnight €280/550 per person) are available, and include accommodation in a 'tent mansion'.

Igalo Spa   HOTEL €€

(031-658 555; www.igalospa.com; Sava Ilića 5, Igalo; r €41-53, ste from €60) More than just a Yugoslavia-era behemoth, this is also a health clinic, where guests can take advantage of the curative powers of Igalo's famous therapeutic mud (among other treatments). While the rooms haven't been as well cared for as visitors' health, caring staff, top views and the old-school bowling alley are top notch. Half- and full-board rates are also available.

Palmon Bay Hotel and Spa   RESORT €€€

(031-332 442; www.palmonbayspa.com; Sava Ilića 7, Igalo; d €150-240, ste €440; P ❄ 🛜 🏊) This sparkling new upscale resort is gorgeous inside and out. Looming from manicured grounds over a pretty pebbled beach, the hotel houses modern, clean rooms (some with exceptional views), four restaurants and a beautifully designed indoor pool/spa area. As befitting Igalo's reputation as a healing centre, the resort has numerous treatments, massages and saunas for guests to choose from.

Eating

Restoran Olimpija   SEAFOOD, MONTENEGRIN €€

(031-580 235; Kumbor; mains €4-15; 8am-11pm) The locals love this family-run place for its stupendous mama-cooked meals, down-home atmosphere and enormous portion sizes. *Meso ispod sača* (meat cooked under a metal lid with hot coals on top) is the speciality here, though the flavourful fish soup is more than worth loosening your belt for.

Leut   SEAFOOD €€

(Braće Pedišić 59-61, Meljine; mains €6.50-20) You'll need to make an effort to find this local favourite, but the pay-off comes in the form of excellent Bokelj-style seafood served on a large terrace facing the water. To get here, follow the sign to Savina at the giant Meljine roundabout and then take the first left.

Getting There & Around

To truly explore this area, it's best to have your own wheels, though there are tons of buses running between Herceg Novi and Igalo (€1.50, 10 minutes) and in the other direction through all the villages en route to Kamenari (€2, 30 minutes).

The **ferry** (031-673 522; www.ferry.co.me; car/motorcycle/bicycle/passenger €4.50/2/1/free; 24hr) between Kamenari and Lepetane runs 24 hours a day.

CYCLE THE SHORELINE

Cyclists should consider leaving the highway at Igalo and pedalling along the waterfront. In summer you'll be slowed by foot traffic but it's a much flatter, safer and more picturesque route than the highway. Apart from a few stretches where you'll be forced back on to the main road, you can travel most of the way to Kamenari alongside the water.

Morinj

032 / POP 230

Secluded in the first bend of the inner bay, the fishing village of Morinj (Морињ) is divided into *gornji* (upper) and *donji* (lower) sections, like many of the coastal villages. The silver dome of St Petka Church (Crkva Sv Petke) sparkles above, but the main attraction here is the pretty beach. It's a sheltered nook so you may see algae in places, but the water's mainly clear and the views down the bay are amazing.

Morinj is a peaceful place now, but between 1991 and 1992, 300 Croatian POWs and civilians were incarcerated at a prison camp here.

◉ Sights

Lipci Prehistoric Drawings   ARCHAEOLOGICAL SITE
You'd never know it – thanks to a distinct (and puzzling) lack of hype – but 3km up the road from Morinj, a quick hike will bring you to the Balkans' most comprehensive collection of prehistoric drawings. Created in the 8th century BC, the drawings – which include mystical animal and sun symbols – have been largely left alone: there's no signage bar a token street sign, no admission fee and no fences. If you're the Indiana Jones type, this one's for you.

To get here, head up the small single-lane road leading uphill after the lone Lipci road sign. Where the asphalt ends, follow the arrow up a rocky path (keep going past the cave) until you reach a cliff face. Look up. See paintings. Commence goosebumps.

🛏 Sleeping & Eating

Autocamp Naluka   CAMPGROUND €
(☑ 069-346 346; www.naluka.montenegro.com; campsites per adult/child €5/1, per tent/car/campervan €4/3.50/10; ☺ May-Sep) Pitch your tent under the mandarin and olive trees and next to the stream that bubbles out of a spring at a constant 10°C – the water's too cold for mosquitoes but perfect for keeping your beer cold! There are only squat toilets but the site is kept immaculate by its English-speaking owner.

★ Konoba Ćatovića Mlini   SEAFOOD €€€
(☑ 032-373 030; www.catovica-mlini.com; mains €12-25; ☺ 11am-11pm) This rustic former mill masquerades as a humble *konoba* (simple family-run establishment), but they doth protest too much: this is one of Montenegro's best restaurants. Watch the geese waddle while you sample the magical bread and olive oil, which appears unbidden at the table. Fish is the focus, but give the traditional Njeguši specialities a go. Whatever you

order, you will dream – while drooling – of it for years to come.

❶ Getting There & Away

Morinj is a 30-minute bus ride from either Herceg Novi or Kotor.

Risan
🎵 032 / POP 2040
While sunseekers still head to its small beaches, Risan (Рисан) has a rundown feel, not helped by the port and large (now-abandoned) hotel hogging its sea frontage. But Montenegro is booming, and with the explosion of mega-resorts, one can't help but believe Risan's ramshackle days are numbered.

It wouldn't be the first time Risan has risen from a slump. This is the oldest town on the bay, dating to at least the 3rd century BC when it was a fortified Illyrian town. After the Romans took over, the town exploded to a population of about 10,000, and its seaside was lined with sumptuous mansions.

Apart from the town's famous mosaics, not much remains from Risan's glory days, but those with a taste for history should take a stroll up Gabela, an atmospheric lane with interesting patterned cobbling dating from the Ottoman occupation.

◉ Sights

Mosaics   RUINS
(admission €2; ☺ 8am-5pm) In 1930, the foundations of a grand villa were discovered in Risan, complete with wonderfully preserved Roman mosaics from the 2nd century AD. The building's not much to look at from the outside, but within, you'll find a dining-room floor decorated with flowers, herbs, grapevines and squid, while other rooms have intricate geometric patterns. Best of all is the bedroom, with its glorious depiction of Hypnos, the Greek god of sleep, reclining on a pillow.

🛏 Sleeping & Eating

Risan is a good option for those with wheels who are keen to explore the region without the price tag of the more popular towns. Private apartments are your best bet. Many advertise online, or look for signs reading '*sobe*' (rooms).

Apartmani Risan   APARTMENT €
(☑ 032-371 077; www.apartmani-risan.com; Stara Slanica bb; apt from €35; P ❄ 🛜) Perched up

a precarious hill, the two great-value apartments here offer majestic views over the sea and to the brooding mountains beyond. Both apartments have plenty of space and good facilities; the larger one has a sleeping loft. The owners – Sasha and Radan – live on-site, and are happy to be as hands-on (or off) as you'd like.

Restoran Risan SEAFOOD, MONTENEGRIN €€

(☑ 032 371 805; mains €5-17; ☺ 7am-11pm) Looking across the bay from Risan's main drag, the town's eponymous restaurant ladles out large portions of fresh seafood (including scrumptious local mussels) and heartier fare (it's renowned for its beef stroganoff).

ⓘ Getting There & Away

Buses running between Herceg Novi (30 minutes, €2.50) and Kotor (20 minutes, €2) stop in Risan.

Just out of Risan, a road climbs up, up, up to Nikšić and Žabljak, branching out west to Trebinje in Herzegovina.

Perast

☑ 032 / POP 350

Looking like a chunk of Venice that has floated down the Adriatic and anchored itself onto the bay, Perast (Пераст) hums with melancholy memories of the days when it was rich and powerful. Despite having only one main street, this tiny town boasts 16 churches and 17 formerly grand palazzos. While some are just enigmatic ruins sprouting bougainvillea and wild fig, others are caught up in the whirlwind of renovation that has hit the town.

The town slopes down from the highway to a narrow waterfront road (Obala Marka Martinovića) that runs along its length. At its heart is St Nicholas' Church, set on a small square lined with date palms and the bronze busts of famous citizens.

Perast's most famous landmarks aren't on land at all: two peculiarly picturesque islands with equally peculiar histories.

⊙ Sights

Gospa od Škrpjela ISLAND

(Our-Lady-of-the-Rock Island) This iconic island was artificially created (on 22 July 1452, to be precise) around a rock where an image of the Madonna was found; every year on that same day, the locals row over with stones to continue the task. The magnificent church was erected in 1630 and has sumptuous Venetian paintings, hundreds of silver votive tablets and a small museum (€1). The most unusual – and famous – exhibit is an embroidered icon of the Madonna and Child partly made with the hair of its maker.

Boats (€5 return) run between Perast and the island during summer.

Sveti Djordje ISLAND

(St George's Island) Sveti Djordje, rising from a natural reef, is the smaller of Perast's two islands. It houses a Benedictine monastery shaded by cypresses, and a large cemetery, earning it the local nickname 'Island of the Dead'. Legend has it that the island is cursed...but it looks pretty heavenly to us.

St Nicholas' Church CHURCH

(Crkva Sv Nikole; treasury €1; ☺ 8am-6pm) This large church has never been completed, and given that it was commenced in the 17th century and the bay's Catholic community has declined markedly since then, one suspects it never will be. Its treasury contains beautifully embroidered vestments and the remains of various saints. Climb the imposing 55m bell tower for stunning views over the bay.

Perast Museum MUSEUM

(Muzej grada Perasta; adult/child €2/1; ☺ 9am-7pm) The Bujović Palace, dating from 1694, has been lovingly preserved and converted into a museum showcasing the town's proud seafaring history. It's worth visiting for the building alone and for the wondrous photo opportunities afforded by its balcony.

✦ Festivals & Events

Fašinada CULTURAL

(www.fasinada-cup.com; ☺ 22 Jul) In this traditional annual event, male descendents of Perast's leading families row a convoy of decorated and roped-together boats to deposit stones on Gospa od Škrpjela island. It's now accompanied by a two-day yachting regatta, the Fašinada Cup, with participants racing to Tivat and back.

Gadjanje Kokota CULTURAL

(☺ 15 May) Possibly even more distasteful than it sounds (Gadjanje Kokota translates as 'Shooting a Cock'), this tradition commemorates a 1654 victory by the people of Perast over the Turks. A competition is held to shoot a rooster, a gory event best avoided by animal lovers. Less distressing parts of proceedings include a Catholic procession, solemn Mass and members of the Boka

ℹ KAMENARI–LEPETANE CAR FERRY

The Bay of Kotor is a very peculiar shape. The entrance is guarded by two peninsulas that shelter the first section of the bay incorporating Herceg Novi and Tivat. The waters then narrow into a thin channel before the spectacular inner bay opens up. **Car ferries** (p40) wend their way across the narrowest point (the Verige Strait) from Kamenari (15km east of Herceg Novi) to Lepetane (5km north of Tivat). They depart roughly every 15 minutes (hourly after 10pm) and the journey only takes about five minutes.

The alternative, the coastal road along the bay to Kotor, is truly spectacular and should be travelled at least once, whether by car or bus. The distance between Herceg Novi and Kotor is only 43km, but it can easily take an hour, longer if you get stuck behind a truck on the narrow winding road.

There's no doubt that the ferry is quicker for Tivat or Budva, but in the height of summer there can be horrendous queues, sometimes stretching for kilometres. For Kotor, the benefit is more marginal. If there are no queues and you've already travelled the scenic route, you might consider catching the ferry and heading to Kotor via the tunnel south of the town. You're unlikely to gain more than about 10 minutes but you will save on petrol. Buses from Herceg Novi to Budva take both routes.

Long-held plans for a bridge spanning the Verige Strait may be edging closer to fruition. If completed, the four-lane cable-stayed Verige Bridge (981m) would cross between the two current ferry points, and significantly reduce traffic around the Bay. Watch this space...

Navy dancing the *kolo* (wheel dance) in the square.

🛏 Sleeping

Bogišić Rooms and Apartments APARTMENT €
(☑ 067-440 062; www.bogisicroomsapartment.com; Obala Marka Martinovića bb; s €25, d without bathroom €42, apt €70; P❄🛜) This welcoming place offers great value for money. The rooms aren't massive, but they're comfortable, cute and right on the waterfront. The hosts have Montenegrin hospitality down pat; you'll want for naught here. The single room and two-bedroom apartment have kitchenettes.

★**Palace Jelena** BOUTIQUE HOTEL €€€
(☑ 032-373 549; www.palacejelena-perast.com; Obala Marka Martinovića bb; d €80-140; ❄🛜) This quaint, family-run hotel isn't suffering from delusions of grandeur; its four atmospheric rooms and lovely restaurant are actually located within a palace (the Lučić-Kolović-Matikola Palace to be precise). It's so close to the shore that you can hear waves lapping from your room. All rooms have gorgeous sea and island views; the most expensive has a balcony.

Hotel Conte APARTMENT €€€
(☑ 032-373 687; www.hotelconte.me; apt €130-290; ❄🛜) Conte is not so much a hotel as a series of deluxe studio to two-bedroom apartments in historic buildings scattered around St Nicholas' Church. The sense of age resonating from the stone walls is palpable, even with the distinctly nontraditional addition of a Jacuzzi and sauna in the flashest apartment. It's worth paying extra for a sea view.

🍴 Eating & Drinking

★**Konoba Školji** SEAFOOD, MONTENEGRIN €€
(☑ 069-419 745; Obala Marka Martinovića bb; mains €7-17; ⊙11am-11pm) This cute, traditional waterfront restaurant is all about the thrill of the grill; fresh seafood and falling-off-the-bone meats are barbecued to perfection in full view of salivating diners. Thankfully, they're not shy with the portion sizes; the delightful/maddening smell of the cooking and the sea air will have you ravenous by the time your meal arrives.

★**Restaurant Conte** SEAFOOD €€€
(☑ 032-373 687; Hotel Conte; mains €9-25; ⊙8am-midnight; 🛜) If you don't fall in love here – with Perast, with your dining partner, with a random waiter – consider your heart stone; with its idyllic island views, lashings of flowers and super-fresh oysters (hello, aphrodisiacs) on the menu, this place is ridiculously romantic. You'll be presented with platters of whole fish to select from; the chosen one will return, cooked and silver-served, to your table.

Beach Bar Pirates BAR
(recliner/umbrella €2.50/1.50; ⊙Jun-Sep) Tucked under the road on the Risan edge

of Perast, this little beach bar serves beers, cocktails and coffees. It often hosts live music acts and beach parties. It's also the best spot in Perast for a swim.

ⓘ Information

There are no banks or ATMs in Perast (though credit cards are accepted almost everywhere).

ⓘ Getting There & Away

Paid parking is available on either approach to town; car access into the town itself is restricted.

There's no bus station but buses to and from Kotor (€1.50, 25 minutes) stop at least every 30 minutes on the main road at the top of town.

Water taxis zoom around Boka Bay during summer and call into all ports, including Perast.

Dobrota

🕿 032 / POP 8170

Dobrota (Доброта) is effectively a residential suburb of Kotor, starting north of Kotor's Old Town and stretching along the shoreline for 5km. Despite the close proximity to its famous neighbour, it retains a distinctive feel. While Kotor looks inwards from its walls, Dobrota gazes out to sea.

Foreign investors have renovated many of the decaying palazzos, some of which are much grander than those you'll find in Perast or Kotor. Soak it all up with an evening sashay along the elegant paved boardwalk tracing the water's edge.

⊙ Sights

St Eustace's Church CHURCH
(Crkva Sv Eustahija) Cavernous St Eustace's dates from 1773 but has a 19th-century steeple and a little walled graveyard. It houses a valuable collection of paintings, including by Bellini and baroque master Carlo Dolci. Opening hours are iffy: you may be able to get in on Sundays.

Žuta Plaža BEACH
Private swimming platforms take up much of the waterline, but this pebbly stretch closest to Kotor is open to everybody. It's a beautiful spot for a swim, with the sheer mountain walls looming above, but it should be noted that there have been problems with water quality here.

🛏 Sleeping

Dobrota is a perfect base for exploring Kotor at arm's length from the noise and flurry

of the Old Town. During summer, there are hundreds of private rooms and apartments available. Seek them out online or ask around; whomever you ask will invariably have a cousin (or a cousin's cousin) with accommodation to rent.

Montenegro Hostel 4U HOSTEL €
(🕿067-675 070; Donji put bb; dm €10-13; ❄🤖) This buzzy hostel may be away from the clamour of the Old Town, but that doesn't mean sleep will come easy. If drinking games, nightly knees-ups and beach parties are your thing, you're unlikely to be interested in catching any zzzzs anyway. The fun-loving staff here somehow find the time to keep the place spotless.

★Palazzo Radomiri HOTEL €€€
(🕿032-333 172; www.palazzoradomiri.com; Dobrota 220; s/d/ste from €160/180/240; ☺Apr-Oct; 🅿❄🤖⛱) This honey-coloured early-18th-century palazzo on the Dobrota waterfront, 4km north of Kotor's Old Town, has been transformed into a first-rate boutique hotel. Some rooms are bigger and grander than others, but all 10 have sea views and luxurious furnishings. Guests can avail themselves of a small workout area, sauna, pool, private jetty, bar and restaurant.

✕ Eating

Caffe del Mare INTERNATIONAL €
(🕿067-279 189; Donji put bb; mains €4.80-12; ☺8am-11pm) Pasta, burgers, pizzas; they've got all the classics here and do them remarkably well (the spicy *Diavolo* pizza is bliss for those with a taste for the hot stuff). Best of all, it does free deliveries all over Dobrota and Kotor for those nights you can't face another restaurant.

Restoran Stari Mlini SEAFOOD €€€
(🕿032-333 555; www.starimlini.com; Ljuta bb; mains €10-22) It's well worth making the trip to Ljuta, just north of Dobrota, to this magical restaurant set in and around an 18th-century flour mill by the edge of the bay. It's pricier than most and the service is variable, but the food is excellent and the setting wonderfully romantic.

ⓘ Information

Kotor Health Centre (Dom zdravlja; 🕿032-334 533; www.www.domzdravljakotor.me; Jadranski Put bb) Kotor's main clinic.

❶ Getting There & Away

A one-way road runs along the waterfront heading south towards Kotor. This road can either be accessed from Jadranski Put at the top end or from a side road about halfway along. Expect an extremely slow crawl along here in summer.

Kotor

🎵 032 / POP 5340

Wedged between brooding mountains and a moody corner of the bay, the achingly atmospheric Kotor (Котор) is perfectly at one with its setting. Hemmed in by staunch walls snaking improbably up the surrounding slopes, the town is a medieval Middle-Ages maze of museums, churches, cafe-strewn squares and Venetian palaces and pillories. It's a dramatic and delightful place where the past coexists with the present; its cobblestones ring with the sound of children racing to school in centuries-old buildings, lines of laundry flutter from wrought-iron balconies, and hundreds of cats – the descendants of seafaring felines – loll in marble laneways. Come nightfall, Kotor's spectacularly lit-up walls glow as serenely as a halo; behind the bulwarks, the streets buzz with bars, live music – from soul to serenades – and castle-top clubbing.

Budva's got the beaches, and nearby Dubrovnik's got the bling, but for romance, ambience and living history, this Old Town outflanks them all.

History

It's thought that Kotor began as Acruvium, part of the Roman province of Dalmatia. Its present look owes much to nearly 400 years of Venetian rule when it was known as Cattaro. In 1813 it briefly joined with Montenegro for the first time, but the Great Powers decided to hand it back to Austria, where it remained until after WWI. There's a strong history of Catholic and Orthodox cooperation in the area.

◉ Sights

The best thing to do in Kotor is to let yourself get lost and found again in the maze of winding streets. You'll soon know every nook and cranny, but there are plenty of old churches to pop into, palaces to ogle, and many coffees and/or vinos to be drunk in the shady squares.

Sea Gate   GATE

(Vrata od Mora; Map p46) The main entrance to the town was constructed in 1555 when it

was under Venetian rule (1420–1797). Look out for the winged lion of St Mark, Venice's symbol, which is displayed prominently on the walls here and in several other spots around the town. Above the gate, the date of the city's liberation from the Nazis is remembered with a communist star and a quote from Tito. An enormous (and inexplicable) bench outside the entrance makes for amusing happy snaps.

As you pass through the gate, look for the 15th-century stone relief of the Madonna and Child flanked by St Tryphon and St Bernard. Stepping through onto Trg od Oružja (Weapons Sq), you'll see a strange stone pyramid in front of the **clock tower** (Map p46) (1602); it was once used as a pillory to shame wayward citizens.

Town Walls   FORTRESS

(Map p46; admission €3; ⏱ 24hr, fees apply 8am-8pm May-Sep) Kotor's fortifications started to head up St John's Hill in the 9th century and by the 14th century a protective loop was completed, which was added to right up until the 19th century. The energetic can make a 1200m ascent up the fortifications via 1350 steps to a height of 260m above sea level; the views from up here are glorious. There are entry points near the North Gate and behind Trg od Salate; avoid the heat of the day and bring lots of water.

St Tryphon's Cathedral   CHURCH

(Katedrala Sv Tripuna; Map p46; Trg Sv Tripuna; admission €2.50; ⏱ 8am-7pm) Kotor's most impressive building, this Catholic cathedral was consecrated in the 12th century but reconstructed after several earthquakes. When the entire frontage was destroyed in 1667, the baroque bell towers were added; the left one remains unfinished. The cathedral's gently hued interior is a masterpiece of Romanesque architecture with slender Corinthian columns alternating with pillars of pink stone, thrusting upwards to support a series of vaulted roofs. Its gilded silver bas-relief altar screen is considered Kotor's most valuable treasure.

Maritime Museum of Montenegro   MUSEUM

(Pomorski muzej Crne Gore; Map p46; www.museummaritimum.com; Trg Bokeljske Mornarice; adult/child €4/1; ⏱ 8am-6.30pm Mon-Sat, 9am-1pm Sun Apr-Oct, 9am-5pm Mon-Sat, to noon Sun Nov-Mar) Kotor's proud history as a naval power is celebrated in three storeys of displays housed in a wonderful early-18th-century palace. An audio guide helps

Kotor

N
0 _____ 200 m
0 _____ 0.1 miles

To Dobrota (1.1km);
Kotor Health Centre (1.1km);
Perast (13km); Risan (17km);
Herceg Novi (43km)

25

18 Tabačina

Ladder of
Cattaro
(150m)

12

Jadranski Put

Škurda River

5
Trg
od Drva
8

11

13

9

22

17 27

Entry to
Town Walls

23

15

Trg
od Mljeka

24

Trg
Sv Luke
7

14

Tourist
Information
Booth

6

2

Trg
od Kina

Trg
od Oružja

4
Trg
Bokeljske
Mornarice

Croatian
Consulate

26

Trg
od Brašna

Trg Sv
Tripuna
10

Jadranski Put

Trg od
Salata

Entry to
Town Walls

Bay of
Kotor

16
21

19

20

3

Gurdič
Spring

ŠURANJ

ŠKALJARI

Limili (200m);
Prčanj (4km)

(250m); Tivat (11km);
Budva (23km)

Kotor

BAY OF KOTOR KOTOR

explain the collection of photographs, paintings, uniforms, exquisitely decorated weapons and models of ships.

St Nicholas' Church CHURCH
(Crkva Sv Nikole; Map p46; Trg Sv Luke) Breathe in the smell of incense and beeswax in this relatively unadorned Orthodox church (1909). The silence, the iconostasis with its silver bas-relief panels, the dark wood against bare grey walls, the filtered light through the dome and the simple stained glass conspire to create a mystical atmosphere.

St Luke's Church CHURCH
(Crkva Sv Luke; Map p46; Trg Sv Luke) Sweet little St Luke's speaks volumes about the history of Croat-Serb relations in Kotor. It was constructed in 1195 as a Catholic church, but from 1657 until 1812 Catholic and Orthodox altars stood side by side, with each faith taking turns to hold services here. It was then given to the Orthodox Church. Fragments of 12th-century frescoes still survive along with two wonderfully painted iconostases: a 17th-century one in the main church and one from the 18th-century in the chapel of St Spiridon, another saint venerated by both faiths.

St Mary's Collegiate Church CHURCH
(Crkva Sv Marije Koleđate; Map p46; Trg od Drva) Built in 1221 on the site of a 6th-century basilica, this Catholic church is distinguished by impressive 20th-century bronze doors covered in bas-reliefs, a particularly gruesome larger-than-life crucifix, and a glass coffin

containing the body of Blessed Osanna of Cattaro (1493–1565). She was what is known as an anchoress, choosing to be walled into a small cell attached to a church so as to devote her life to prayer.

Cats Museum MUSEUM
(Map p46; www.catsmuseum.org; near Trg od Kina; admission €1; ⊙10am-6pm) Crazy cat people and those with a fondness for whimsical vintage art will adore this charming museum, home to thousands of moggie-themed ye olde postcards, lithographs, prints, jewellery and beautiful antique advertisements. The small admission fee goes towards taking care of Kotor's famous felines.

⚓ Activities & Tours

Various tour boats leave from opposite the Old Town to explore the bay; expect to pay upwards of €15 for a day tour. If you're keen to potter around the Boka on a boat of your own, you'll be disappointed unless you have a boat licence. Most hire companies supply skippers and cater firmly to the top end.

Ladder of Cattaro HIKING
FREE The truly vigorous can climb the ancient caravan trail known as the Ladder of Cattaro, which starts near the Škurda River and zigzags up the mountain to join the Coastal Mountain Traversal in Lovćen National Park. The usual requirements for water/sturdy shoes/strong lungs apply.

BACK ROAD TO MT LOVĆEN

The journey from Kotor to Mt Lovćen, the ancient core of the country, is one of Montenegro's great drives. Take the road heading towards the Tivat tunnel and turn right just past the graveyard. After 5km, follow the sign to Cetinje on your left opposite the fort. From here, there's 17km of good but narrow road snaking up 25 hairpin turns, each one revealing a vista more spectacular than the last. Take your time and keep your wits about you; you'll need to pull over and be prepared to reverse if you meet oncoming traffic. From the top, the views stretch over the entire bay to the Adriatic. At the entrance to Lovćen National Park you can continue straight ahead through Njeguši for the shortest route to Cetinje or turn right and continue on the scenic route through the park.

Adventure Montenegro   KAYAKING

(☑ 069-049 733; www.adventuremontenegro.com) Who needs a noisy speedboat when you can paddle in peace? Rent a kayak (per day single/double kayak €20/25) and explore the bay on your own terms. The group also runs eight-day kayaking holidays (€700) if you just can't get your land-legs back.

Kotor Open Tour   BUS

(tickets €20; ⊙ 9am-5pm, departing every 30min) On sunny days during summer, these open-top, hop-on-hop-off sightseeing buses ply the busy road between Kotor, Perast and Risan, showing off the hot spots (apart from the pedestrian-free Stari Grad, of course) and providing histories and explanations via multi-language audio guides. The ticket price includes admission to the museums in Perast and Risan.

You can't pre-book a ticket; just look out for the women wearing red T-shirts near the Sea Gate, or ask at the tourism information booth.

Kotor Bay Tours   TOURS

(☑ 069-152 015; www.kotorbaytours.com) This well-organised group offers tons of tours and activities, from sunset hikes and village visits up the Town Walls (€40, three hours) to boat/kayak/cycle trips around Kotor, Perast and Dobrota (€60). Gourmands won't want to miss their 'All about Mussels' tour (€50): in addition to the requisite walk around Kotor's Stari Grad and a jaunt out to Perast's islands, the junket includes hours of eating and drinking your fill at a local mussel farm.

Montenegro Submarine   BOATING

(Map p46; ☑ 069-576 355; www.montenegrosubmarine.me; Central Park; adult/child from €12/8; ⊙ 9am-8pm March-Nov) Want to find out if Kotor Bay is as beautiful down below as it is on top? Hop aboard one of these really quite adorable semi-submersibles and find out. Hour-long day and night tours cruise the bay, while three-hour jaunts explore Perast's magical Sveti Đorđe and Gospa od Škrpjela islands. There's above-water seating as well if you prefer your scenery not entirely blue.

Škurda Canyon   ADVENTURE SPORTS

The much-photographed St John's Hill hides a secret: the magnificent Škurda Canyon. In addition to the obviously splendid views of the Old Town, the canyon – about an hour's clamber from Kotor – is riddled with sheer, smooth drops, tunnels and waterfalls. Canyoning trips (average €80) are run by Kotor Bay Tours and Montenegro+ (p53). Whoever you go with, expect to spend about an hour getting to the canyon plus anywhere from two to four hours making the descent.

★☆ Festivals & Events

Camellia Day   CULTURAL

(⊙ mid-Mar) A celebration of the bloom that enlivens many Kotor gardens in mid-March. Includes the Camellia Ball, where a prominent local woman is chosen as the Lady of the Camellia.

Summer Carnival   CARNIVAL

(⊙ Aug) A condensed version of the main (winter) carnival staged at a more tourist-friendly time.

Kotor Art   PERFORMING ARTS

(www.kotorart.me) Kotor's summer arts festival acts as an umbrella for several established events, including the Children's Theatre Festival (www.kotorskifestival.me; ⊙ early Jul), Don Branko's Music Days (featuring international artists performing classical music in Kotor's squares and churches from mid-July to mid-August), Perast's Klapa Festival, and assorted workshops, lectures and touring productions.

Traditional Winter Carnival CARNIVAL
(☺ Feb) Carrying on the Venetian Renaissance tradition with two weeks of masked balls, parades and performances.

Boka Night CULTURAL
(☺ mid-Aug) Decorated boats light up the bay, fireworks explode in the sky and the populace parties like there's no tomorrow.

Boka Navy Day CULTURAL
(☺ 26 Jun) Dating back to 1420, on 26 June the traditionally clad sailors are presented with the flag and keys of the city and perform the *kolo* (circle dance).

🛏 Sleeping

Although the Stari Grad is a charming place to stay, you'd better pack earplugs. In summer, the bars blast music onto the streets until 1am every night, rubbish collectors clank around at 6am and the chattering starts at the cafes by 8am. Enquire about private accommodation at the tourist information booth.

★ Old Town Hostel HOSTEL €
(Map p46; ☎ 032-325 317; www.hostel-kotor.me; near Trg od Salata; dm €18-22, d €50, without bathroom €30, apt €55; ✳ 🖨) If the ghosts of the Bisanti family had any concerns when their 13th-century palazzo was converted into a hostel, they must be overjoyed now. Sympathetic renovations have brought the place to life, and the ancient stone walls now echo with the cheerful chatter of happy travellers, mixing and mingling beneath the Bisanti coat of arms.

★ Palazzo Drusko GUESTHOUSE €€
(Map p46; ☎ 032-325 257; www.palazzodrusko.me; near Trg od Mljeka; s/d from €50/88; ✳ 🖨) Loaded with character and filled with antiques, this venerable 600-year-old palazzo is a memorable place to stay, right in the heart of the old town. Thoughtful extras include a guest kitchen, 3D TVs and old-fashioned radios rigged to play Montenegrin music.

Hotel Marija HOTEL €€
(Map p46; ☎ 032-325 062; www.hotelmarija.me; Stari Grad; r €65-130; ✳) This charming little hotel occupies a beautiful palazzo in the centre of the Old Town and although the decor of the rooms is a little old-fashioned, it's very comfortable, clean and has a romantic feel, despite its dated furnishings. One room has a balcony for those Juliet moments. The location is unbeatable, but be warned: the walls aren't soundproofed.

Tianis APARTMENT €€
(Map p46; ☎ 032-302 178; www.tianis.net; Tabačina 569; apt €105-160; 🅿 ✳ 🖨) Well located without being in the midst of the melee, this friendly establishment has a clutch of clean, comfortable apartments of varying sizes, some of which have magical views across the Škurda River to the Old Town from their terraces.

★ Hotel Hippocampus BOUTIQUE HOTEL €€€
(Map p46; ☎ 068-889 862; www.hotelhippocampus.com; near Trg od Mljeka; d €140-260; ✳ 🖨) The hippocampus is the part of the brain responsible for memories, and you'll have plenty of those after a stay at this gorgeous boutique hotel. The owner is an architect, and it shows: every inch of the place is elegant, interesting and evocative. They haven't placed style over substance, though: the beds are comfortable, the rooms are spacious and the staff attentive.

Hotel Cattaro BOUTIQUE HOTEL €€€
(Map p46; ☎ 032-311 000; www.cattarohotel.com; near Trg od Oružja; d €150-200, ste €259-300; ✳ 🖨) Perched up in the Town Walls, Cattaro looks down over the bay, Old Town and mountain battlements, offering a vista that's tough to beat. Within, the rooms are spacious and elegant but don't tend to let in a lot of light. The popular Citadela bar is attached to the hotel, and Kotor's king of clubs – Maximus – is a stagger away. Thankfully, rooms are soundproofed.

🍴 Eating

There are dozens of restaurants, bakeries and takeaway joints on Kotor's cobbled lanes. Most restaurants stick to the tried-and-true Montenegrin/seafood theme; just pick a place that grabs you and dive in. For the sweet-toothed, cherry-filled strudel is a speciality of the region. Self-caterers can stock up at the **market** (Map p46; ☺ 7am-2pm) under the town walls, or at the big supermarket within the **Kamelija** (Map p46; www.kamelija.me; Jadranski Put; ☺ 8am-11pm) shopping centre, about a five-minute walk from the Old Town.

Restoran Galerija MONTENEGRIN, SEAFOOD €€
(Map p46; ☎ 068-825 956; www.restorangalerija.com; Šuranj bb; mains €7-20; ☺ 11am-11.30pm) This bustling place on the waterfront excels in both meat and seafood, as well as fast and attentive service (along the coast, you'll often find these things are mutually exclusive).

Try the prawns or mixed seafood in buzara sauce, a deceptively simple – yet spectacularly sublime – blend of olive oil, wine, garlic and mild spices.

Galion
SEAFOOD €€€

(Map p46; ☑ 032-325 054; Šuranj bb; meals €12-23; ⊘ noon-midnight) With an achingly romantic setting, extremely upmarket Galion gazes directly at the Old Town across the millionaire yachts in the marina. Fresh fish is the focus, but you'll also find steaks and pasta. It usually closes in winter.

Drinking & Nightlife

Kotor is full of cafe-bars that spill onto its squares and fill them with the buzz of conversation. Take your pick.

Bokun Wine Bar
WINE BAR

(Map p46; Trg Sv Luke; ⊘ 8am-1am) This evocative little nook is an ideal place to sample local wines (and perfectly paired meats and cheeses), all to the accompaniment of live music (think jazz, soul and samba) on weekends.

Bandiera
BAR

(Map p46; near Trg od Salata) Tourists don't tend to venture down this darker end of town; their loss, your gain. This cluttered, cavernous old-school bar is a top hang-out, where laid-back conversations and rock music take precedence over texting and techno.

Maximus
CLUB

(Map p46; ☑ 067-216 767; www.discomaximus.me; near Trg od Oružja; free-€5; ⊘ 11pm-5am Thu-Sat, nightly in summer) Montenegro's most pumping club comes into its own in summer, hosting big-name international DJs and local starlets.

Shopping

There are almost as many antique and souvenir shops as there are cats in the Stari Grad.

Cats of Kotor
ARTS & CRAFTS, CLOTHING

(Map p46; www.catsofkotor.com; near Trg od Mljeka; ⊘ 10am-6pm) Though you can't bundle them into your backpack (tempting though it may be), you can bring home the cats of Kotor in the form of beautiful, locally made handicrafts with a feline flavour. Part gallery, part boutique, this quirky shop sells everything from cat-themed jewellery and clothes to original artworks.

Mon Ami Wine House
WINE

(Map p46; near Trg od Mljeka; ⊘ 9am-3pm & 5pm-midnight) Local boutique wine producers rarely get a look-in on restaurant menus. If you'd like to sample a broader selection of Montenegro's output, this cute little shop offers tasting flights of five wines and three types of *rakija* (fruit brandy). Otherwise, just pick a pretty hand-painted bottle and take your chances.

ℹ Information

The post office and a choice of ATMs are on the main square, Trg od Oružja. There's a **medical clinic** (p44) in Dobrota.

Tourist Information Booth (Map p46; ☑ 032-325 950; www.tokotor.me; outside Vrata od Mora; ⊘ 8am-8pm Apr-Nov, 8am-5pm Dec-Mar) Stocks free maps and brochures, and can help with contacts for private accommodation.

ℹ Getting There & Away

The main road to Tivat and Budva turns off the waterfront road at a baffling intersection south of the Stari Grad and heads through a long tunnel.

The **bus station** (☑ 032-325 809; ⊘ ticket sales 6am-8pm) is to the south of town, just off the road leading to the tunnel. Buses to Herceg Novi (€4, one hour), Budva (€4, 55 minutes), Tivat (€2.50, 20 minutes) and Podgorica (€7.50, two hours) are at least hourly. Further flung destinations include Kolašin (€10.50, four hours), Dubrovnik (€14, two hours, six daily) and Belgrade (€30, 12 hours, seven daily). Find more fares and timetables at www.busticket4.me.

A taxi to Tivat airport should cost €7 to €10.

There's talk of building a 15km cable car between Kotor and Montenegro's historic capital of Cetinje. It's an extremely ambitious (and expensive) plan; if it comes to fruition, the super-scenic journey will take 40 minutes and pass near Njegoš Mausoleum (Mt Lovćen).

Prčanj

☑ 032 / POP 1200

A formerly prosperous maritime town, Prčanj (Прчањ) has lots of old stone buildings, a couple of restaurants, a bakery, a minimarket, a post office and Catholic churches that come in a choice of small, medium and XXL.

⊙ Sights

St Nicholas' Church
CHURCH

(Crkva Sv Nikole) Built in the baroque style in 1735, this medium-sized church has a

Franciscan monastery attached, although the last monks left in 1908. The church was badly damaged in the 1979 earthquake but wasn't fully restored until 2011. It contains a grand Venetian-built high altar containing an oil painting of St Nicholas flanked by wooden carvings of St Peter and St Paul.

Church of the Birth of the Blessed Virgin Mary CHURCH
(Crkva Rođenja Blažene Djevice Marije; ⊙7-9pm Mon-Sat, 9-11am Sun) Even the name of this whopping church is outsized. It's said to be the biggest religious building on the Adriatic coast and it certainly dominates this little town in a God-is-watching-you kind of way. It was begun in 1789 but not completed until 1908, when Catholics were in the majority in Prčanj.

St John the Baptist's Church CHURCH
(Crkva Sv Ivana Krstitelja) Simple, solid and semi-derelict, this tiny church dates from 1221 or 1397, depending on which resource you believe.

🛏 Sleeping & Eating
The hotels have good-quality restaurants with the obligatory bay views. The waterfront is dotted with local eateries selling grilled meats and fish.

Hotel Splendido HOTEL €€€
(☑032-301 700; www.splendido-hotel.com; Jadranska Magistrala; r €100-130, apt €130-180; P❋@🛰🏊) Splendido is magnifico. Completely gutted and fitted with comfortable modern rooms, this large stone palazzo still surveys the bay as solidly as it's ever done, although there's now a blissful terrace and swimming pool separating it from the water's edge. Its restaurant, Tramontana, is excellent and open to nonguests.

🛈 Getting There & Away
Heading north along the bay from Kotor to Prčanj, the road narrows to a single lane despite it being two-way, which makes for lots of fun and plenty of honking when a bus meets a truck coming in the opposite direction. Prčanj is 5km from Kotor.

Stoliv
☑032 / POP 350
Donji Stoliv (Lower Stoliv; Столив) is a pleasant seaside village with a huddle of stone houses surmounted by a grand church, 9.5km from Kotor. It's worth stopping here

to take the idyllic but steep half-hour's walk through the olive and chestnut trees to the upper village, Gornji Stoliv. Most of the families who lived here for centuries have now left, with only a few houses remaining in use and the rest in varying states of picturesque ruin. A church dedicated to the prophet Elijah (Crkva Sv Ilije), dating from 1553, keeps a lonely vigil. At 250m, the views over the bay to Perast are sublime.

Down in Donji Stoliv, several houses offer camping in July and August under their fig and olive trees for around €10 for two people with a car and tent. Facilities are basic (squat toilets with a basket for toilet paper) and water supplies sometimes run out. Keep an eye out for signs reading *auto kamp*. If you prefer to be out of the elements, ask around for private rooms *(sobe)* to let.

During summer, buses to and from Kotor stop at Stoliv.

Lastva
☑032 / POP 750
Lastva (Ластва) is a divided village, and the *gornja* (upper) section has been actively promoted to tourists for its rustic ambience. There's a decent road for starters, leading 3km up the hill. Gornja Lastva doesn't offer the same off-the-beaten-track satisfaction as Stoliv, but it's nice to see that this village has been kept alive, with kids darting about and old ladies dressed in black pottering about gathering wild herbs.

The best time to visit is the first Saturday in August, when a village fair is held.

🛈 Sights
St Mary's Church CHURCH
(Crkva Sv Marije) If you're lucky, the parish priest will be around to unlock this 15th-century village church, which reputedly has some accomplished Italian paintings inside.

🛏 Sleeping & Eating
Eco Hotel Carrubba BOUTIQUE HOTEL €€€
(☑032-540 153; www.septemberhotels.com; Donja Lastva; r from €130) Enjoy dreamy views from the terraces of this elegant 19th-century building, a mere step from the sea. It's a good option if you wish to be near Tivat while enjoying a tranquil remove. The attached restaurant is no slouch in the seafood department.

Waikiki Restaurant
& Beach Club
INTERNATIONAL €€

(☏069-141 710; www.waikikibeach-tivat.com; Donja Lastva; mains €7-20; ⊙7am-1am) Sprawling, sunny and scene-y, this complex tends more towards Tivat (or its namesake) than Donja Lastva. The seafood restaurant here is excellent; the very swimmable private beach, cocktail bar, sunbed service, squeal-inducing kids' playground and typically Mediterranean beach posturing offer good reasons to make a day of it.

ⓘ Information

Tourist Office (⊙8am-noon & 5-8pm Mon-Sat, 8am-noon Sun)

ⓘ Getting There & Away

From Stoliv, the road rounds the tip of the Vrmac Peninsula and passes the ferry terminal at Lepetane before popping out in the front section of the bay; Lastva is another 2km up the road.

Tivat

♪ 032 / POP 14,100

With bobbing super yachts, a posh promenade and rows of elegant edifices, visitors to Tivat (Тиват) could be forgiven for wondering if they're in Monaco or Montenegro. The erstwhile-mediocre seaside town has undergone a major makeover – courtesy of the multimillion-dollar redevelopment of its old naval base into a first-class marina – and while it bears zero resemblance to anywhere else in the country, Tivat is now attracting the uber-wealthy (and less-loaded rubber-neckers) in droves.

The town has a reputation as being one of the sunniest spots in Boka Kotorska. While Tivat will never rival Kotor for charm, it makes a pleasant stop on a trip around the bay, and is a useful base for exploring the sweet villages of the Vrmac and Luština Peninsulas.

⊙ Sights

Porto Montenegro
MARINA, VILLAGE

(Map p54; www.portomontenegro.com) Single-handedly responsible for Tivat's transformation, this surreal 24-hectare town-within-a-town occupies the former Arsenal shipyard and naval base. Primped, preening and planned right down to the last polished pebble, the almost impossibly glamorous complex includes five upmarket apartment buildings, a 'lifestyle village' of fancy boutiques, bars, restaurants and

leisure facilities, a museum, and berths for 450 yachts (with a total of 850 berths planned by completion). The Regent resort is situated in Porto's heart.

Porto is a phased development – at the time of research, construction was underway of another huge residential block and pool – but the works don't detract from the surreal feeling of finding yourself in a place usually reserved for those of otherworldly wealth.

Unsurprisingly, the project hasn't been without controversy: 3500 locals took to the streets to protest the sale of the shipyard – a state asset – to foreign investors (an international consortium of the exceedingly rich led by Candian businessman Peter Munk, who has since sold the complex to the government of Dubai) and the loss of 480 jobs. Yet many naysayers have been silenced by the improvements that are evident in the town.

The complex is open to the public and it's a pleasant place to stroll and ogle opulent yachts – if you're not prone to fits of rage at the injustices of contemporary economics.

The success of such of a venture relies partially on enticing yacht crews to dock here for the winter, so bars, restaurants and activity providers operate year-round (unlike most of the Montenegrin coast). Prices are generally geared more towards crew-members than oligarchs and, while expensive for Montenegro, are reasonable by European standards. It appears the strategy is having no small amount of success: the marina was named Superyacht Marina of the Year (2015) by the international Yacht Harbour Association and, in 2016, was recognised as one of the world's three best marinas.

Naval Heritage Collection
MUSEUM

(Zbirka Pomorskog Nasljeđa; Map p54; Porto Montenegro; adult/child €2/1; ⊙9am-4pm Mon-Fri, 1-5pm Sat) Porto Montenegro doffs its hat to its past with this well-curated display (in Montenegrin and English) devoted to the history of the Arsenal shipyard and naval base, housed in one of the site's beautiful old boat sheds. The star exhibits are too big for the museum: the two Yugoslav navy submarines drydocked outside (tours €5).

Parents can let the kids off the leash at an aptly nautical-themed playground right next to the museum.

Buća-Luković Museum & Gallery
MUSEUM

(Muzej i Galerija Buća-Luković; Map p54; ☏032-674 591; www.czktivat.me; Trg od kulture; ⊙8am-10pm Mon-Sat, 4-10pm Sun) FREE Aristocratic families from Perast, Dobrota and Kotor once built their summer residences at Tivat to take advantage of its sunnier outlook. One of the few survivors is this 500-year-old fortified enclosure with its own Catholic chapel, which once belonged to Kotor's Buća family.

The solid stone defensive tower houses a collection of Roman bits and bobs; next door is a well-presented ethnographical museum with fishing and farming artefacts. Head upstairs for beautiful jewellery and folk costumes. The gallery focuses on modern painting and sculpture and often hosts exhibitions.

Town Beach
BEACH

(Gradska Plaža; Map p54) You're better off heading to the Luštica Peninsula for a proper swim, but Tivat does offer a couple of options if you're desperate for a dip. Town Beach is a long concrete platform with a 20m pebbly section right by the main promenade. There's another pebbly beach, Belani (Plaža Belane; Map p54), just past the marina.

🏃 Activities

Montenegro+
WATER SPORTS

(Map p54; ☑069-190 190; www.montenegro plus.me; Jetty 1, Porto Montenegro; ☉9am-7pm) This well-organised group has active pursuits in Tivat covered. It rents stand-up paddleboards (two hours/half-day/full day €15/25/35), kayaks (half-/full day €40/60) and mountain bikes (€30 per day), plus it offers wakeboard sessions (from €75 for 30 minutes; lessons also available), PADI dive courses (enquire online) and tours, including guided kayak trips to hot spots including the Blue Grotto (€56), and a mountain-biking tour along the Vrmac ridge (€45).

Pura Vida
SPA

(Map p54; ☑032-540 356; www.puravida-spa.com; Porto Montenegro; massage from €30; ☉9am-9pm Mon-Sat, noon-8pm Sun) Of course Porto has a day spa, offering all the plucking, pummelling and pampering treatments you'd expect from a luxury resort.

Montenegro Cruising
CRUISE

(Map p54; ☑068-821 300; cruise €20; ☉10am May-Sep) Offers daily cruises during the tourist season on boats named *Vesna,* stopping at Žanjic beach, Herceg Novi, Perast's islands and Kotor; the boat returns to Tivat at 6pm. Budva-based travel agents commonly sell this cruise inclusive of bus transfers, with their clients finishing the cruise at Kotor.

⭐ Festivals & Events

Žućenica Fest
FOOD & DRINK

(☉early Jun) Unusual but popular festival celebrating all the weird and wonderful dishes that can be made from wild dandelion (and other local ingredients).

Carnival
CARNIVAL

(☉Feb) Like the other bay towns, Tivat's residents don their Venetian masks in February.

🛏 Sleeping

⭐ Hostel Anton
HOSTEL €

(Map p54; ☑069-261 182; www.hostelanton. com; Mažina bb; dm/r €11/27; 🛜) It's a 10-minute hike from Tivat town, but your weary legs will be forgotten once you arrive at this wonderful hilltop hostel. It's a hostel of the old-school: family-run, oddball art on the walls, instruments waiting to be picked up, and a very friendly, communal vibe. If glam is your bag, keep moving; amenities are functional but far from flash. Otherwise, prepare for a memorable stay.

Hotel Palma
HOTEL €€

(Map p54; ☑032-672 288; www.primorje.me; Šetalište Kapetana Iva Vizina; d €80-120, ste €300; ❄🛜) Recently renovated and fairly sparkling, the Palma ticks all the seaside-holiday boxes: it's got a private beach, a good restaurant, ocean views, comfortable beds and amiable staff. It's not quite Porto Montenegro...but then again, nor are the prices.

⭐ Regent Porto Montenegro
RESORT €€€

(Map p54; ☑032-660 660; www.regenthotels. com/regent-portomontenegro; Porto Montenegro; r €350-550, ste €930-1200; ❄🛜💺) A sparkling new hideout for the rich and famous (or lesser mortals having a serious splurge), this is the kind of place you can imagine seeing in the background of paparazzi shots. Utter luxury is the name of the game here, and not a euro has been spared in making this resort a world-beater in terms of glamour, design and services.

Though the resort has been modelled on opulent Italian palazzos, the neutral-palette room and suite decor is remarkably restrained; the designers have left the bay and mountain balcony views to speak for themselves. Facilities – including four gourmet restaurants, a 20m infinity pool and a first-class spa – are as chic as you'd expect, and staff are achingly professional.

Tivat

The resort is in the heart of the Porto Montenegro complex, meaning you can park your yacht (or just drool at someone else's), drop your bags and have the whole complex at your topsiders.

✗ Eating

You'll find Tivat's finest restaurants at Porto Montenegro. It's also a great place to check out if you're hankering after something other than the usual seafood or Montenegrin mixed grills, with Asian, Lebanese and Italian eateries all finding a place along the marina.

Self-caterers will find gourmet goods at the excellent **Bonella** (Map p54; Porto Montenegro; ☉ 8am-11pm) supermarket.

Prova   MEDITERRANEAN €€
(Map p54; ☎ 032-671 468; www.prova.co.me; Šetalište Iva Vizina 1; mains €7.50-18; ☉ 8am-1am) Shaped like a boat with chandeliers that look like mutant alien jellyfish, this upmarket eatery is the very epitome of chichi Tivat. All the outlandish trappings are not just subterfuge; the food, particularly the pasta, is excellent.

Tivat

★ **Byblos**   LEBANESE €€€
(Map p54; ☎063-222 023; www.byblos.me; Porto Montenegro; mains €8-27; ⊗7am-1am) This stunning new restaurant is one of those rare places that satisfies both the stomach and the spirit. The inside is heavy on atmosphere – all lanterns and elegant exotica – while the outdoor Mezze and Shisa Terrace is a billowy hideaway of posh private 'tents'. The food is sublime; the Lebanese chefs have taken their national classics and given them an upmarket spin. You won't find food like this anywhere else in Montenegro.

★ **One**   ITALIAN €€€
(Map p54; ☎067-486 045; Porto Montenegro; mains €9-25; ⊗8.30am-midnight) It bills its terrace view as 'the most expensive in the country', and considering said vista takes in trillions of euros worth of mega-yachts, it's probably right. But the pricey panorama isn't all this popular brasserie is about: One's authentic, excellent take on Adriatic cuisine is worth splashing out for. It also does magnificent Western-style breakfasts (from €6).

Mitsu   JAPANESE €€€
(Map p54; ☎032-540 230; Porto Montenegro; mains €11-21; ⊗9am-11pm) This hip eatery is the perfect remedy if you're starting to suffer from an overdose of pasta and grilled seafood. Sushi and sashimi are prepared in an open kitchen on the side of the dining room, and the menu stretches to the odd Chinese and Vietnamese (and – randomly – Indian) classic.

🍷 **Drinking & Nightlife**

Black Sheep   PUB
(Map p54; Ribarski put; ⊗8am-2am) This wonderful little gastropub swims against

Montenegro's tsunami of wines and *rakija*, serving up lashings of craft beers and cool cocktails. Hip, happening and occasionally hectic (weekends go off with live music and DJs), a night out here is as far from yachtie yahooing as you can get. On Sundays until 4pm, it dishes up sinfully fatty hangover brunches.

Clubhouse   BAR
(Map p54; www.facebook.com/TheClubhouse PortoMontenegro; Porto Montenegro; ⊗9am-1am Sun-Thu, to 2am Fri & Sat) Doing its very best to keep the yacht crews entertained, this lively little Aussie-run bar hosts live music and kooky themed nights, and screens international football and rugby matches. There's a good selection of imported beer, and visiting Antipodeans can drown their homesickness in 'flat white' coffee, Australian shiraz and New Zealand sauvignon blanc.

🛍 **Shopping**

As might be expected of a place designed with the mega-wealthy in mind, Porto Montenegro is busting at the designer seams with luxury-brand boutiques and speciality shops including an English-language **bookstore** (Map p54; www.novaknjiga. com; Porto Montenegro; ⊗8am-9pm, closed Wed & Sun).

ℹ **Information**

Tourist Office (Map p54; ☎032-671 324; www. tivat.travel; Palih Boraca 8; ⊗8am-3pm Mon-Fri, to noon Sat) Accommodation contacts and information about local sights and walks.

ⓘ Getting There & Around

AIR

Tivat airport (p172) is 3km south of town and 8km through the tunnel from Kotor. Taxis charge around €5 to €7 for Tivat, €10 for Kotor and €15 to €20 for Budva. As of 2016, there are direct flights between Tivat and Manchester and Gatwick.

You'll find car-hire counters at the airport.

BICYCLE

Bike Tivat (www.biketivat.com; subscription per day/week €5/30) has four automated docking stations scattered around Tivat and two in Donja Lastva. You'll need to purchase a subscription at the tourist office and then use an electronic card to unlock the bikes. Bikes are free for the first half-hour and then charged at 50c for up to an hour; subscriptions include up to four hours of use.

Mountain bikes can be rented through **Montenegro+** (p53).

BUS

Buses to Kotor (€2.50, 20 minutes) stop outside a silver kiosk on Palih Boraca. The main bus station is inconveniently located halfway between Tivat and the airport. From there, buses head to Herceg Novi (€3.50, 10 daily), Kotor (€2.50, seven daily), Budva (€3.50, at least hourly), Bar (€6.50, seven daily), Cetinje (€5, at least hourly), Podgorica (€7, at least hourly) and Belgrade (€28, at least five daily).

CAR

Tivat sits on the western side of the Vrmac Peninsula, which juts out into the Bay of Kotor and divides it in two. The quickest route to Kotor is to take the main road southeast in the direction of Budva, turn left at the major intersection past the airport and take the tunnel. The alternative is the narrow coastal road. For Herceg Novi, take the ferry from Lepetane, 5km northwest of town.

Around Tivat

Tivat town may be a mecca for the moneyed, but its surrounds are rich in natural and historic attractions. Three unspoiled islands, each with its own unusual tale to tell, are within easy reach of Tivat and all make for a pleasant day of exploring.

⊙ Sights

Ostrvo Cvijeća   ISLAND
(Island of Flowers) The overly poetically named Ostrvo Cvijeća (Island of Flowers) is accessed by an unlikely looking road that heads behind the airport and through a rundown area where a former tourist complex shelters people displaced by the region's most recent wars. At the very end of the pot-holed road is **St Michael the Archangel's Monastery** (Manastir Sv Arhanđela Mihaila). This is the area's most historically significant site. The sweet little 19th-century **Holy Trinity Church** (Crkva Sv Trojice) stands nearby, shaded by trees and protected by stone walls.

The remains of Roman mosaics have been discovered here, along with the ruins of a 9th-century church and Benedictine monastery. From the early 13th century, St Michael's was the seat of the Orthodox bishop of Zeta until it was destroyed by the Venetians in 1452.

Sveti Marko   ISLAND
(St Mark's Island) The larger of two islands stretching out in a line from Ostrvo Cvijeća, the heavily forested Sveti Marko (St Mark) has run wonderfully wild since its stint as a Club Med came to an end with the Yugoslav wars. Plans for the construction of a six-star resort come and go; for now, it lies green, glorious and abandoned.

Gospa od Milosti   ISLAND
(Our-Lady-of-Mercy Island) The diminutive Gospa od Milosti was once the residence of Kotor's Catholic bishops and is now a convent. A wooden statue of the Madonna kept in the church is said to have miraculous powers.

ⓘ Getting There & Around

Sveti Marko and Gospa od Milosti can be reached via water taxi – or by hitching a ride with a friendly yachtie – from either Tivat or Herceg Novi.

Luština Peninsula

Reaching out to form the southern headland of the Bay of Kotor, the lovely Luština Peninsula (Луштица) hides secluded beaches and a dusting of idyllic villages scattered among the olive groves of its remote southern edge. If you want to enjoy this magical area while it's still relatively untouched, you'd better get in quick: developers are snapping up Luština in droves.

The first section of the peninsula facing Tivat is already quite developed, with works on five-star resorts underway around Radovići and Pržno. At **Krtoli** the pebbly beaches look over the green swathe of St Mark's Island and the picturesque Our-Lady-of-Mercy Island, which are immediately offshore. If you're looking for a spot to chill out and relax by the water, you could do a lot worse. This area is cheaper and less frantic than most of the coast and some excellent midsized apartment hotels have sprung up. Further west, Bjelila is a cute little fishing village comprising a cluster of old stone houses dipping their feet in the water.

Continuing along the peninsula, the houses stop, the road gets narrower and the scenery gets greener and prettier. Climbing up the ridge on the way to Rose, a panorama of the bay opens up before you. If you're in the mood for a leisurely drive with a high probability of getting at least temporarily lost, continue on the narrow back roads from Rose that meander through the bucolic olive groves of the southern half of the peninsula. If you see signs for Radovići, you're still heading in the right direction.

Along the southern coastline is a string of clean beaches that are popular with day trippers travelling from Herceg Novi by taxi boat.

⊙ Sights

★ Blue Grotto
CAVE

(Plava Špilja) A popular cruise stop, the Blue Grotto gets its name from the mesmerising effect of the light reflecting through the clear water. Boats head into the 9m-high cave and allow you an opportunity for an iridescent swim. Most boat and kayak tour operators in the region offer trips out here; opt for one that arrives early, before the crowds descend.

Uvala Veslo
BEACH

It's rougher and rockier than most other peninsula beaches, but with super-clear water and steep rugged drop-offs, this secluded bay offers adventure galore for strong swimmers keen on snorkelling and cliff jumping. It's not one for the kids, but those seeking splendid isolation might just find their paradise here. There's a little signposted campground in an olive grove nearby.

Žanjic
BEACH

Sitting in a sheltered cove below the olive groves, Žanjic's 300m-long white pebbly beach, restaurants and bars attracts up to 1000 people a day in the height of summer. Come by car or water taxi or paddle over in a kayak.

Mirišta
BEACH

This beach may be smaller than neighbouring Žanjic, but it's every bit as popular. The Austro-Hungarian Arza fortress lies abandoned (for how long remains to be seen along this development-crazed coastline) at the tip of Mirišta; it's not in the best condition and safety isn't guaranteed, but if you simply can't help yourself, it's there for the exploring.

There's an excellent seafood **restaurant** (☑ 069-515485; www.restoranmirista.com; Mirišta; mains €8-22) right on the beach.

Plavi Horizont
BEACH

(Blue Horizon) Located in the little town of Pržno (not to be confused with the other Pržno near Sveti Stefan), Plavi Horizont is – for now – a definite candidate for the title of Montenegro's best beach; a gorgeous scallop of white sand, it sits within a green horseshoe of scrub, pines and olive trees. Alas, its days as relatively unspoiled paradise are numbered: at the time of research, construction of the Qatari-owned Beyond Horizon five-star resort was about to get underway.

BAY OF KOTOR LUŠTICA PENINSULA

MAMULA ISLAND

Lapped on all sides by the sparkling Adriatic and dominated by a photogenic Austro-Hungarian fortress, Mamula island is one of the most stunning spots in the Bay. But its beauty is a haunted one; in 1942, the fortress was commandeered as a concentration camp by Mussolini's fascists, holding an estimated 2000 mostly local prisoners, of whom more than 130 were tortured or starved to death. While such grim reminders of man's inhumanity to man are usually left to rot or turned into memorials, no such future awaits Mamula: the former death camp is set to be transformed into an elite resort.

Approved by the Montenegrin government in 2016, construction of the luxury hotel – complete with marina, nightclub and spa – has unsurprisingly provoked intense outrage, particularly among families of those killed or interned at Mamula. So too has advertising for the project, which billed the future resort as being steeped in a 'party ambience'. Promises of a museum and memorial honouring the victims have done little to appease the rage.

Dobreč
BEACH

Blue-flagged Dobreč is reported to have some of the cleanest waters in Montenegro and is only accessible by sea – usually by taxi boat from Herceg Novi, though tours with Kayak Herceg Novi (p38) also stop in here. Make a day of it, as there's a good restaurant, hammocks to laze in and a little water park for the kids.

Rose
VILLAGE

At the peninsula's very tip you'll find this sleepy fishing village (pronounced with two syllables: ro-seh), a blissful stand of stone houses gazing at Herceg Novi across the sparkling waters of the bay. Outside summer, village life winds down to near inertia, but from May to September a handful of waterside eateries open their doors to day trippers. If you fancy staying over, ask a local about private accommodation.

Rose is easily reached by taxi boat from Herceg Novi (€10 to €15). Kayak Herceg Novi (p38) stops here on its guided paddle tours or you can hire a kayak and go it alone; it takes about 30 minutes each way.

Oblatno
BEACH

It was inevitable that the virtually untouched paradise of green headlands and blue waters at Trašte Bay would attract the attention of developers. It's now home to the chic Almara Beach Club (www.almara.me), with a restaurant, day beds, DJs and live music – attracting a young crowd of sunseekers and partygoers. Five minutes away, work on the Luštica Bay development – an entirely new town complete with seven hotels, countless private residences, a golf course and marina – is well underway.

🛏 Sleeping

Forte Rose
B&B €€

(☏ 067-377 311; www.forterose.me; Rose; apt from €90; P ❄ 🛜) This charming old stone fortress still serves a protective purpose; a stay here guards against the intrusion of rude reality. It's a world unto itself with a private beach, top restaurant and discreet, personal service. The apartments aren't huge, but they're clean and the sea views are outlandish. Chartered tours of nearby hot spots are available on the owners' yacht.

Apartments Briv
APARTMENT €€

(☏ 032-680 110; Obala Đuraševića bb, Krtoli; apt from €80; P ❄ @) Step down from the sun deck of this modern block and straight into the water. There are 24 attractive apartments of differing sizes and configurations on offer. Try for the ones on the ground floor that have large terraces facing the water. You can rent a jet ski or borrow a kayak to paddle out to the islands.

★ Klinci Village Resort
B&B €€€

(☏ 063-200 050; www.klincivillageresort.me; Klinci; apt from €115; P ❄ 🛜 🍽) Tucked away on a 300-year-old olive farm with views to the Adriatic, this gorgeous B&B is one of Montenegro's most romantic getaways. The spick-and-span one- and two-bedroom apartments are divided between three old stone cottages; all have balconies, kitchens and tons of space. The sense of privacy and intimacy here is palpable; the staff are there when you need them, invisible when you don't.

The resort has an exceptional restaurant attached.

Klinci village is 3km from Rose.

🍴 Eating

★ Ribarsko Selo
SEAFOOD €€

(Fishing Village; ☏ 069-149 119; www.ribarskoselo.com; Žanjic; mains €8-26; ⊙ 9am-1am; 🛜) Wherever you're staying and whatever you're doing, make a stop at Ribarsko Selo a priority. Less a mere eatery than an all-encompassing experience, this fantastic new waterfront 'village' has no menu, basing its daily meals on whatever the local fishermen bring in (and whatever organic veggies the chefs have picked from their garden).

The owners have made this a destination in its own right: there are day beds by the beach, kayaks for rent, massages available and impeccable accommodation (apartments €280, bungalows €110 to €150) for those needing to sleep off their meals (or are rightfully entranced by the unbeatable location and dégagé ambience).

★ Vino Santo
SEAFOOD €€€

(☏ 067-851 662; www.vinosanto.me; Obala Đuraševića bb, Krtoli; mains €9-22; ⊙ noon-midnight) If different-restaurant-same-menu fatigue is starting to set in, the deceptively humble-looking Vino Santo offers the antidote. The traditional seafood favourites are all present and accounted for, but acclaimed chef and author Dragan Peričić adds a creative French twist in the delivery. The bayside views are almost as sublime as the food.

DAVOR LOVINCIC / GETTY IMAGES ©

Naturally Gifted

When you're this little it's easy to be overlooked, so Montenegro overcompensates by being rammed full of extraordinary sights. The coastline is so beautiful that not even the mountains can resist dipping their toes in the clear waters.

Contents
➔ **Sundrenched Coast**
➔ **Mountain Majesty**

Above Lake Skadar National Park (p97)

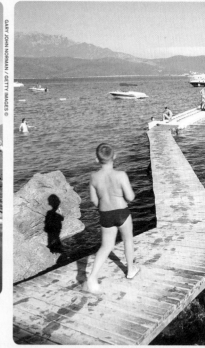

GARY JOHN NORMAN / GETTY IMAGES ©

1. Fishermen, Bay of Kotor (p34) 2. Oblatno Beach (p58)
3. Buljarica Beach (p76) 4. Sveti Stefan (p74)

LAURIE NOBLE / GETTY IMAGES ©

Sundrenched Coast

Lord Byron described this coastline as 'the most beautiful encounter between the land and the sea'. Wherever you choose to splash about in the crystalline waters, chances are there will be a mountainous backdrop proving the great Romantic poet right.

Bay of Kotor

The combination of Mediterranean vegetation, historic towns, cute-as-a-button villages and rugged mountains plunging to an opalescent sea makes the Bay of Kotor pretty hard to beat. More fragrant than the ground floor of a department store, the Bay is subtly infused with the scent of wild herbs, perfumed flowers and aromatic trees.

It's little wonder that the inner part of the bay was the first site in Montenegro to be inscribed on the Unesco World Heritage List – recognising both its natural and cultural value.

Walled Towns

For centuries the people of the coast have protected their towns with stone walls, creating a picturesque counterpoint to the natural beauty surrounding them.

At Budva and Ulcinj the ancient fortifications jut out over the azure blue of the Adriatic. Kotor's walls arch high up on the cliffs behind the town. At night they are spectacularly illuminated, forming a halo from their reflections in the still, dark waters of the bay.

Most striking of all is Sveti Stefan, a picture-perfect island village anchored to the coast by the narrowest of causeways. While off-limits to the general public it has survived its transformation into a luxury resort with all of its historic charm intact.

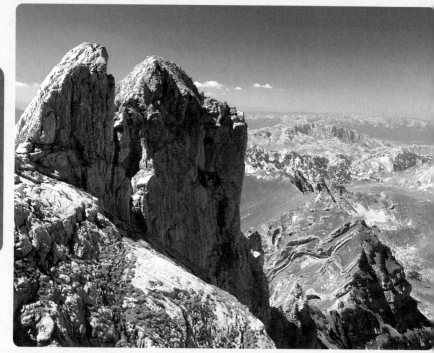

Durmitor National Park (p115)

Mountain Majesty

Much of Montenegro's surface looks like it's been dug up by a giant puppy out of freshly laid concrete. Montenegro's mountains push up behind each other, filling most of the land, with only a scattering of sparkling lakes and deeply cut river canyons to give them breathing space.

Durmitor National Park

A lunar landscape of craggy peaks gives way to high plains and twinkling glacial lakes known as 'mountain eyes' – this is the second of Montenegro's World Heritage Sites. The Tara River slices deeply through the Durmitor range, providing one of the world's most dramatic rafting routes and the nation's most popular active attraction. Savin Kuk never quite sheds its cap of snow and in the winter its 3.5km run is adored by enthusiastic skiers and snowboarders.

Biogradska Gora National Park

If you're on the hunt for wood nymphs or satyrs, the 1600 hectares of virgin forest at the heart of the Bjelasica Mountains would be a good place to start.

Mountaintop Monuments

Seemingly sprouting out of the surrounding cliffs, gleaming white Ostrog Monastery is the country's spiritual heart for its Orthodox population and a popular pilgrimage site. At the top of one of Mt Lovćen's highest peaks stands the Njegoš Mausoleum. This tomb for a national hero echoes the grandeur of the black mountain itself, through imposing sculpture, solemn architecture and awe-inspiring views.

Adriatic Coast

Best Places to Eat

➡ Konoba Zago (p73)

➡ Miško (p89)

➡ Kaldrma (p84)

➡ Grill Bistro Parma (p70)

➡ Mercur (p70)

➡ Paštrovića Dvori (p75)

Best Places to Sleep

➡ Hostel Pirate (p85)

➡ Aman Sveti Stefan (p75)

➡ Avala Resort & Villas (p68)

➡ Hotel Poseidon (p68)

➡ Palata Venezija (p86)

➡ Le Petit Chateau (p81)

Why Go?

Beautiful places often get slugged with the tedious tagline, 'The pearl of...', and the southern coastline of Montenegro is no exception: in this case, it's '...the Adriatic'. But this 80km stretch is less milky dewdrop than eye-popping opal; the malachite greens of the looming mountains and the intense blues of the reflecting waters are dazzling enough to cause hallucinations.

Budva – the so-called 'Montenegrin Miami' – is the country's most visited destination, thanks to its alluring Old Town, buzzy bars and a bevy of Blue Flag beaches. Nearby, elegant Sveti Stefan offers million-dollar ogling, while Bečići, Pržno and Petrovac burst at the seams with sun-seeking families come summertime. Further south, the evocative cliffside ruins of Stari Bar provide a peep into the past, while eastern-flavoured Ulcinj is the gateway to a 12km succession of sandy beaches running to the Albanian border; perhaps surprisingly, you'll find Montenegro's best nudist beach here.

When to Go

➡ Enjoy the beaches and balmy weather in May and June before the crowds descend.

➡ July and August see soaring temperatures, crowded beaches, peak prices – but this is the best time to party.

➡ In September and October you may get some rain, but the air and water temperatures are still warm.

Climate

'Gorgeously Mediterranean' is the best way to describe it. Ulcinj is said to be one of the sunniest spots on the Adriatic, notching up 218 sunny days a year.

ℹ Getting There & Away

Budva is connected to the Bay of Kotor by the Jadranski Put (Adriatic highway; also known as 'Jadranska magistrala'). The main route to Cetinje and Podgorica leaves Jadranski Put between Budva and Bečići and climbs steeply into the mountains. Petrovac is connected to Podgorica via a highway leading through Virpazar and the

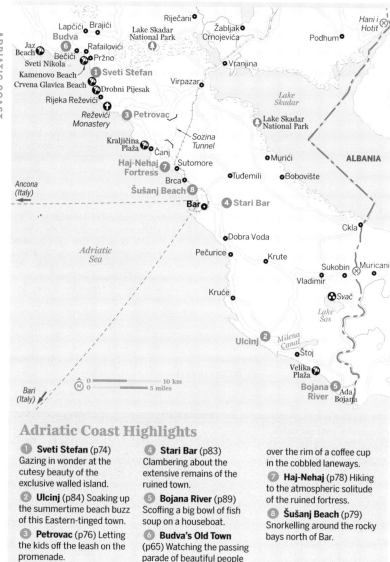

Adriatic Coast Highlights

1 **Sveti Stefan** (p74) Gazing in wonder at the cutesy beauty of the exclusive walled island.

2 **Ulcinj** (p84) Soaking up the summertime beach buzz of this Eastern-tinged town.

3 **Petrovac** (p76) Letting the kids off the leash on the promenade.

4 **Stari Bar** (p83) Clambering about the extensive remains of the ruined town.

5 **Bojana River** (p89) Scoffing a big bowl of fish soup on a houseboat.

6 **Budva's Old Town** (p65) Watching the passing parade of beautiful people

over the rim of a coffee cup in the cobbled laneways.

7 **Haj-Nehaj** (p78) Hiking to the atmospheric solitude of the ruined fortress.

8 **Šušanj Beach** (p79) Snorkelling around the rocky bays north of Bar.

western edge of Lake Skadar. This route can also be reached by a tunnel starting near Sutomore, north of Bar (toll €3.50). A scenic back road links Ulcinj to the southern edge of Montenegro's section of Lake Skadar.

Regular buses connect all the coastal towns with the Bay of Kotor and Podgorica. A railway line links Bar with the centre of the country, including Lake Skadar and Podgorica. There are ferries from Bar to Italy and bus connections to Albania from Ulcinj.

❶ Getting Around

Jadranski Put is the main road connecting all coastal towns and is well served by buses. In summer, taxi boats are a useful option for short trips between beaches.

Budva

🗹 033 / POP 13,400

Budva (Будва) is the poster child of Montenegrin tourism. Easily the country's most-visited destination, it attracts hordes of holidaymakers intent on exploring its atmospheric Stari Grad (Old Town), sunning themselves on the bonny beaches of the Budva Riviera and partying until dawn; with scores of buzzy bars and clanging clubs, it's not nicknamed 'the Montenegrin Miami' for nothing.

Though Budva has been settled since the 5th century BC, you'll be hard-pressed finding much – outside of the Old Town – that isn't shiny and relatively new. Development has run rampant here, and not all of it appears to be particularly well thought out. In the height of the season, Budva's sands are blanketed with package holidaymakers from Russia and Ukraine, while the nouveau riche park their multimillion-dollar yachts in the town's guarded marina. That said, Budva has a hectic, happy charm all its own, and is a must-stay stop on any Montenegrin itinerary.

❍ Sights

◉ Stari Grad

Budva's best feature and star attraction is the Stari Grad (Old Town) – a mini-Dubrovnik with marbled streets and Venetian walls rising from the clear waters below. You can still see the remains of Venice's emblem, the winged lion of St Mark, over the **main gate** (Map p69). Much of the Old Town was ruined by two earthquakes in 1979, but it has since been completely rebuilt and now houses more shops, bars and restaurants than residences. At its seaward end, the **Citadela** (Map p69; admission €2.50; ⊙9am-midnight May-Oct, to 5pm Nov-Apr) offers striking views, a small museum and a library full of rare tomes and maps. In the square in front of the citadel is a cluster of interesting churches. Nearby is the entry to the **town walls** (Map p69; admission €1.50).

Trg Između Crkava   SQUARE
(Map p69) Literally the 'square between the churches', this open area below the citadel provides a visual reminder of the once-cosy relationship between Orthodox and Catholic Christians in this area.

Beautiful frescoes cover the walls and ceiling of **Holy Trinity Church** (Crkva Sv Trojice; Map p69; ⊙8am-noon & 5pm-midnight summer, 8am-noon & 4-7pm winter), in the centre of the square. Built in 1804 out of stripes of pink and honey-coloured stone, this Orthodox church is the only one of the square's interesting cluster of churches that is regularly open.

The largest of the churches is Catholic **St John's Church** (Crkva Sv Ivana; Map p69), which served as a cathedral until 1828 (Budva is now part of the diocese of Kotor). A side chapel houses the Madonna of Budva – a 12th-century icon venerated by Catholic and Orthodox Budvans alike.

Built into the city walls are two tiny churches, which are rarely open. Budva's oldest church is Catholic **St Mary's in Punta** (Crkva Sv Marije; Map p69), dating from 840. **St Sava's Church** (Crkva Sv Save; Map p69), named after the founder of the Serbian Orthodox Church, once had both Orthodox and Catholic altars.

Archaeological Museum   MUSEUM
(Arheološki muzej; Map p69; 🗹033-453 308; Petra I Petrovića 11; adult/child €2.50/1.50; ⊙9am-9pm Tue-Fri, 2-9pm Sat & Sun) The Archaeological Museum shows off the town's ancient and complicated history – dating back to at least 500 BC – over four floors of exhibits. There's an impressive collection of Greek and Roman jewellery, ceramics and glassware (how it survived in a town so prone to earthquakes and war is anyone's guess) and an ancient helmet with holes in the back, which suggest that the former owner had at least one very bad day.

Budva

Ričardova Glava BEACH

(Richard's Head; Map p69) Immediately south of the Old Town, this little beach has the ancient walls as an impressive backdrop. Wander around the headland and you'll come to a statue of a naked dancer, one of Budva's most-photographed landmarks. Carry on and you'll find the quiet, double-bayed Mogren Beach. There's a spot near here where the fearless or foolhardy leap from the cliffs into the waters below.

Rest of Budva

Slovenska Plaža BEACH

(Map p66) After the marina, the long sweep of Budva's main beach commences, heralded by blaring local pop and endless rows of sun umbrellas and loungers (available for hire at about €3 for each). If you can't get your head around this typically Mediterranean concept, there's no charge for spreading out your towel on the patches of beach set aside for the purpose.

Budva

⊙ **Sights**
1 Slovenska Obala B4
2 Slovenska Plaža C4

🛏 **Sleeping**
3 Hotel Kangaroo C3
4 Hotel Lučić A4
5 Hotel Slovenska Plaža C3
6 Saki Hostel & Apartmani D1

🍽 **Eating**
7 Farmers' Market A4
8 Grill Bistro Parma C1
9 Jadran kod Krsta B5
10 Mercur B2
11 Porto A5

🍷 **Drinking & Nightlife**
12 Discoteque Trocadero A5
13 Torch Beach Club C4

Slovenska Obala   WATERFRONT
(Map p66) In summer, Budva's main beachside promenade morphs into a bustling, hustling strip of fast-food outlets, beach bars in the guise of pirate ships and famous landmarks, travel agencies hawking tours, market stalls and a fun fair.

Podmaine Monastery   CHRISTIAN MONASTERY
(www.manastirpodmaine.org) On the surprisingly peaceful northern slopes of town, this Serbian Orthodox monastery features the same stripes of pink and honey-coloured stone as the Stari Grad's Holy Trinity Church. Interesting frescoes inside the church include a Judgement Day scene showing the fate to befall the damned (look for the communist officer with the red star on his military uniform), including being eaten alive by fish and what appears to be a chicken.

From here, a walking track leads up the mountains for 2km to the fortified **Podostrog Monastery**. It was here that Njegoš wrote *The Mountain Wreath* and also here that his predecessor Danilo is said to have instigated the savage events that inspired it.

🏃 Activities & Tours

Travel agencies on Slovenska Obala peddle every kind of day tour, including the following (with indicative prices): Ostrog (€17); Bay of Kotor cruise (€25); Dubrovnik (€25 to €35); Cetinje and Mt Lovćen (€23); Lake Skadar (€35); Albania (€50); rafting on the Tara River (€60 to €75).

You can hire a kayak (€5 per hour) or paddle boat (€6 per hour) from Mogren Beach. A huge range of boats with skippers are available for hire from the marina. A midsized launch might charge €400 for a day's fishing, while a flash one could be €1200 or more.

For underwater thrills, contact **Budva Diving** (Map p69; ☎ 069-060 416; www.budvadiving.com).

Montenegro Adventure Centre   PARAGLIDING
(☎ 067-580 664; www.montenegrofly.com; ⊙ Apr-Sep) The Montenegro Adventure Centre offers plenty of action from its perch high above Budva. Rafting, hiking, mountain biking and accommodation can all be arranged, as well as paragliding from launch sites around the country. An unforgettable tandem flight landing 750m below at Bečići beach costs €65.

Aqua Park Budva   WATER PARK
(☎ 069-554 444; www.aquaparkbudva.me; Topliški Put; 4hr adult/child €16/12, all day €20/15; ⊙10am-7pm summer) Screamy, splashy good times await at this gigantic new water park. Looking down over Budva from Topliš Hill (2km from town), it's home to some truly bonkers waterslides, a wave pool and loads of places for the littlies to paddle and play. Make a day of it; there are also restaurants, bars and a kids' cafe. The park can accommodate up to 6000 people, so don't come expecting calm.

🎉 Festivals & Events

Carnival of Budva   CULTURAL
Venetian-masked high jinks in April or early May.

Theatre City   PERFORMING ARTS
(www.gradteatar.com) Renowned arts festival happening largely in and around the Old Town for six weeks from mid-June.

★ **Sea Dance Festival**   MUSIC
(www.seadancefestival.me; ⊙ mid-Jul) Three huge days of international music acts on Jaz Beach.

Days of Širun FOOD, CULTURAL

(⊘Oct) A one-day celebration of wine, fish and song on the first Saturday of October.

🛌 Sleeping

The tourist office can provide you with information on renting private rooms, or have a look at www.booking-budva.com.

Stari Grad

★**Montenegro Freedom Hostel** HOSTEL €

(Map p69; 📋 067-523 496; montenegro freedom@gmail.com; Cara Dušana 21; dm/tw/d €18/50/66; ❄️🛜) In a quieter section of the Old Town, this beloved, sociable hostel has tidy little rooms scattered between three buildings. The terraces and small courtyard are popular spots for impromptu guitar-led singalongs.

Sailor House GUESTHOUSE €€

(Map p69; www.sailor-house-guest-house-budva. bedspro.com; Vuka Karadžića 25; r from €50; ❄️🛜) Come for the budget prices and great Old Town location, stay for the warm hospitality. The five cosy rooms are kept immaculate, and there's a shared kitchen for socialising. Bike rentals available. Online bookings only.

★**Hotel Astoria** BOUTIQUE HOTEL €€€

(Map p69; 📋 033-451 110; www.astoriamonte negro.com; Njegoševa 4; d/ste from €185/225; ❄️🛜) Water shimmers down the corridor wall as you enter this chic boutique hotel hidden in the Old Town's fortifications. The rooms are on the small side but they're beautifully furnished; the sea-view suite is spectacular. To top it all off, the wonderful roof terrace is home to Budva's most magnificent dining space, **La Bocca** (mains €6.50-20).

★**Avala Resort & Villas** RESORT €€€

(Map p69; www.avalaresort.com; Mediteranska 2; d/villa/ste from €225/316/360; 🅿️❄️🛜🏊) Stunning, breathtaking, luxurious: and that's just the views from the sea-facing rooms. This modern resort is a decadent delight, with a prime location right on Ričardova Glava, and an array of simple yet elegant rooms and sumptuous suites to choose from. The eye-smartingly blue outdoor pool makes direct eye contact with the Old Town and Sveti Nikola; you'd better waterproof your camera, as this is prime selfie-scenery.

Rest of Budva

Saki Hostel & Apartmani HOSTEL, APARTMENTS €

(Map p66; 📋 067-368 065; www.saki-apartmani. com; IV Proleterska bb; dm €12, apt from €40; 🅿️❄️🛜) Not quite a hostel and not quite an apartment hotel, this friendly family-run block on the outskirts of town offers elements of both. Individual beds are rented, hostel-style, in a rambling set of rooms. Private apartments have large balconies, all beds have been crammed in where kitchens might otherwise be. Grape and kiwifruit vines shade the pleasant communal terrace.

Hotel Lučić HOTEL €€

(Map p66; 📋 033-403-320; www.hotellucic.com; Jadranski put 37; d/apt from €70/110; 🅿️❄️🛜) The Lučić is fairly generic, but who needs zany themed rooms when your digs are clean, comfortable, spacious and central? The staff here are helpful, and the restaurant isn't shy with serving sizes. It's about 400m from both the beach and the Old Town.

Hotel Kangaroo HOTEL €€

(Map p66; 📋 033-458 653; www.hotelkangaroo. me; Velji Vinogradi bb; s/d €40/65; 🅿️❄️@🛜) Bounce into a large clean room with a desk and terrace at this minimal-frills midsized hotel that's a hop, skip and jump from the beach. The owners once lived in Australia, which explains the name and the large 3D mural of Captain Cook's *Endeavour* in the popular restaurant below.

★**Hotel Poseidon** HOTEL €€€

(📋 033-463 134; www.poseidon-jaz.com; Jaz Beach; d/apt per person €59/47; 🅿️❄️🛜) This glorious seaside hotel has been sitting by the sands of Jaz Beach since 1967, and while the clean, spacious rooms don't show their age, its excellent service certainly echoes decades of experience. The views from every room – many of which have kitchens – are picture-perfect, and the hotel has its own small slice of private beach with sunbeds and umbrellas free for guests' use.

The wonderful terrace restaurant is open to nonguests as well.

Hotel Slovenska Plaža RESORT €€€

(Map p66; 📋 033-451 654; www.hgbudvanska rivijera.com; 1 Trg Slobode; d/ste from €105/130; ⊘May-Oct) With more than a thousand rooms, two pools, 11 tennis courts, four restaurants, salons, a cinema, galleries and markets on-site, this recently renovated resort is less a hotel than a rambling, raucous village

Budva Old Town

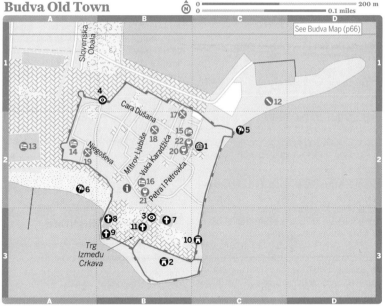

Budva Old Town

⊙ Sights
1 Archaeological Museum	C2
2 Citadela	B3
3 Holy Trinity Church	B3
4 Main Gate	B1
5 Plaža Pizana	C2
6 Ričardova Glava	A2
7 St John's Church	B3
8 St Mary's in Punta	B3
9 St Sava's Church	B3
10 Town Walls	C3
11 Trg Između Crkava	B3

🏃 Activities, Courses & Tours
12 Budva Diving	C1

🛏 Sleeping
13 Avala Resort & Villas	A2
14 Hotel Astoria	A2
15 Montenegro Freedom Hostel	B2
16 Sailor House	B2

🍴 Eating
17 Hong Kong	B2
18 Konoba Portun	B2
19 Konoba Stari Grad	A2

🍷 Drinking & Nightlife
20 Casper	B2
21 Greco	B2
22 The Prince	B2

(or – with its nightly entertainment schedules and karaoke parties – a beached cruise ship). Fans of Yugoslav architecture will find its spacious socialism-meets-Spanish-Mission aesthetic fascinating. Some facilities are also open to nonguests.

🍴 Eating

For cheap fast food and delicious gelato, you need only stroll along Slovenska Obala. Self-caterers will find plenty of supermarkets around Budva, or check out the **farmers market** (Zelena Pijaca; Map p66; Mediteranska bb;

☺ from 6am) for fresh produce and domestic cheese, meats and fish.

🍴 Stari Grad

Hong Kong CHINESE **€**

(Map p69; ☎ 033-452 725; www.kineski-restoran. me; Vuka Karadzica 1; dishes €3.50-10; ☺ 11am-11pm) It's not the most authentic Chinese food in the world, but if your taste buds are craving a change from the Montenegrin menu, you could do far worse than hoist your chopsticks at this Old Town eatery that's been running for almost a quarter of a century. All the classics are here, and they do great local-seafood sweet-and-sours. They also deliver.

Konoba Portun MONTENEGRIN, SEAFOOD €€
(Map p69; ☑068-412 536; Mitrov Ljubiše 5; mains €7-20; ☺noon-midnight) Hidden within the Old Town's tiny lanes, this atmospheric eatery has only three outdoor tables and a handful inside; it feels like you're eating in a long-lost relative's home. The traditional dishes are beautifully presented. Don't miss out on their house speciality, *hobotnica ispod sača* (octopus cooked under a metal lid with hot coals on top).

Konoba Stari Grad SEAFOOD €€
(Map p69; ☑033-454 443; www.konoba starigrad.me; Njegoševa 12; mains €8-22; ☺11am-11pm) With an attractive stone-walled interior and a sunny terrace sandwiched between the Stari Grad's walls and beach, this *konoba* (family-run establishment) isn't short on atmosphere. It's a touch touristy, but the seafood's very good and there's live music most nights.

Rest of Budva

★**Mercur** MONTENEGRIN €€
(Katunska Trpeza; Map p66; ☑067-570 483; Budva bus station; mains €3-12) Bus stations and top nosh are usually mutually exclusive territories, but this marvellous restaurant is the exception to the rule. For starters, it sits in a gorgeous green oasis populated by peacocks, deer and goats; there's also a playground. The menu is Montenegrin to the core, with superb grilled and baked *(ispod sač)* meats, spicy soups and local seafood. The prices are ridiculously low.

★**Grill Bistro Parma** MONTENEGRIN €€
(Map p66; ☑069-028 076; Mainski Put 70; mains €3-10; ☺24hr) A good grill *(roštilj)* is easy to find in meat-loving Montenegro, but if you're looking for one that's great, get your carnivorous self to Parma post-haste. Everything from *ćevapi* to chicken is barbecued to perfection here; their *punjena pljeskavica* (stuffed spicy hamburger) will inspire daydreams and drooling for months after your meal. Portions are massive. The restaurant is friendly and often packed; they also do deliveries.

Jadran kod Krsta MONTENEGRIN, SEAFOOD €€
(Map p66; ☑069-030 180; www.restaurantjadran. com; Šetalište bb; mains €6-20; ☺7am-1am; 🛜)

With candlelit tables directly over the water, this extremely popular, long-standing restaurant offers all the usual seafood suspects along with classic Montenegrin dishes from the interior. It may seem incongruous, but there's a rip-roaring bar – the Beer & Bike Club – out the back.

Porto MONTENEGRIN, SEAFOOD €€
(Map p66; ☑069-025 850; www.restoranporto. com; City Marina, Šetalište bb; mains €7-18; ☺10am-1am) From the waterfront promenade a little bridge arches over a fish pond and into this romantic restaurant where jocular bow-tied waiters flit about with plates laden with fresh seafood. The food's excellent and the wine list offers plenty of choice from around the region.

🍸 Drinking & Nightlife

Stari Grad

Greco BAR
(Map p69; Njegoševa bb; ☺9am-2am) On summer nights, the little square that Greco shares with its neighbour/rival Cafe Jef is packed from wall to wall with revellers. It's easily the busiest spot in the Old Town.

Casper BAR
(Map p69; www.facebook.com/casper.budva; Petra I Petrovića bb; ☺9am-1am Jun-Sep, 5pm-1am Oct-May; 🛜) Chill out under the pine tree in this picturesque Old Town cafe-bar. DJs kick off from July, spinning everything from soul to house. Casper hosts its own jazz festival in September.

Prince PUB
(Map p69; Petra i Petrovića bb; ☺8am-midnight) If you're hankering for something slightly more stout than Montenegro's light lagers, pop down to this friendly little hang-out. It bills itself as an 'English pub', and while the inside is indeed dim and cosy, you'd never mistake its sunny, mega-Mediterranean outdoor area for anything you'd find along the Thames. Yes, they show football on the telly.

Rest of Budva

Top Hill CLUB
(www.tophill.me; Topliški Put; events €10-25; ☺11pm-5am Jul & Aug) The top cat of Montenegro's summer party scene attracts up to 5000 revellers to its open-air club atop Topliš Hill, offering them top-notch sound

and lighting, sea views, big-name touring DJs and performances by local pop stars.

Discoteque Trocadero   CLUB
(Map p66; ☑ 069-069 086; www.trocaderobudva. com; Mediteranska 4; men €5, women free; ☺ 11pm-5am Jun-Sep) It's not nightclubbing as we know it (where's the dance floor?) but Trocadero is the best of Budva's indoor clubs. From the mezzanine you can gaze down at punters propping up the little circular tables that are scattered throughout the large oval space. Music ranges from techno to turbo folk, with regular live performances by local starlets.

Torch Beach Club   BAR
(Map p66; ☑ 033-683 683; www.budvabeach.com; Slovenksa Plaža; ☺ 8am-midnight summer) It's totally scene-y, but Torch is a fun, over-the-top outdoor party palace that epitomises summertime Mediterranean madness. Pool parties, sun-lounge cocktails and light noshing are the order of the day; come sundown, DJs hit the decks and the carousing kicks off in earnest.

ℹ Information

Accident & Emergency Clinic (Map p66; ☑ 033-427 200; www.dialysiscenter.me; Popa Jola Zeca bb)

Tourist Office (Map p69; ☑ 033-452 750; www.budva.travel; Njegoševa 28; ☺ 9am-9pm Mon-Sat, 5-9pm Sun Jun-Aug, 8am-8pm Mon-Sat Sep-May) Small but helpful office in the old town.

ℹ Getting There & Around

BUS
The **bus station** (Map p66; ☑ 033-456 000; Popa Jola Zeca bb) has frequent services to Herceg Novi (€6.50, 1¾ hours), Cetinje (€3.75, 40 minutes), Kotor (€3.75, 40 minutes), Bar (€5, 1¼ hours), Ulcinj (€7.50, two hours) and Podgorica (€6.50, 1½ hours), around six buses a day to Kolašin (€10, three hours) and one to Žabljak (€16, five hours). International destinations include Belgrade (from €26, 11 hours, 15 daily) and Sarajevo (€22, 7½ hours, four daily).

You can flag down the Mediteran Express (€1.50) from the bus stops on Jadranski Put to head to Bečići (five minutes) or Sveti Stefan (20 minutes). They depart every 10 minutes in summer and hourly in winter.

CAR
There are plenty of well-marked parking areas; expect to pay about €5 per day or around €2 per hour. Tow trucks earn steady business from the Mediteranska shopping strip.

Opposite the bus station, **Meridian Rentacar** (Map p66; ☑ 033-454 105; www.meridian-rentacar.com; Popa Jola Zeca bb) offers one-day hire from €36. For something a bit zippier, **Rent A Scooter Montenegro** (☑ 068-201 095; www.rentascooter.me) has mopeds from €23 per day.

TAXI
Taxis are in ready supply in Budva, but many of those that hang around the nightspots in the early hours are prone to overcharging. You're better off calling a reputable company. Otherwise check that the taxi has a meter and check what rate they charge; €4 per kilometre is *not* the going rate.

Eco Taxi (☑ 19567; www.taxibudva.com)

Terrae-Taxi (☑ 19717; www.terraecar.com) Advertises set fares to the following airports: Tivat (€15), Podgorica (€40) and Ćilipi, Dubrovnik (€90).

Around Budva

⊙ Sights

Jaz Beach   BEACH
The blue waters and broad sands of Jaz Beach look spectacular when viewed from high up on the Tivat road. While it's not built-up like Budva and Bečići, the beach is still lined with loungers, sun umbrellas and noisy beach bars; head down the Budva end of the beach for a little more seclusion. If peace and privacy is what you're after, steer clear in mid-July, when Jaz is overrun by more than 100,000 merrymakers boogeying it up at the Sea Dance Festival (p67).

Sveti Nikola   ISLAND
Known locally as 'Hawaii', Sveti Nikola is Montenegro's largest island, stretching to nearly 2km. Fallow deer wander about on this uninhabited green spot, which is only a nautical mile away from Budva or Bečići Beach. Its rocky beaches make it a popular destination in summer when taxi boats regularly ferry sunseekers to and fro; those leaving from Slovenska Plaža charge about €3 per person each way (charter your own for €15 to €20).

Krapina   VILLAGE
(☑ 033-40 25 22) If the smell of suntan lotion is getting a bit cloying, head for the hills and the lovely oasis of Krapina. Just 6km from town, this clean, green escape offers a sweet taste of village life that's great fun for the whole family; there are donkeys and rabbits for the littlies to cuddle, a zipline (€5) over

DON'T MISS

SEA DANCE FESTIVAL

Ever since the Rolling Stones served up satisfaction to a 40,000-strong crowd in 2007, Jaz Beach has become renowned as one of Europe's best open-air music venues. Though Mick, Keef and co were followed by the big-name likes of Madonna and Lenny Kravitz, it's the annual Sea Dance festival (p67) that's kept the sands of Jaz tamped down by hundreds of thousands of boogying feet.

A rip-roaring three-day celebration of electronic and alternative music, Sea Dance was established in 2014 as an extension of Serbia's award-winning EXIT festival for revellers reluctant to end the party. Since then, Sea Dance has attracted 300,000 merrymakers (and counting), and has been named 'Best medium-sized European festival'. Previous acts include Jamiroquai, Underworld, Prodigy, Skrillex and Montenegro's favourite musical maverick, Rambo Amadeus.

Most festivalgoers camp on-site, though Jaz is within walking distance of Budva if sandy sleeps aren't your thing (be sure to book far, far ahead). If you're keen to make a dancey, delirious week of it, EXIT organisers run transfers between the festivals; check online at www.exitfest.org for details.

a canyon for the older kids and a gorgeous waterfall-splashed natural pool for everyone to swim in. The delightful restaurant (mains €5 to €18) serves fish straight from its own farm; you can snooze it off on one of the lawn lounges.

Krapina is a 6km winding and well-signposted drive from Budva.

Bečići & Rafailovići

📞 033

Welcome to the Benidorm of Montenegro! Like the Spanish tourist town, Bečići (Бечићи) has been completely swallowed by large resort complexes, complete with swimming pools, nightclubs and casinos. If the primary objective of your trip is to flit between the pool, pokies and sand, cocktail in hand, this is the place to do it. Just don't expect any actual engagement with Montenegrin culture.

Bečići and its neighbour Rafailovići (Рафаиловићи) share a 1950m-long sandy beach immediately east of Budva. In 1935 it won a Parisian prize and was named the most beautiful beach in Europe, although it's unlikely to win that prize today. It does, however, have a Blue Flag rating for cleanliness and water quality.

Rafailovići is equally built up but retains the vaguest remnants of a village feel. Older-style apartment hotels hug the cliffs and restaurants line the shore. It's a popular spot for families, but at high tide there's hardly any beach.

🏃 Activities

During summer there's usually someone hiring jet skis, pedal boats, banana boats and kayaks from the beach, and taxi boats ply the shore for the trip to Sveti Nikola (p71). If you fancy a spot of parasailing you'll need to keep your eyes open to watch where the boats dock. A short ride costs around €25. If the kids are getting restless, there's a large water park attached to the Hotel Mediteran (📞 033-424 383; www.mediteran.me; Jadranski Put; 🅿️ ❄️ 🛜 🏊).

🛏️ Sleeping & Eating

Hotel Aleksandar   BOUTIQUE HOTEL €€
(📞 033-560 290; www.hotel-aleksandar.me; Rafailovići; d €85-95, ste €270-350; 🅿️ ❄️ 🛜 🏊) Elegant and surprisingly understated, this new designer hotel is a delight. It's already winning die-hard devotees, thanks to an exceptionally accommodating staff, posh restaurant–wine bar and prime location smack on the beach. The rooms are sparkling and large. It also has a detox centre attached, which may come in handy for those getting a little too fond of the local *rakija* (fruit brandy).

Hotel Obala   HOTEL €€
(📞 033-471 045; www.hotelobala.me; Rafailovići; d/ste from €80/160; 🅿️ ❄️ 🛜) The Obala may not have the razzamatazz of its flashier neighbours, but this clean, understated, beachfront hotel is run by some of the friendliest people you'll meet along the coast. If the hotel is full, they also have apartments and rooms in other locations around Rafailovići.

Hotel Splendid RESORT €€€
(☑033-773 777; www.montenegrostars.com;
Jadranski put, Bečići; s €244-290, d €490-580;
P❈@☎≋) The rooms are luxurious, but
the real star of this mammoth resort is the
pool complex. Three outdoor pools (there's
another one inside) swirl around palm trees
and manicured slices of lawn leading down
to the large chunk of beach that the hotel
consumes. There's also a kids club, lavish
health and beauty spa and various spots to
eat and drink.

In a smart – or cynical – move, the Splendid's attached Casino Royale was named after the James Bond film of the same name,
which was purportedly filmed in nearby
Petrovac. It wasn't, but that hasn't stopped
punters looking to soak up a bit of 007's luck
on the tables (or, ahem, otherwise).

Porat SEAFOOD €€
(☑069-028 279; Rafailovići; mains €7-23;
⊙8am-1am) Romantic (but sans soppiness)
and nautical (without the naff), this excellent restaurant has 'atmosphere' down pat.
Sitting on the promenade, Porat has been
in continuous business since 1980, and the
experience shows in their attentive staff
and top-notch fish dishes. They also have a
superb wine list.

❶ Getting There & Away

Regular buses run between Budva and Bečići
(50c) or Rafailovići (€1).

Pržno

☑033 / POP 320
Charming little Pržno (Пржно) offers a
cramped, family-friendly, red-sand beach
and a surprisingly good selection of restaurants. An enigmatic ruin rests on a craggy
island offshore, and just enough old stone
houses remain to counterbalance the large-
scale resort at the northern end of the beach.
The walk from here through the woods to
Sveti Stefan is exceedingly beautiful.

◉ Sights

Kamenovo BEACH
If you're feeling the squeeze on Pržno's
beach, take a wander up to lovely little
Kamenovo. There are no hotels here and
while you'll find a couple of beach bars and
a handful of umbrella renters, it feels positively deserted after the mayhem of nearby
resort towns. It's 1km north of Pržno. Don't

go barefoot: *kamen* means 'stone' and there
are plenty around.

In late May every year, calm little Kamenovo gets all amped up for the Spring Break
electronic music festival (www.springbreak
montenegro.me).

✈ Activities

Pro Diving Montenegro DIVING
(☑069-013 985; www.prodiving.me; Hotel Maestral) This well-established outfit offers shore
dives (€20) and diving trips to various wrecks
(€45), caves (€40 to €100) and various reefs.
PADI diving courses are €300.

🛏 Sleeping

Apartmani Kažanegra APARTMENT €€
(☑033-468 429; www.kazanegra.com; Obala 12;
per person €50-60; P❈☎) This stone villa is
as close as you can get to the beach without
ending up with sandy toes. It houses a range
of tidy one- and two-bedroom apartments
with private terraces overlooking the sea.

Hotel Residence Miločer HOTEL €€€
(☑033-427 100; www.residencemontenegro.com;
Jadranski Put; r €122, apt €140-208; P❈☎≋)
Maybe it's because it's linked to an
award-winning hospitality school that this
hotel ticks all the right boxes. The decor's
fresh and modern, there's secure parking,
the breakfast buffets are excellent, and the
staff aren't afraid to smile. The rooftop pool
is tiny, but has brilliant views (and a cocktail
bar).

Maestral Resort & Casino RESORT €€€
(☑033-410 100; www.maestral.info; s/d/apt from
€150/200/250; P❈☎≋) The Maestral offers
everything you'd expect from a large seaside
resort; luxurious rooms (ask for one facing
the sea), private beach, spa centre, plenty
of pools, good restaurants and live entertainment in summer. The attentive staff
somehow keep the whole place running like
clockwork.

✖ Eating

★**Konoba Zago** MONTENEGRIN, SEAFOOD €€€
(☑033-468 463; www.zago-przno.com; Obala 5;
mains €8-24; ⊙9am-midnight) 'If it ain't broke,
why fix it?' seems to be the adage adhered
to by the owners of Zago, one of Pržno's first
restaurants, and still one of its best. The traditional menu is as authentic as you can get
(they make their own olive oil, catch their
own fish and bake their own bread), as is

the restaurant's setting in an old stone villa overlooking the Adriatic.

They also have apartments to rent for those who can't get enough of the calm, far-from-the-madding-crowds location (or food).

★ **Konoba Langust**   SEAFOOD €€€
(☑ 033-468 369; Obala 34; mains €9-22) This highly rated fish restaurant has been serving traditional seafood meals from its stretch of the Pržno promenade for more than 20 years. Take it from their many guests who have been returning here year after year: you can certainly find these dishes cheaper elsewhere, but you're unlikely to find them better.

ⓘ Information

There's an ATM in the lobby of the large Maestral resort at the northern end of town.

The **post office** is at the southern end by the main bus stop and taxi stand.

ⓘ Getting There & Away

Budva and Sveti Stefan are 10 minutes in either direction from Pržno. The Mediteran Express bus running between the two stops here (€1.50).

Sveti Stefan

☑ 033 / POP 370

Of all the stupefying sights along the Adriatic shoreline, Sveti Stefan (Свети Стефан) is the coast's money shot. A fortified island village connected to the mainland by a narrow causeway, its photogenic jumble of 15th-century stone villas overlook an impeccable pink-sand beach and tempting turquoise waters. The island was nationalised in the 1950s and is now part of – and owned by – the luxurious Aman resort, meaning it's off-limits to all but paying guests. But ogling comes for free; Sveti Stefan has unsurprisingly been named as Montenegro's most-photographed site.

Sveti Stefan is also the name of the township that's sprung up onshore. From its steep slopes, you can admire the iconic island to your heart's content. On the downside, parking is difficult, there are lots of steps and there's little in the way of shops. Families staying at or day tripping to Sveti Stefan will be delighted to discover an excellent (and free!) playground near Olive restaurant.

⊙ Sights

Sveti Stefan Beach   BEACH
The main point of coming to Sveti Stefan is to spend as much time horizontal as possible, with occasional breaks for a cooling dip. The water here gets deep quickly, as if the surrounding mountains couldn't be bothered adjusting their slope. The sands are pinkish and pebbly, but it's difficult to care about a stray rock in your bathers when you've got a jaw-dropping view of the islands – the famous one and the submarine-shaped one populated solely by birds – to squint at from behind your sunnies.

The uncrowded beach on the Budva side of the causeway belongs to the resort. If you don't fancy shelling out €30 for the day-use fee (ie you're not completely insane), the deckchairs on the other side of the causeway get cheaper the further along the beach you go, and there's plenty of rocky – but free – space near the end.

Miločer Beach   BEACH
(King's Beach, Kraljeva Plaža) At the northern end of Sveti Stefan Beach, a path leads over a headland draped in pine and olive trees to the turquoise waters and pink sands of Miločer Beach. Set back from the tranquil bay and fronted by a loggia draped in sweet-scented wisteria is the Villa Miločer. This grand two-storey stone building was built in 1934 as the summer residence of the Karađorđević royal family, the Serbian monarchs who headed the first Yugoslavia.

The whole area is now part of the Aman resort and while you're welcome to walk through, access to the beach will cost you a hefty €75.

Queen's Beach   BEACH
(Kraljičina Plaža) Around the headland from Miločer Beach, Queen's Beach was a favourite of Queen Marija Karađorđević, and it's easy to see why. Cypresses and olive trees provide the backdrop to a pretty 120m curve of reddish sand. You won't get much of a view though, as this beach is set aside exclusively for Aman guests. The public path skirts behind the resort's large spa centre, and then up through the trees to Pržno.

Crvena Glavica   BEACH
A 2km hike south of Sveti Stefan will bring you to this collection of seven small and gorgeous beaches with rocky red sand (*crvena glavica* means 'red head'). It's a steep and bumpy path, but if you're intent on seeking

out some peace and quiet (or are a dedicated nudist; you can get your gear off with impunity here), it's worth the journey.

Praskvica Monastery   CHRISTIAN MONASTERY
Just off the highway in the hills slightly north of Sveti Stefan, this humble 600-year-old monastery, named after the peach-scented water of a brook that flows nearby, rests amid an ancient olive grove. It was an important political centre for the Paštrovići, a local tribe of Serbian origin whose distinctive cultural traditions have survived along this section of the coast despite numerous foreign occupations.

The monastery is well signposted from the main road and an easy walk from either Sveti Stefan or Pržno. It's a working monastery; visitors are welcome, but be sure to dress accordingly.

🛏 Sleeping

Crvena Glavica Auto Kamp   CAMPGROUND €
(☑069-468 070; per adult/child/tent/car €3/1.50/4/3; ⊙Jun-Sep) You don't need to be a movie star or oligarch to enjoy those million-dollar views. Pitch your tent under the olive trees and stroll past the roving chickens down to the rocky but peaceful shoreline. The outdoor showers and squat toilets are very basic.

★Vila Drago   GUESTHOUSE €€
(☑033-468 477; www.viladrago.com; Slobode 32; r €82-115, apt €155-165; ❄ 🛜) The only problem with this place is that you may never want to leave your terrace; the views are *that* sublime. The super-comfy pillows and fully stocked bathrooms are a nice touch. Some rooms and both apartments have kitchens, but it's unlikely you'll use them; the stupendous on-site restaurant (mains €5 to 20) dishes up specialities from the local Paštrovići clan, including roast suckling pig and melt-in-the-mouth baked lamb.

Apartments Dijana   APARTMENT €€
(☑069-256 101; www.dijana-montenegro.com; Slobode bb; studio €75-120, apt €150-200; P❄🛜🏊) Be sure to book far, far ahead if you want to snag one of these comfortable, extremely clean apartments; word of Dijana's warm welcomes has gotten around and it's a popular place. The apartments all have kitchens, balconies and impeccable views to the sea; the flower-strewn communal terrace makes for a beautiful spot to wind down with a vino or three.

★Aman Sveti Stefan   RESORT €€€
(☑033-420 000; www.aman.com; ste €770-3356; P❄🛜🏊) This superlatives-defying resort is one-of-a-kind. Occupying the entire island of Sveti Stefan, it offers 50 luxurious suites that showcase the stone walls and wooden beams of the ancient houses. Amazingly, there's still a village feel here – albeit an *exclusive* village; it's closed to the public – with cobbled lanes, churches, lots of indigenous foliage and an open-air cafe on the main piazza.

Back on the shore, Villa Miločer has a further eight suites by the beach.

🍴 Eating

★Paštrovića Dvori   MONTENEGRIN €€
(☑033-468 162; Blizikuće; mains €5-16) With its authentic, homemade Paštrovići cuisine and nightly traditional entertainment, this happy, hospitable family-run restaurant ought to be on every traveller's to-try list. It is less flash than most of the other choices in oh-so-shiny Sveti Stefan (though it does tick the 'divine views' box), but therein lies its charm. The restaurant is well signposted on the main road just above Sveti Stefan.

Olive   INTERNATIONAL €€
(☑069-133 133; www.olivetaste.com; mains €6-16) Right off the causeway and at the foot of the Miločer pathway, Olive has a prime view of the island and hotel beach. The menu features the usual array of traditional fish, meat and pasta dishes; they also do a mean souvlaki. Parents find it a pleasant place to sip a coffee and catch their breath while the kids run amok on the next-door playground.

ℹ Information

There's an ATM by the strip of shops before the causeway.

ℹ Getting There & Away

Mediteran Express buses head to and from Budva (€1.50, 20 minutes) every 10 minutes in summer and hourly in winter, stopping on the hill about halfway down to the beach.

Sveti Stefan is all windy, narrow roads, which of course the locals tear down with gay abandon; visitors should exercise a touch more caution on the many blind bends. Parking at the beach costs €2 per hour.

Rijeka Reževići

🎵 033 / POP 40

The traditional Paštrović-style architecture of Rijeka Reževići (Ријека Режевићи) differs from the rest of Montenegro, favouring rows of terrace houses with stone walls, small windows, single-pitched roofs and 'hog's back' curved terracotta tiles. This charming village offers some lovely examples and although gentrification is evident, the focus has been on restoration rather than demolition.

Rijeka Reževići is an easy 5km drive from Petrovac.

🔘 Sights

Presjek   BEACH

This quiet, boulder-strewn beach is great for snorkelling (bring your own gear) or simply slipping off and finding your own secluded swimming spot. Get here by following the footpath that starts at the car park below the village church and onwards through the woods.

Reževići Monastery   CHRISTIAN MONASTERY

Hospitality has always been important at this atmospheric stone complex, just 2km south of Rijeka Reževići. Until the 19th century, the Paštrovići would leave a bottle of wine here for passers-by, one of whom in 1226 was King Stefan the First-Crowned of the Serbian Nemanjić dynasty, who founded the **Church of the Dormition** (Crkva Uspenja Bogorodice), the smaller church of the complex. There are fine frescoes covering the walls, though the frescoes in the larger **Church of the Holy Trinity** (Crkva Sv Trojice; 1770) – repainted in the 1970s – are more vivid.

Drobni Pijesak   BEACH

Hidden in a secluded cove three minutes north of Rijeka Reževići, Drobni Pijesak is a 240m stretch of 'ground sand' (the literal translation of the name) surrounded by green hills and turquoise waters. Every year on 28 June, the elders of the 12 Paštrović clans hold the Bankada here, a community court with origins in the 16th century. Nowadays its main focus is the restoration and preservation of the tribe's traditions, environmental and cultural conservation and economic development. The day ends with a folk and arts festival.

🛏 Sleeping & Eating

Reževići Apartments   APARTMENT €€

(🎵 033-468 181; www.rezevici-apartmani.com; Reževići Rijeka bb; d €50, apt €65-110; 🅿 ❄ 🛜 🏊)

If a day trip to Rijeka Reževići just isn't enough, you can drop your bags at this lovely family-run property overlooking the village and the sea. It's clean, quiet and a couple of minutes to the beach; the hosts have lavish hospitality down pat.

Balun   SEAFOOD €€

(🎵 069-285 652; mains €9-20) This beachside restaurant is comparatively pricey, but it's highly rated by the locals. If you're on a budget but keen on million-dollar views, you can always just order a coffee and gaze over the oleanders to the clear waters below.

Petrovac

🎵 033 / POP 1400

The Romans had the right idea, building their summer villas on this lovely bay. If only the new crop of developers had a scrap of their classic good taste. Still, once you get down to the pretty beachside promenade where lush Mediterranean plants perfume the air and a 16th-century Venetian fortress guards a tiny stone harbour, the aberrations up the hill are barely visible. This is one of the best places on the coast for families: the accommodation is reasonably priced, the water is clear and kids roam the esplanade at night with impunity.

Petrovac (Петровац) enjoyed a few minutes of Hollywood fame in 2006 when the town was billed as the location for the Casino Royale in the James Bond film of the same name. Tourists and developers arrived in droves; many of them still haven't discovered that all 'Petrovac' scenes were actually filmed in the Czech Republic.

🔘 Sights

In July and August you'll be lucky to find an inch of space on the fine reddish pebbles of the **town beach**, but wander south and there's cypress- and oleander-lined **Lučice Beach**, with a kids' waterslide on its far end. Continue over the leafy headland for another 30 minutes and the 2.4km-long sweep of **Buljarica Beach** comes into view, most of which is blissfully undeveloped – at least for now.

The small **Katič** and **Sveta Nedjelja** (Holy Sunday) islets just offshore can be

ČANJ & SUTOMORE

If you're on a budget, or simply have a yen for a seaside holiday that's more splash, less flash, give Budva the bump and head south to **Čanj** or **Sutomore**. Located roughly midway between Petrovac and Bar, the two beach towns attract hordes of Montenegrin and Serbian families and young 'uns intent on spending their summers swimming, sunning and staggering between beach bars and nightclubs. Neither spot is particularly upmarket, but the beaches are beautiful with water clear enough for snorkelling, and both towns have a carefree nostalgic feel. The best beach in the region is the pink-sanded **Kraljičina Plaža**, just around the headland from Čanj. It can only be reached by boat; you'll find them running from Čanj in the peak season, or from Bar for as little as €3.

There are plenty of hotels in Sutomore – none of them is exceptional, but they are cheap – and a few in Čanj. In both towns, you'll find a plethora of *sobe* or *apartmani* signs; many also advertise online. Private apartments hover around the €30 to €40 range, while a double room in a beachfront hotel goes from €35 up.

visited by kayak or by arranging a lift from Petrovac's small harbour.

★ Kastio   FORTRESS

Clamber up the steps of this small Venetian fortress for photogenic views of the beach and the dramatic diagonal stratification of the limestone cliffs melting into the turquoise water below. An interesting socialist-realist bas-relief remembering the 'socialist revolution' is partly obscured in the foliage. The entrance is by the small Petrovac harbour.

Roman Mosaics   RUINS

(Kasnoantički mozaik) Apart from the beaches, Petrovac's most interesting attraction is also its least heralded. In 1902, the foundations of a Roman building complete with mosaics, probably dating from the 4th century, were discovered in an olive grove and here they remain in a precarious state of preservation. A glass shed covers a section of mosaic roughly 10m by 15m; it's invariably locked but you can peer through the windows. Around the shed, extensive brick foundations can be seen.

The site is a little tricky to find: take the path leading through private land opposite the 500-year-old **St Thomas' Church** then make your way through the olive grove to the dig site; you'll need to watch your footing.

The site has the potential to be a huge drawcard for Petrovac; whether this is ever acted upon remains to be seen.

Gradište Monastery   CHRISTIAN MONASTERY

Perched on a hill overlooking Buljarica Beach, Gradište Monastery is a tranquil collection of stone buildings facing onto a central courtyard. The monastery was first mentioned in documents from 1305, although it's believed to date from 1116. Like many Montenegrin monasteries, it's had a rough time over the years at the hands of invading armies and has been rebuilt several times.

The three churches on the site are renowned for their frescoes, some of which date back to 1620.

Taking the main road south of Petrovac, turn left after the tunnel and take the steep road up to the monastery (park at the bottom if you're not sure if your car is up to it).

🏃 Activities

Petrovac Kayak Club   KAYAKING

(📞 067-803 684; www.montekayak.com; 46 Nika Anđusa) This friendly group offers guided kayaking trips, including two-hour journeys to Katič and Sveta Nedjelja islands (from €20) and full-day customised paddles (from €80). Kayak hire is available for those who want to go it alone (30 minutes/one hour/half-day/full day from €7/10/24/40). They can also organise kayak fishing trips (from €30).

🎉 Festivals & Events

Petrovac Night   MUSIC, FOOD

(🕙 late Aug) Free fish, wine and beer, majorette parades, performances by Eurovision contestants... Who could ask for anything more?

🛏 Sleeping

For private accommodation in and around Petrovac, try **Mornar Travel Agency** (📞 033-461 410; www.mornartravel.me).

★ **Rakočević Apartments** APARTMENT €
(☑ 067-626 795; www.rakocevic-apartments.com; apt from €30-80) These apartments offer possibly the best high-season value in Petrovac. The 10 apartments in two locations (in the centre beside the promenade, or by the bus station near the top of town) range in size from studios to family-size units. If uber-trendy digs are what you're after, look elsewhere (and pay more), but if comfortable, clean and well appointed floats your boat, book now.

Camping Maslina CAMPGROUND €
(☑ 033-461 215; www.campingmaslina.com; Buljarica bb; per adult/child/tent/car/caravan €3.50/1.50/3/3/5; 🅿 🛜) As Montenegrin campsites go, this is one of the best, with more than 100 camping spots under centuries-old olive trees, working wi-fi and a tidy ablutions block with proper sit-down toilets and solar-powered hot water. You'll find it just off the road to Buljarica Beach.

Hotel Đurić HOTEL €€
(☑ 033-461 814; www.hoteldjuric.com; Brežine bb; d/ste/apt from €80/100/180; ⊖ May-Sep; ❄ 🛜 🐾) There's a vaguely Spanish Mission feel to this smart boutique hotel. All rooms have kitchen facilities and there's a restaurant at the back under a canopy of kiwifruit and grape vines.

Vile Olivia RESORT €€€
(☑ 033-461 194; www.vileoliva.com; d from €150, apt from €210) Set on a large olive grove and just metres from the beach, Petrovac's largest hotel complex is a favourite with families for its kids club, shady playground, two pools and nightly traditional entertainment programs. The staff here are professional, and the buffet restaurant is up to scratch. Rooms and apartments are fairly generic but very spacious and clean; all have balconies.

🍴 Eating

The esplanade is lined with fast-food joints, ice-cream stands, restaurants and cafe-bars. In the midst of it all, you'll find some excellent full-service restaurants.

The **Voli** (Nika Anđusa 22; ⊖ 6am-11pm) supermarket has everything for self-caterers. It's attached to a small fresh-produce market.

Oskar SEAFOOD €€
(mains €5-17) There are loads of seafood joints to choose from along the esplanade, and pretty much all of them are good. Oskar takes it up a notch, with consistently brisk service, ginormous portions of fresh seafood, and a lively ambience courtesy of a buzzy crowd. As per its location, the views are sensational.

Balkan MONTENEGRIN €€
(☑ 068-540 569; Nika Andjusa 18; ⊖ 7am-midnight) One street behind the main seaside drag, Balkan is a cosy, traditional place that – for families, anyway – makes up for its lack of ocean views with a good playground. They do offer seafood, but Balkan is best for its heaped servings of beautifully barbecued meats.

Konoba Bonaca MONTENEGRIN, SEAFOOD €€
(☑ 069-084 735; Barski Put bb; mains €6-17) Favoured by Petrovacians, this restaurant focuses mainly on seafood but the local cheeses and olives are also excellent. Grab a table under the grapevines on the terrace and make yourself comfortable; service isn't the speediest, but there's some prime people-watching and wine sipping to be done as you wait.

🍷 Drinking & Nightlife

Terasa Castelo BAR, CLUB
(terrace/club free/€2; ⊖ 8am-1am) Sip a cocktail and enjoy the romantic panorama from the parapets of the Venetian fortress. DJs spark up both on the terrace and downstairs in the club Castelo on summer nights. Whether you plan to stay for the late-night shenanigans or not, it's also a great place for a fine meal to match the view.

Ponta Beach Bar BAR
(⊖ 8am-1am) With a sea-level terrace built into the stone at the south end of the beach, this is a great location for a sunset cocktail. Later on, local rock bands get the joint jumping.

ℹ Information

Accident & Emergency Clinic (Zdravstvena stanica; ☑ 069-680 741) At the top of town; follow the road from the bus station.

ℹ Getting There & Away

Petrovac's **bus station** (☑ 068-503 399) is near the top of town. There are regular services to Budva (€2.75, 30 minutes) and Bar (€3, 30 minutes), as well as Herceg Novi (€6, two hours, five daily), Kotor (€5, 1¼ hours, nine daily) and Ulcinj (€5, one hour, eight daily). International destinations include Dubrovnik (€20, 3½ hours,

HAJ-NEHAJ FORTRESS

If you wasted your youth playing Dungeons & Dragons or you just like poking around old ruins, the lonely battlements of **Haj-Nehaj Fortress** should be added to your itinerary. Haj-Nehaj was built in the 15th century by the Venetians to defend their southern border from the Ottoman Turks, whose conquests had brought them as far as the river that runs into Šušanj Beach in modern Bar.

To get here from Bar, follow the highway north for 6.5km and turn left where the fortress is signposted. At the intersection of the first sealed road to the right, a rough unsealed road heads hard right through the houses. Walk straight up this road with the castle directly in front of you and turn right at the end into a rough car park. Look for the start of the track among the bushes on the slope. From here it's a steep but attractive walk through the pines for 30 minutes on a stony path that's often hard to distinguish.

When the gate finally does come into view, the fortifications rise so precipitously from the stone that you'll be left wondering how it was ever built. Once you're inside, there are extensive ruins to explore, rising charismatically from a blanket of wild sage and flowers. At the very top, looking over Bar, is the shell of the 13th-century **St Demetrius' Church** (Crkva Sv Dimitrija), easily recognised by its vaulted roof and stone altar. It predates the fort itself and once had separate Catholic and Orthodox altars.

ADRIATIC COAST BAR

one daily) and Belgrade (€24, 10 hours, five daily).

Don Street Taxi Service (☑ 069-437 966; www.taxi-transfer.me) has metered cabs and advertises the following set fares: Tivat (€35), Budva (€15), Bar (€15), Ulcinj (€35) and Podgorica (€40).

Bar

☑ 030 / POP 17,000

Dominated by Montenegro's main port and a large industrial area, Bar (Бар) is unlikely to be anyone's holiday highlight, but it is a handy transport hub welcoming trains from Belgrade and ferries from Italy. Otherwise, the only real reason to come is to use the city as a base for visiting the fascinating ruins of Stari Bar (Old Bar) in the mountains behind.

Unlike the northern part of the coast, which remained largely under the rule of Venice and then Austria, the areas from Bar southwards spent 300 years under Turkish control. 'New' Bar itself – founded in 1908 – has a fairly modern feel to it, but once you start heading towards the Albanian border, you'll notice more mosques and Ottoman-esque buildings.

◉ Sights

With a large industrial port and marina on its doorstep, Bar's **City Beach** (Map p80) is not the most appealing option for swimming. Heading north, **Šušanj Beach** (Map p80) is popular with Serbian holidaymakers. Beat the crowds in the succession of rocky coves that follow; they're perfect for snorkelling and sheltered swimming. If you're concerned about the Speedos chafing, you can go the full monty at a stony bay just before the rustic ruins of the 11th-century Benedictine monastery of the **Mother of God of Ratac** (Bogorodica Ratac). Destroyed by the Turks in 1571, the remains of its chapel now have a congregation consisting of wild figs and the occasional *baba* (grandma) in black.

King Nikola's Palace   MUSEUM
(Dvorac Kralja Nikole; Map p80; ☑ 030-314 079; Šetalište Kralje Nikole; adult/child €1.50/1; ☺ 8am-2pm & 5-11pm) Presenting an elegant facade to the water, King Nikola's Palace was built in 1885 and now houses a collection of antiquities, folk costumes and royal furniture. Its shady gardens contain plants cultivated from seeds and cuttings collected from around the world by Montenegro's sailors.

Church of St Jovan Vladimir   CATHEDRAL
(Hram Sv Jovana Vladimira; Map p80; Bul Revolucije) This huge, modern, gold-topped cathedral can be seen from all across Bar. It's dedicated to Jovan Vladimir, the patron saint of Bar, who is considered to be the first Serbian saint.

🕺 Activities

Canyoning   ADVENTURE SPORTS
Just outside of Bar, two relatively unknown canyons have recently opened up for exploration with day trips run by Active Travels

Bar

⊚ Sights
1 Church of St Jovan Vladimir	B2
2 City Beach	B2
3 King Nikola's Palace	B2
4 Šušanj Beach	A1

⊙ Activities, Courses & Tours
5 Montenegro Yacht Excursions	B2
6 Scuba Quest Diving Centre	B2

⊜ Sleeping
7 Le Petit Chateau	B2
8 Villa Jadran	B1

⊗ Eating
9 Knjaževu Baštu	B2

⊖ Drinking & Nightlife
10 Green Mill	B3
11 Salsa Familia	B2

Montenegro (p38). Rikavac (€75) is a small canyon with a gentle three-hour program of hiking, abseiling and swimming suitable for beginners (including kids over eight); the remote Medjurečje canyon (€115) offers more hard-core adventure, with six hours of hiking through water, abseiling down waterfalls (15–30m) and plenty of sliding down the slippery canyon walls.

Scuba Quest Diving Centre   DIVING
(Map p80; ☏ 069-495 604; www.divemontenegro.com; Bar Marina; intro dive €60) Based in Bar, this highly regarded group nevertheless covers the entire coast with an extensive choice of dive sites, which include wrecks, reefs and caves. Two-dive trips for certified divers are €60; PADI open-water courses are €300. They also rent snorkelling equipment (€5

BAR–BELGRADE TRAIN

Chugging over 435 bridges, into 254 tunnels and up steep, 1000m-plus mountains, a ride on the Bar–Belgrade train is no mere A-to-B commute. A marvel of engineering and one of Europe's most spectacular train trips, the railway runs through the heartlands of Montenegro and Serbia, taking in vistas and villages impossible to catch by car. Make sure your camera is charged; the journey from Serbia's landlocked capital to the Adriatic Sea twists and turns past massifs, monasteries, canyons, rivers and serene Lake Skadar. Those suffering vertigo may wish to avert their eyes during the crossing of the 500m-long Mala Rijeka bridge; swooning 200m above the river of the same name, the viaduct was – until 2001 – the highest railway bridge in the world.

The journey is more than just a series of scenic photo-ops: it's a social event. For 11 hours (or more, depending on border formalities), locals and travellers are banded to-gether in close confines, with not much else to do but indulge in the Balkan propensity for banter. Combine the fact that there's no dining car with Slavic hospitality (and a tendency to pack way, way too much food...not to mention bottles of *rakija*), and voila! Instant party.

A major project of the former Yugoslavia, construction of the 476km line began in the 1950s, though it wasn't until 1976 that President Tito cut the ribbon. Josip Broz was such a fan of riding these rails that he had his own luxury train built, complete with sumptuous bedrooms, Turkish rugs and a full-sized bath-tub. To follow in his (somewhat less luxuri-ous) footsteps, a 2nd-class ticket costs €21; trains run twice a day. Check with Montene-gro Railways (www.cg-prevoz.me) for updated timetables and fares.

day) and can organise yacht charters (half-/full day €300/450).

Montenegro Yacht Excursions BOATING
(Map p80; ☑ 067-109 109; www.utjeha.me; half-/full day cruise €380/760; ☺May-Sep) These boat cruises take in some of the Adriatic's prime panoramas, including Sveta Nedjelja to the north and south to Ulcinj.

🛏 Sleeping & Eating

Given it's a major transport hub, it's surpris-ingly difficult to find decent accommodation in Bar, though the situation is slowly improv-ing with a glut of private rentals appearing on the market. Hunt them down online or ask at the tourist office.

★**Le Petit Chateau** BOUTIQUE HOTEL €€
(Map p80; ☑ 030-314 400; Šetalište Kralja Nikole bb; d €90) This pretty little hotel is as cute – and almost as twee – as the name might suggest. Located in a beautifully restored, former royal residence within the walls of King Nikola's Palace, its handful of quaint but spacious rooms sit above an equally en-chanting restaurant and bar. For ambience and location in Bar, this little house is un-beatable.

Villa Jadran B&B €€
(Map p80; ☑ 030-350 330; www.vilajadran.net; Ilino bb; d/apt from €44/61; P❄🛜) The rooms

and apartments here may be humble, but for this price, they're a steal. The overall cleanliness and comfort don't suffer for the price, and you can expect a warmer welcome than what you'd get at many of the pricier places in town.

Knjaževu Baštu MONTENEGRIN €€€
(Duke's Garden; Map p80; ☑ 030-312 601; www.knjazevabasta.com; King Nikola's Palace; mains €9-24; ☺9am-11pm) While the region-al specialities, service and exhaustive wine list here are indeed excellent, it's the pal-ace location that makes Knjaževu Baštu so special. It's as lush and as opulent as you'd expect from such a regal setting, with tre-mendous chandeliers, luxurious furniture and – of course – divine views of the royal gardens.

🍷 Drinking & Nightlife

The one thing Bar isn't short of is bars. There are heaps of them along and just off Ulica Vladimira Rolovića.

Green Mill BAR
(Map p80; Vladimira Rolovića bb) The 'best place to party in town' gong surely goes to Green Mill (and its friendly neighbour Bar Varade-ro), with exuberant crowds, thumping good-time music and occasional live acts. Nothing fancy, just tons of fun.

WORTH A TRIP

THE OLD OLIVE TREE

There are more than 100,000 olive trees in the Bar area, many of which have seen more than a millennium. At Mirovica near Stari Bar is a living witness that has stood and mutely waved symbols of peace while the armies of consecutive empires have swept through the land. With 2000 birthdays under its belt, **stara maslina** (old olive tree; adult/child €1/50c) is possibly the oldest tree in Continental Europe and one of the oldest of its species in the world.

A ring of white stone protects its personal space from tree-huggers and there's a nominal charge to visit (adult/child €1/50c), but it can be admired nearly as well from the road. Look for the signpost on the Bar–Ulcinj road; at the end of this road, look for the stone wall slightly to the right.

Salsa Familia   BAR
(Map p80; Maršala Tita bb; ⊙10am-midnight) Salsa in Crna Gora? Somehow, this unusual place works an absolute treat, with lively Cuban dance parties (and lessons), zingy cocktails and – perhaps strangest of all, for Montenegro – a nonsmoking interior. They also do food, and while Cuban food is not in abundance, the great pizzas and superb Russian *pelmeni* (dumplings) are worth a try. Great coffee too.

❶ Information

There are several banks with ATMs around Ulica Maršala Tita and Ulica Vladimira Rolovića.
Accident & Emergency Clinic (Map p80; ✆030-311 001; www.domzdravljabar.com; Jovana Tomaševića 42)
Tourist Information Centre (Map p80; ✆030-311 633; www.visitbar.org; Obala 13 Jula bb; ⊙8am-8pm Mon-Sat, to 2pm Sun Jul-Sep, 8am-4pm Mon-Fri Oct-Jun) Stocks city maps and useful brochures listing sights and private accommodation.

❶ Getting There & Away

BOAT
Ferries to Bari (deck/cabin/car from €48/67/78, nine hours) and Ancona (deck/cabin/car from €60/80/90, 16 hours) in Italy leave from the ferry terminal (*putnički terminal*) near the centre of town. You can book your **Montenegro Lines** (Map p80; ✆030-311 164; www.montenegrolines.net)

ferry tickets here, and there's a post office branch and an ATM.

In summer you can hail a taxi boat from the marina or beach for a short trip up the coast (from about €3 to €5).

BUS
The **bus station** (Map p80; ✆030-346 141; Beogradska bb) is adjacent to the train station, 1km southeast of the centre. Frequent buses head to Kotor (€6.50, two hours), Budva (€5, one hour), Ulcinj (€3, 30 minutes) and Podgorica (€4.50, 1¼ hours), and five daily go to Kolašin (€6.50, three hours).

Local buses stop in the centre on Ulica Jovana Tomaševića and head to Stari Bar and north along the coast as far as Čanj.

CAR
From Bar, the fastest route to Podgorica is via a toll road (€3.50 each way) and the 4km-long Sozina tunnel that leaves the highway just past Sutomore, northwest of Bar. The journey takes about 45 minutes.
Meridian Rentacar (Map p80; ✆069-318 666; www.meridian-rentacar.com; Jovana Tomaševića 30; per day from €37) has a branch in the centre of town.

TRAIN
The **train station** (Map p80; ✆030-301 622; www.zpcg.me; Beogradska bb) has services to Virpazar (€1.20, 25 minutes, seven daily), Podgorica (€2.40, one hour, 12 daily), Kolašin (€5.40, 2½ hours, four daily), Mojkovac (€6.20, 2¾ hours, five daily), Bijelo Polje (€7.20, 3¼ hours, five daily) and Belgrade (€21, 11 hours, two daily).

Stari Bar
✆030 / POP 1870
The gloriously dilapidated Stari Bar (Стари Бар) – Bar's original settlement – teeters on a bluff at the foot of Mt Rumija, offering jaw-dropping views and enough enigmatic rubble to get even the dullest imagination running rampant. While it's not quite the 'Montenegrin Pompeii' – as some silver-tongued locals insist on calling it – Stari Bar is a wonderful place to spend a day exploring.

A steep, cobbled hill climbs past a cluster of old houses and shops to the fortified entrance, where a short dark passage leads to a large expanse of vine-clad ruins and abandoned streets overgrown with grass and wild flowers. Alas, visiting Stari Bar is – for now – not suitable for those in wheelchairs.

History

Discoveries of pottery and metal suggest that the Illyrians founded the city around 800 BC. In the 10th century, the Byzantine town was known as Antivarium as it's opposite the Italian city of Bari. It passed in and out of Slavic and Byzantine rule until the Venetians took it in 1443 (note the lion of St Mark in the entryway) and held it until it was taken by the Ottomans in 1571. Nearly all the 240 buildings now lie in ruins, a result of Montenegrin shelling when they captured the town in 1878.

◉ Sights

★ Stari Bar   RUINS
(Old Bar; adult/child €2/1; ☺8am-10pm) A small museum just inside the entrance explains the site and its history. From here, follow the green arrows around the major points of interest. In the western part of the town are the remains of St Nicholas' Church (Crkva Sv Nikole) offering glimpses of Serbo-Byzantine frescoes.

The northern corner has an 11th-century fortress with much-photographed views showcasing Stari Bar's isolated setting amid mountains and olive groves. Nearby are the foundations of St George's Cathedral (Katedrala Sv Đorđa). Originally a Romanesque church, it was converted into a mosque in the 17th century by the Turks, but the unlucky edifice was yet again in ruins after an accidental explosion of gunpowder.

If you're wondering why St John's Church (Crkva Sv Jovana) is in such good nick, it's because it's been completely reconstructed by one of the families associated with the original church. One of the few other buildings to have an intact roof is St Verenada's Church (Crkva Sv Verenade), which contains a display of photography from the greater Bar area.

Ottoman constructions include a solid and charming Turkish bathhouse from the 17th or 18th century, the clock tower (1752) and the 17th-century aqueduct that carried water from a spring 3km away; it was reconstructed after the 1979 earthquake.

Omerbašića Mosque   MOSQUE
(Omerbašića džamija) Just outside Stari Bar's main gate, this simple construction (dating from 1662) has a square stone base and an elegant minaret enclosed by a stone wall. The domed structure near the entrance is the tomb of Dervish Hasan. Many of the Roma people who make a significant proportion of Stari Bar's remaining population practise Islam.

✷ Festivals & Events

Maslinijada   FOOD, CULTURAL
(☺late Nov) Celebrating the annual olive harvest with free olive-everything tastings, lashings of (thankfully not olive) wine and traditional performances.

ADRIATIC COAST STARI BAR

PIRATES OF THE MEDITERRANEAN

Listen up, me hearties, to a swashbuckling tale of murder, theft and slavery. Even before the Venetians took over in 1405, Ulcinj (p84) had a reputation as a pirate's lair. That didn't change when the Ottomans wrested control (nominally at least) in 1571. Quite the opposite, in fact. By the end of the 16th century, as many as 400 pirates, mainly from Malta, Tunisia and Algeria, made Ulcinj their main port of call – wreaking havoc on passing vessels and then returning to party up large on Mala Plaža.

Pirate captains became celebrities across the eastern Mediterranean, with stories of the Karamindžoja brothers, Lika Ceni, Ali Hodža and the like fuelling the imaginations of avid listeners. Spanish writer Cervantes was one victim; he's said to have spent five years in the vaults by the main square before being ransomed. Legend has it that he appropriated the town's name for his character Dulcinea in *Don Quixote*. Others were less lucky, like the pilgrims bound for Mecca robbed then drowned by Lika Ceni – an act that outraged the sultan and landed the pirate a hefty price on his head.

Along with their usual business of pirating, Ulcinj's crews had a lucrative sideline in slavery. Ulcinj became the centre of a thriving slave trade, with people (mainly from North Africa and some as young as two or three) paraded for sale on the town's main square. Ulcinj is perhaps the only place in the Western Balkans to have had a significant black minority.

ADRIATIC COAST ULCINJ

🛏 Sleeping & Eating

There are no hotels in Stari Bar, but if you ask around, you might be able to find someone willing to take you in for the night. Some of the restaurants also offer very simple accommodation.

At the time of writing, a new hostel-cum-arts-centre was being built in an old olive mill by the fortress and was due for completion in spring 2017. Check for updates at www.thegrovemontenegro.blogspot.com.au.

★ **Kaldrma**   MONTENEGRIN €€
(☑030-304 208; mains €5-13; ⊙10am-10pm; 🍴) 🥾 Located on the steep road leading to Stari Bar's main gate (the restaurant's name means 'cobblestone'), this wonderful little eatery manages to be simultaneously very traditional and slightly twee. The focus is on the cuisine of Stari Bar itself, including tender lamb dishes and tons of seasonal vegetarian/vegan options. The *japrak* (stuffed vine leaves) are made to a family recipe and absolutely must be tasted to be believed.

Sleep it all off in a sweet little room upstairs with mattresses laid on woven rugs (€20).

ℹ Getting There & Away

Stari Bar is 4km northeast of Bar, off the Ulcinj road. Buses marked Stari Bar depart from Ulica Jovana Tomaševića in the centre of 'new' Bar every hour (€1). *Apparently* every hour, that is: if you're in a rush, you can get a taxi for about €6.

Ulcinj

☑030 / POP 10,800

For a taste of Albania without actually crossing the border, head down to buzzy, beautiful Ulcinj (Улцињ; pronounced 'ul-tsin-ye'). The population is 61% Albanian (68% Muslim), and in summertime it swells with Kosovar holidaymakers for the simple reason that it's a lot nicer than the Albanian seaside towns. The elegant minarets of numerous mosques give Ulcinj (Ulqin in Albanian) a distinctly Eastern feel, as does the lively music echoing out of the kebab stands around Mala Plaža (Small Beach). Ulcinj's ramshackle Old Town looms above the heaving beach and is a fantastic spot for people-watching without being surrounded by people; if you'd rather take in an entirely different species, the nearby Ulcinj Salinas is home to thousands of birds, including – surprisingly – flamingos.

◉ Sights

Ulcinj is dotted with plenty of swimming spots; **Mala Plaža** (Little Beach; Map p86) is the town's main beach.

Each beach has a commercial license, with seasonal beach bars and eateries. If you value your eardrums, avoid those with names like Ibiza and **Aquarius** (Map p86) and head somewhere like **Sapore di Mare** (Map p86) where you can either plant yourself on a concrete terrace or find a patch of grass under the pines. **Ladies' Beach** (Map p86; admission €2), true to its name, has a strict women-only policy, while a section of the beach in front of the **Hotel Albatros** (Map p86) is clothing-optional.

Stari Grad   AREA
(Map p86) The ancient Stari Grad overlooking Mala Plaža is largely residential and somewhat dilapidated, a legacy of the 1979 earthquake. This is part of its charm – this Old Town really *does* feel old, with its uneven cobblestones and the paucity of street lighting. A steep slope leads to the Upper Gate, where just inside the walls there's a small **museum** (Map p86; www.ul-museum.me; admission €2; ⊙9am-8pm Tue-Sun summer, 8am-3pm winter) containing Roman and Ottoman artefacts and a relief map of the town. On the site is a 1510 church that was converted to a mosque in 1693; you can still see the ruined minaret.

Just outside the museum is a **fountain** (Map p86) (these days, it's more like a tap) with an Arabic inscription, crescent moon and flowers carved into the stone.

The best way to spend an afternoon here is to simply ramble to your heart's content. Whatever else you find, mind-blowing views of Ulcinj and the beach below are guaranteed.

There has been talk for time immemorial about installing an elevator from Ulcinj's little harbour up to the Old Town, so that others – rather than just able-bodied types – can enjoy its ambience as well. Locals have stopped holding their breath...

St Nicholas' Cathedral   CHURCH
(Saborna crkva Sv Nikole; Map p86; Buda Tomovića bb) Set among a picturesque grove of gnarled olive trees just below the Upper Gate is this Orthodox cathedral. It's a relative newbie, having been built in 1890 shortly after the Ottomans were booted out, although it's believed to stand on the site of a 15th-century monastery.

THE MOSQUES OF ULCINJ

One of Ulcinj's most distinct features is its plethora of mosques (p88). Most are fairly simple structures that are usually more interesting from the inside than out. An exception is the **Sailor's Mosque** (Džamija Pomoraca; Map p86; Detarët e Ulqinit bb), an imposing stone structure right on the waterfront; it was once used as a lighthouse. The mosque was completed in 2012, replacing one (destroyed 1931) that predated the Ottomans. There are some interesting frescoes inside. Three minutes up the road, the 1719 **Pasha's Mosque** (Pašina džamija; Map p86; Buda Tomovića bb) is an elegant complex with a *hammam* (Turkish bathhouse) attached.

Kryepazarit Mosque (Džamija Vrhpazara; Map p86; Gjergj Kastrioti Skënderbeu bb) was built in 1749 at the intersection of the main streets; its name means 'Top of the Market'. Within the same block but set slightly back from the road is the 1728 **Mezjah Mosque** (Džamija Namaždjah; Map p86; Hazif Ali Ulqinaku 71). It's Ulcinj's main Islamic place of worship. Further north, **Lamit Mosque** (Džamija Ljamit; Map p86; Kadi Hysen Mujali bb) dates from 1689 but was substantially rebuilt after the 1979 earthquake. The ceiling has interesting green-painted geometric wood panelling.

🏃 Activities

Ulcinj Salinas
BIRDWATCHING

If birds get you all aflutter, you've come to the right place. The marshy Ulcinj Salinas (saltpans) – a 1500-hectare private reserve – attract more than 250 species of migratory birds (half of the birds registered in all of Europe), including Dalmatian pelicans, Eurasian spoonbills, various birds of prey and – believe it or not – flamingos.

Environmental groups have been fighting to prevent development of the salinas and have them officially protected by the government, and while a disused museum hasn't yet been revamped as hoped, the reserve does have a birdwatching tower, signposts and information boards.

The salinas are about a 15-minute drive out of town (head in the direction of Velika Plaža and follow the signs), though just showing up here isn't recommended; you'll likely be turned away at the gate if you show up without warning. Contact the Ulcinj Tourism Information Centre (p88) or Real Estate Travel Agency and they'll make arrangements for you.

Read more about the birds of the salinas (and elsewhere in Montenegro) at www.birdwatchingmn.org.

D'Olcinium Diving Club
DIVING

(Map p86; ☑067-319 100; uldiving@gmail.com; Detarët e Ulqinit bb) Local dive sites include various wrecks (this is pirate territory, after all) and the remains of a submerged town. If you've got up-to-date qualifications you can rent gear (€20) here, or head out on their boat for a day's diving (from €40). Night dives are also offered (from €25).

🛏 Sleeping

At **Real Estate Travel Agency** (Map p86; ☑069 124 140; www.realestate-travel.com; Hazif Ali Ulqinaku bb; r per person from €15), obliging English-speaking staff can help you find private rooms, apartments or hotels. They also rent bikes and cars, run tours and sell maps of Ulcinj.

★ Olive Tree Glamping
TENTED CAMP €

(Map p86; ☑069-060 026; www.facebook.com/montenegroluxtent; tent €40; ☉ Jun-Sep) The tents may be new, but they're dotted across a centuries-old olive grove – one tree is more than 1300 years old – that produces some of Montenegro's finest oil. It's an absolutely wonderful place to get away from the bustle of the beaches below, with hammocks tied between the trees, perfect sea views and engaging hosts only too happy to welcome you into the family.

The pretty, raised tents come with either two singles or a queen, outdoor relaxing areas, barbecues, and solar lanterns and phone chargers (there's no electricity, and that's a good thing).

★ Hostel Pirate
HOSTEL €

(Map p86; ☑068-212 552; www.hostel-pirate.com; 28 Dhjetori bb; dm €9-11, d with shared bathroom from €25; P❋🛇) Just because it's Ulcinj's only hostel doesn't mean this jolly Pirate rests on its laurels. This is an immaculate, friendly, comfortable and flat-out wonderful place that installs fierce

Ulcinj

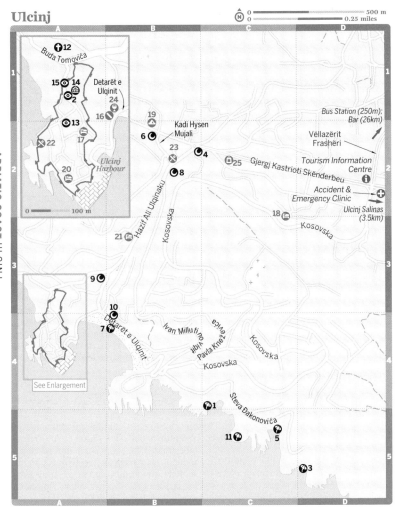

love and loyalty in its guests; it's easily one of the best in Montenegro. The hostel organises bike rentals, tours, kitesurfing and rafting expeditions; they also turn on free barbecue dinners fuelled by shots of equally gratis *rakija*.

Apartments Kalaja   HOTEL **€**
(Map p86; ☏ 069-037 076; www.ulqin-kalaja.com; Stari Grad; d €33, apt €39-55; ☎) The views are expansive, but expensive this friendly place is not. Perched up in Ulcinj's Stari Grad, Kalaja's nine decent – if unthrillingly furnished – rooms and apartments are housed in an

old, rambling stone house that overlooks the sea and the gorgeous hodgepodge of Ulcinj city below. The excellent attached restaurant is open to – and whoppingly popular with – nonguests.

★**Palata Venezija**   HOTEL **€€**
(Map p86; ☏ 030-421 004; www.hotel-palata venezia-montenegro.com; Stari Grad; r/apt from €90/110; ❄☎☎) Situated within a centuries-old palazzo with ridiculous views of Mala Plaža and out to sea, this gorgeously reno-vated place is the best choice for Old Town digs. While the attentive multilingual staff,

Ulcinj

excellent facilities and large rooms and apartments are all very modern, the hotel is steeped in history: be sure to ask them to unlock the small museum (Bey's House) near the restaurant.

In addition to the usual holidaymakers, the hotel is regularly booked out by international birdwatchers; if you're a twitcher, enquire at the front desk about tours and sightings.

Call as you arrive and they'll send a porter down to help you with your bags up the Upper Gate slope.

✖ Eating

If you're keen to cook, hit the traditional market (Map p86; Gjergj Kastrioti Skënderbeu bb) at the top end of town.

During summer, uncountable kebab stalls, *pekare* (bakeries) and other fast-food joints operate hand over fist all along Mala Plaža.

Restaurant Pizzeria Bazar PIZZERIA, SEAFOOD €
(Map p86; Hazif Ali Ulqinaku bb; mains €4-10; ☺6am-midnight) This upstairs restaurant is a great people-watching perch when the streets below are heaving with tourists. Though the name gives pizza top billing, it's their seafood that drags in the locals; the owners catch their own fish every morning. Be sure to try a plate of *lignje na žaru* (grilled squid), one of the restaurant's specialities.

Antigona SEAFOOD €€
(Map p86; ☏ 069-154 117; Stari Grad bb; mains €6-27) Antigona's clifftop terrace offers perhaps

the most romantic aspect of any eatery in Ulcinj, and handsome waiters in bow ties only add to the impression. The seafood is excellent too – but be sure to check the price and weight of the fish in advance if you wish to avoid any nasty surprises come bill time. It also rents rooms (from €35 per night).

☙ Drinking & Nightlife

Provocateur BAR
(Map p86; Mala Plaža; ☺10am-2am summer) This behemoth of a beachside bar is actually a lot more relaxed than its intimidating size would have you believe. It's an ideal spot to

> ### ❶ A SURFEIT OF STREET NAMES
>
> You're unlikely to a find a single street sign in many Montenegrin towns but in Ulcinj, you'll sometimes find three different ones per street: a Montenegrin name, an Albanian version of the Yugoslav-era name, and a new Albanian name. Thus the main boulevard leading east–west at the top of town is either Maršala Tita or Gjergj Kastrioti Skënderbeu, and the main street heading down to the beach is either Ulica 26 Novembra or Rruga Hazif Ali Ulqinaku. We've used the names that were most prominently displayed at the time of research (usually the new Albanian names), but be aware that there is a push to return to the old names.

ℹ️ VISITING MOSQUES

Unlike in some parts of the Islamic world, respectful non-Muslims are usually welcome to visit mosques in Montenegro, although some mosques don't allow women or have separate areas set aside for them (if you're unsure, ask for permission before entering). Mosques are primarily a place for prayer and most are kept purposefully plain so as not to distract the faithful – so there's usually not a lot to see inside anyway. The interiors of some are decorated with geometric patterns or Arabic calligraphy but the representation of people or animals is strictly forbidden. What they all have in common is a prayer niche aligned at the centre of the wall facing Mecca.

If you're keen to visit, a few simple protocols should be followed. Clothing should be loose and should cover the body: shorts, singlets, short skirts and tight jeans are a no-no and women will often cover their heads. Shoes must be removed and mobile phones switched off.

Devout Muslims are required to ritually cleanse themselves before entering for prayer, so there's usually a fountain or tap near the entrance. Non-Muslims aren't expected to do so. Don't distract anyone praying by wandering around or talking loudly inside the mosque – in fact, don't enter at all if group prayers or other community activities are taking place.

start your night and get the goss on where to head next.

ℹ️ Information

Accident & Emergency Clinic (Map p86; ☑ 030-412 433; Majka Tereza bb) There's a pharmacy attached.

Tourism Information Centre (Map p86; www.ulcinj.travel; Gjergj Kastrioti Skënderbeu bb; ⊙ Mon-Fri 8am-3pm) For information, maps and accommodation advice in Ulcinj, Ada Bojana and Velika Plaža.

ℹ️ Getting There &Away

The **bus station** (☑ 030-413 225; Vëllazërit Frashëri bb) is on the northeastern edge of town. Services head to Bar (€3, 30 minutes, frequent), Kotor (€9, 2½ hours, daily), Budva (€7.50, two hours, eight daily), Podgorica (€5.50, two hours, 12 daily) and Rožaje (€12, six hours, daily). International destinations include Shkodra (€6, 1½ hours, daily), Priština (€16.50, six hours, six daily), Sarajevo (€24.50, seven hours, daily) and Belgrade (€29, 11½ hours, two daily).

A minibus to Velika Plaža or Ada Bojana from Gjergj Kastrioti Skënderbeu will cost around €2 to €3.

Velika Plaža & Ada Bojana

The appropriately named Velika Plaža (Big Beach; Велика Плажа) starts 4km southeast of Ulcinj and stretches for 12 sandy kilometres. It's divided into sections with names such as Miami, Copacabana and Tropicana; these beaches don't always live up to their glamorous names, and the water is mostly too shallow for proper swimming, but it's hard not to have fun when everyone else is clearly having a ball.

A bridge leads over the river to the peculiar Ada Bojana (Ада Бојана). It was formed around a shipwreck between two existing islands in the river mouth, which eventually gathered enough sediment to cover around 520 hectares and create 3km of sandy beach. During its Yugoslav heyday it became one of Europe's premier nudist resorts. If you'd prefer to keep your gear on, stick to the river mouth. In spite of – or because of – its unusualness, Ada Bojana is a favourite holiday spot for modish Montenegrins and hip, sea-starved Serbs.

⦿ Sights

Milena Canal   CANAL

On the drive out to Velika Plaža, keep your eyes out for the murky Milena canal, where local fishermen use nets suspended from long willow rods attached to wooden stilt houses. The effect is remarkably redolent of Southeast Asia. There are more of these contraptions on the banks of the Bojana River at the other end of Velika Plaža.

🏃 Activities

This area is making a name for itself as a prime spot for water and wind sports, especially kitesurfing. There is a handful of well-rated outfits here, including **Kitesfera** (☑ 069-210 249; www.kitesfera.com) and **Kite Loop** (www.kiteloop.net).

LAKE ŠAS

If you've got your own wheels and fancy getting well off the beaten track, this pretty area near the Albanian border makes a pleasant drive. Take the road leading northwest from Ulcinj. After 17km you'll reach the large village of **Vladimir** where a marked turn-off to the right leads to the lake.

After 2km, you'll see to your right the ruins of the once-great Zetan city of **Svač** (Šas). Park here and cut across to the top left corner of the rough football field, where you'll find the beginnings of a rocky path. Wear proper shoes; the track is rough and there are a lot of thorns. There's not much left of Svač apart from the shells of a couple of buildings, one of which was obviously a church. The town was razed by the Mongols in 1242 and the Ottomans in the 16th century, after which it was abandoned. It's now a rustic, beautiful spot, offering broad views over the plains towards the Rumija Mountains.

Jump back in the car and continue to follow the signs to the lake, which is 2.5km further on. **Lake Šas** (Šasko Jezero; Шаско Језеро) covers 364 hectares and is lined with a muddy border of reeds and water lilies; it's an important habitat for 240 species of bird. In winter it attracts both dedicated birdwatchers and Italian hunters.

Character-filled **Restaurant Shasi** (☑ 069-592 873; restorantshasi@gmail.com; mains €7-15; ⊙ 9am-11pm) is a rambling stone complex built into a cliff by the lake. It's a lovely, quiet spot where the staff spring into action when you arrive and fish soup is served with delicious corn damper. Shasi's specialities are eel, mullet and carp, caught from the pier at the bottom of its yard. They also offer simple accommodation (doubles from €30).

Mountain Riders   HORSE RIDING
(www.mountainriders.me; 4hr ride €90; ⊙Oct-May) These four-hour guided horseback tours clip-clop along the entire length of Velika Plaža during the off-season (ie when there's nobody to trample). Suitable for beginners.

★ Festivals & Events

Southern Soul Festival   MUSIC
(www.southernsoulfestival.me; ⊙late Jun–early Jul) Four days of soul, jazz, funk, house and disco on Velika Plaža's Copacabana Beach.

★ Eating

Several memorable fish restaurants jut out over the Bojana River near the Ada Bojana bridge. The local speciality is *riblja čorba* (fish soup). Each of these restaurants is worth making the 14km drive from Ulcinj.

★**Miško**   SEAFOOD €€
(☑069-022 868; www.restoranmisko.com; Bojana River; mains €8-19) The most upmarket of the Bojana River restaurants is focussed completely on seafood, including octopus,

shrimps, shellfish, a big selection of fresh fish, and, of course, delicious *riblja čorba*. Its motto, with apologies to Julius Caesar, is: '*Veni, Vidi, Sjedi, Jedi*', which translates from a mix of Latin and Montenegrin as 'I came. See! Sit! Eat!'

★**Ćićkova Čarda**   SEAFOOD, ITALIAN €€
(Bojana River; mains €5.50-13) Seemingly constructed Robinson Crusoe–style from flotsam and jetsam, this very atmospheric restaurant on the Ada Bojana side of the river serves lots of traditional seafood dishes as well as the usual selection of pasta, risotto, steaks and grills. It's a wonderful spot to watch the sunset from. Add your name to the hundreds scrawled all over its wooden walls.

ℹ Getting There & Away

In summer, there's a day rate to access the island (by car €5, on foot €2). You'll need your own car, as public transport options are few and far between.

Central Montenegro

Best Places to Eat

➡ Stari Most (p97)
➡ Dali (p105)
➡ Konoba Badanj (p99)
➡ Pod Volat (p105)
➡ Pekara (p109)

Best Places to Sleep

➡ Apartments Athos (p104)
➡ Hotel Hemera (p104)
➡ Hotel Trebjesa (p109)
➡ La Vecchia Casa (p96)
➡ Monte Rosa (p92)

Why Go?

Ogle the splendid cap of northern mountains and impeccable drape of glittering coastline by all means, but to truly get to know Montenegro, a visit to the country's core is a must.

Its beating heart is Mt Lovćen, a 1749m-high symbol of national identity and the very black mountain that gives Crna Gora its name. To the south, Lake Skadar is the country's lungs, a clean, green oasis of lily-strewn waterways and rare bird havens. Swoop north to Ostrog to discover the very soul of the nation in a gravity-defying cliff-face monastery that literally brings pilgrims to their knees. And you'll find character galore in Montenegro's two capitals; the modern-day seat of Podgorica is home to hip bars and a happening arts scene, while the royal city of Cetinje proudly preserves its gallant past in a collection of richly endowed museums and galleries.

When to Go

➡ May is late spring and the perfect time to visit the capital, before the sizzling summer.

➡ August offers Great weather for exploring Lake Skadar; Danilovgrad hosts the River Zeta Festival.

➡ September is not as scorching but still warm enough, and a great time to drive the panoramic Circuit Around Korita.

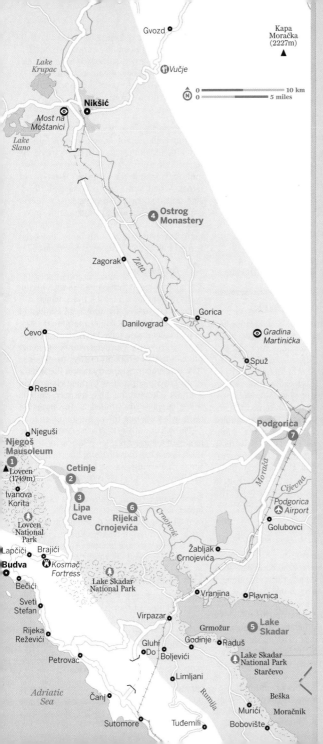

Central Montenegro Highlights

① **Njegoš Mausoleum** (p92) Marvelling at the majesty of both the mountains and the monument at the top.

② **National Museum of Montenegro** (p93) Delving into history, art and culture in the former royal capital Cetinje.

③ **Lipa Cave** (p95) Diving even deeper into the past on a tour of one of the country's largest caves.

④ **Ostrog Monastery** (p107) Gazing in wonder at the improbable cliff-face construction of this holy site.

⑤ **Lake Skadar** (p97) Cruising the sparkling waters to the island monasteries and bird sanctuaries.

⑥ **Rijeka Crnojevića** (p97) Feasting on the sublime seafood and serene setting.

⑦ **Nova Varoš** (p105) Soaking up the nocturnal buzz of Podgorica's party precinct.

Climate

Extremes are more noticeable in this region than on the coast. Podgorica is scorching in summer and can reach above 40°C. In the mountains the climate is considerably cooler. Temperatures can drop below freezing any time from October to March.

❶ Getting There & Away

Podgorica has an international airport and is the country's main bus and train hub. The main highway from the coast starts near Sutomore and takes a 4km-long tunnel (toll charge €3.50) through the mountains to Virpazar and on to Podgorica .

❶ Getting Around

Regular bus services head from Podgorica to Cetinje, Nikšić and Virpazar. Trains connect Podgorica to Virpazar, Danilovgrad and Nikšić.

Lovćen National Park

Directly behind Kotor is **Mt Lovćen** (Ловћен; pronounced '*lov*-chen'; 1749m), the black mountain that gave Crna Gora (Montenegro) its name; *crna/negro* means 'black', and *gora/ monte* means 'mountain' in Montenegrin and Italian respectively. This locale occupies a special place in the hearts of all Montenegrins. For most of its history it represented the entire nation – a rocky island of Slavic resistance in an Ottoman sea. A striking shrine to Montenegro's most famous son, Petar II Petrović Njegoš, peers down from its heights, with views stretching as far as Albania and Croatia.

The park's main hub is **Ivanova Korita** near its centre, where there are a few eateries and accommodation providers and, in winter, a beginners' ski slope.

◉ Sights

★ **Njegoš Mausoleum**   MONUMENT
(Njegošev Mauzolej; admission €3; ☺8am-6pm) Lovćen's star attraction, this magnificent mausoleum (built 1970 to 1974) sits at the top of its second-highest peak, Jezerski Vrh (1657m). Take the 461 steps up to the entry where two granite giantesses guard the tomb of Montenegro's greatest hero. Inside under a golden mosaic canopy, a 28-ton Petar II Petrović Njegoš rests in the wings of an eagle, carved from a single block of black granite.

The actual tomb lies below, and a path at the rear leads to a dramatic circular viewing platform providing the same spectacular views that caused George Bernard Shaw to exclaim, 'Am I in paradise or on the moon?'.

A photographer stationed near the entrance has a stash of folk costumes and a computer set up to print out quirky instant souvenirs (photos from €3.50).

Njeguši   VILLAGE
On the northern edge of the park, this endearing collection of stone houses is famous for being the home village of the Petrović dynasty, Montenegro's most important rulers, and for making the country's best *pršut* (smoke-dried ham) and *sir* (cheese). Roadside stalls sell both, along with honey, *rakija* (fruit brandy), hand-woven mats and souvenirs. In the nearby village of Erakovic, Petar II Petrović Njegoš' birth house has been turned into a small **museum** (admission €2).

☆ Activities

The mountains are criss-crossed with hiking paths and mountain-biking trails, which can be accessed from Kotor, Budva or Cetinje, and the **Coastal Mountain Traversal** (Primorska planinarska transverzala (PPT)) runs straight through. If you're planning on hiking, come prepared; the temperature is, on average, 10°C cooler than on the coast and the weather on Lovćen is prone to sudden changes in summer. Despite the high average rainfall, water supplies are limited as the moisture quickly leeches into the karstic limestone.

The **National Park Visitor Centre** (www. nparkovi.me; Ivanova Korita; ☺9am-5pm) in Ivanova Korita has tons of useful information on the park, its trails and accommodation. They also rent mountain bikes (per hour €2).

Quad Biking   ADVENTURE
(www.globtourmontenegro.com; tour €85; ☺summer) These exhilarating day-long bush-bashing tours leave from Ivanovo Korito, bumping up Mt Lovćen to take in some of Montenegro's best mountain and sea views.

🛏 Sleeping & Eating

The National Park Visitor Centre offers accommodation in four-bed bungalows (€40). Informal camping is possible within the park (small/large tent €3/5, campervan €10), with additional charges for using established campgrounds (€10) or lighting fires in designated places (€5, including wood).

★ **Monte Rosa**   HOTEL €€
(☏069-300 600; www.hotelmonterosa.me; Ivanova Korita; d/ste/apt from €50/85/120; ❄🛜🏊) This

charming chalet makes for a serene mountain getaway. The views from its massive glass windows are extraordinary, and its restaurant is worth stopping into even if you don't plan to stay the night. Rooms are spotless with simple wooden interiors. You'll find it right near the National Park Visitor Centre.

Konoba kod Radonjića MONTENEGRIN €€
(Njeguši; mains €6-12) This atmospheric *konoba* (simple family-run establishment) serves up delicious roast lamb as well as the local specialities, *pršut* (smoke-dried ham; €4.50) and *sir* (cheese; €3.50).

❶ Getting There & Away

If you're driving, the park (entry fee €2) can be approached from either Kotor (20km) or Cetinje (7km). Tour buses are the only buses that head into the park.

Be aware that this is a *very* twisty-turny and narrow road; the large tour buses that hog it in summer don't make the driving experience any easier. Don't be distracted by the beyond-spectacular views.

Cetinje
📱 041 / POP 16,700

Rising from a green vale surrounded by rough grey mountains, Cetinje (Цетиње) is an odd mix of erstwhile capital and overgrown village, where single-storey cottages and stately mansions share the same street. Several of those mansions – dating from the days when European ambassadors rubbed shoulders with Montenegrin princesses – have become museums or schools for art and music.

The city was founded in 1482 by Ivan Crnojević, the ruler of the Zeta state, after abandoning his previous capital near Lake Skadar, Žabljak Crnojevića, to the Ottomans. A large statue of him stands in the main square, Dvorski Trg. Cetinje was the capital of Montenegro until 1946, when it passed the baton – somewhat reluctantly – to Titograd (now Podgorica); today, it's billed as the 'royal capital', and is home to the country's most impressive collection of museums.

◎ Sights

National Museum of Montenegro MUSEUM
(Narodni muzej Crne Gore; Map p94; www.mnmuseum.org; all museums adult/child €10/5; ☺9am-5pm) The National Museum is actually a collection of four museums and two galleries housed in a clump of important buildings. A joint ticket

❶ A ROYAL ROUND TRIP

From Cetinje, a 53km, day-long circular mountain-biking route follows asphalt roads through Lovćen National Park. You'll ascend 890m in your first 20km to the entrance of the Njegoš Mausoleum, where you can stop for the views and a bite to eat. It's mainly downhill from here, heading in the direction of Kotor before looping through Njeguši and back to Cetinje.

will get you into all of them or you can buy individual tickets.

Two are housed within the imposing former Parliament building (1910). On the ground floor, the fascinating **History Museum** (Istorijski muzej; Map p94; 📱041-230 310; Novice Cerovića 7; adult/child €3/1.50; ☺9am-5pm) follows a timeline from the Stone Age to 1955. There are few English signs but the enthusiastic staff will give you an overview. Bullet holes are a theme of some of the most interesting relics: there are three in the back of the tunic that Prince Danilo was wearing when assassinated; Prince Nikola's standard from the battle of Vučji Do has 396; while, in the communist section, there's a big gaping one in the skull of a fallen comrade.

Upstairs you'll find the excellent **Montenegrin Art Gallery** (Crnogorska galerija umjetnosti; Map p94; Novice Cerovića 7; adult/child €4/2; ☺9am-5pm), with a small but important collection of icons. The most precious of them all is the bejewelled 9th-century *Our Lady of Philermos*, traditionally believed to be painted by St Luke himself. It's spectacularly presented in its own blue-lit 'chapel'.

For something more edgy, head to the **Miodrag Dado Đurić Gallery** (Galerija; Map p94; Balšića Pazar; adult/child €4/2; ☺10am-2pm & 6-9pm Tue-Sun). Housed in a striking five-storey concrete and glass building, it promotes and displays 20th-century and contemporary Montenegrin art. One ticket covers both this and the national gallery.

Opposite the History Museum, the wonderfully castle-like **Biljarda** (Njegoš Museum, Njegošev muzej; Map p94; Dvorski Trg; adult/child €3/1.50; ☺9am-5pm) was the residence of Montenegro's favourite son, prince-bishop and poet Petar II Petrović Njegoš. It was built and financed by the Russians in 1838 and housed the nation's first billiard table (hence the name). The bottom floor is devoted to

Cetinje

Cetinje

military costumes, photos of soldiers with outlandish moustaches and exquisitely decorated weapons. Upstairs are Njegoš' personal effects, including his bishop's cross and garments, documents, fabulous furniture and, of course, the famous billiard table.

When you leave Biljarda, turn right and follow the walls to the glass pavilion housing an astonishing large-scale **Relief Map of Montenegro** (Map p94; admission €1), created by the Austrians in 1917. Peek through the windows if it's closed. A **lapidarium** in the courtyard beside it is dotted with ancient inscribed tombstones collected from across Montenegro.

Entry to the **King Nikola Museum** (Muzej kralja Nikole; Map p94; Dvorski Trg; adult/child €5/2.50; ☺9am-5pm) – a stunning 1871 maroon-and-white palace that was home to the last sovereign of Montenegro – is by guided tour (you may need to wait for a group to form). Although looted during WWII, it retains enough plush furnishings, stern portraits and taxidermied animals to capture the spirit of the court.

If you haven't worn yourself out yet, pop into the **Ethnographic Museum** (Etnografski Muzej; Map p94; Dvorski Trg; adult/child €2/1; ☺9am-5pm), where you'll find a well-presented collection of costumes and tools explained by English notations.

Ulica Njegoševa STREET
(Map p94) Cetinje's main street is Njegoševa, a partly pedestrianised thoroughfare lined with interesting buildings, cafes and shops. At the southern end are two shady parks and the elegant **Blue Palace** (Plavi Dvorac; Map p94), built in 1895 for Crown Prince Danilo but recently commandeered by the Montenegrin President – hence the manicured gardens. Its neighbour is the equally graceful former **British Embassy** (Map p94), built in 1912 but Georgian in its sensibilities; it's now a music academy. Just north of the pedestrian-only section is a striking art-nouveau building covered in tiles, which was once the **French Embassy** (Map p94).

Cetinje Monastery CHRISTIAN MONASTERY
(Cetinjski Manastir; Map p94; ☺8am-6pm) It's a case of four times lucky for the Cetinje Monastery, having been repeatedly destroyed during Ottoman attacks and rebuilt. This sturdy incarnation dates from 1786, with its only exterior ornamentation being the capitals of columns recycled from the original building, founded in 1484. The chapel to the right of the courtyard holds the monastery's proudest possessions: a shard of the True Cross (the pièce de résistance of many of Europe's churches) and the mummified right hand of St John the Baptist.

The monastery **treasury** (admission €2) is only open to groups, but if you are persuasive enough and prepared to wait around, you may be able to get in (mornings are the best time to try). It holds a wealth of fascinating objects including the jewel-encrusted crown

of 14th-century Serbian king – and later saint – Stefan Uroš III Dečanski, icons and a copy of the 1494 *Oktoih* (Book of the Eight Voices), the first book printed in Serbian.

Dress modestly or you'll either be denied entry or given an unflattering smock to wear.

Vlach Church CHURCH
(Vlaška crkva; Map p94; Baja Pivljanina bb) While its present appearance dates from the 19th century, this stone church was actually founded around 1450, thus pre-dating the Montenegrin founding of Cetinje. A sumptuous gilded iconostasis (1878) is the centrepiece of current church.

Take a close look at the church's fence: it's made from 1544 barrels of guns taken from the Ottomans during the wars at the end of the 19th century. Two 14th-century *stećci* stand in the churchyard, examples of mysterious carved stone monuments that are found throughout northern Montenegro and neighbouring Bosnia.

Court Church CHURCH
(Dvorska crkva; Map p94; Novice Cerovića bb) Built in 1886 on the ruins of the original Cetinje Monastery, this cute little church has a lovely gilded iconostasis, but its main claim to fame is as the burial place of Cetinje's founder, Ivan Crnojević, and Montenegro's last sovereigns, Nikola I and Milena. The pair may have been unpopular after fleeing the country to Italy during WWI, but they received a hero's welcome in 1989, when their bodies were returned and interred in these white-marble tombs in a three-hour Orthodox service.

★**Lipa Cave** CAVE
(Lipska Pećina; ☎067-003 040; www.lipa-cave.me; ☺9am-6pm May-Oct) Cetinje may indeed be littered with old-time reminders of its days as Montenegro's capital city, but just 4km away lies an attraction that makes the town look positively modern. Millions of years old, Lipa Cave is one of the country's largest caves – and the only one open for organised visits – with 2.5km of passages and halls filled with stalactites, stalagmites and freaky natural pillars. Choose between basic, 45-minute tours (adult/child €7/5), a 100-minute 'adventure' tour (adult/child €20/10) or an 'extreme' exploration (fit adults only, €50).

★ Festivals & Events

Ljeto u Prijestonici PERFORMING ARTS
(Summer in the Old Capital; www.cetinje.travel; ☺Jul-Sep) Summer-long festival, with live music,

art exhibitions, folkloric dancing, classic car displays, literary events, food stalls...if it's cultural, edible or just plain fun, this whopping festival has it going on.

🛏 Sleeping

★ La Vecchia Casa   B&B €
(Map p94; ☑067-629 660; www.lavecchia casa.com; Vojvode Batrica 6; s/d/apt €17/28/40; P ❄ 🛜) With its gorgeous garden, traditional hospitality and pervading sense of tranquility, this remarkably renovated period house wouldn't be out of place in a quaint mountain village. Instead, it's right in the centre of Cetinje, offering a rural-feeling retreat with all of the historical capital's attractions, shops and restaurants a short stroll away. Clean, simple rooms retain a sense of the home's history; good-sized apartments have kitchens.

Royal Square Apartment   APARTMENT €
(Map p94; ☑067-678 206; petrai22@hotmail. com; Njegoševa 52; apt from €39; ❄🛜) Get in quick if you want to snag yourself these cheap, central and colourful digs right in the heart of Cetinje's historic pedestrian zone. It's a popular place, and so it should be: the town's main attractions are but a stumble from the door, the apartments – while they don't look any great shakes from outside – are comfortable and well-equipped, and the host couldn't be more helpful.

✗ Eating

Head to the local market (Map p94; off 13 Novembra) for fresh produce and local specialities.

★ Kole   MONTENEGRIN, EUROPEAN €€
(Map p94; ☑041-231 620; www.restaurantkole. me; Bul Crnogorskih Junaka 12; mains €4-15;

⊙7am-midnight) They serve omelettes and pasta at this snazzy modern eatery, but it's the local specialities that truly shine. Try the memorable Njeguški *ražanj*, smoky spit-roasted meat stuffed with *pršut* and cheese.

Gradska Kafana   INTERNATIONAL €€
(Map p94; Dvorski Trg; mains €4-14; ⊙9am-midnight) Situated within the endearingly rundown old Bulgarian Embassy, this local favourite is a top spot for a good-sized meal (Cetinje may not be by the sea, but Gradska Kafana still whips up excellent fish and chips), a relaxing tipple and watching the world go by.

ℹ Information

Accident & Emergency Clinic (Hitna pomoć; Map p94; ☑041-233 002; Vuka Mićunovića 2)
Tourist Information (Map p94; ☑041-230 250; www.cetinje.travel; Novice Cerovića bb, Njegošev Park; ⊙8am-6pm Mar-Oct, to 4pm Nov-Feb) Offers helpful advice and information, though be aware that they often charge for brochures that might be free elsewhere. The website could use an update, but it's a good place to start your pre-Cetinje research.

ℹ Getting There & Away

Cetinje is on the main Budva–Podgorica highway and can also be reached by a glorious back road from Kotor via Lovćen National Park. The rundown **bus station** (Map p94; Trg Golootočkih Žrtava) has regular services from Herceg Novi (€7, 2½ hours), Budva (€4, 40 minutes), Kotor (€5, 1½ hours) and Podgorica (€3, 30 minutes).

It remains to be seen whether a proposed 15km cable car linking Cetinje and Kotor (via Mt Lovćen) will ever come to pass.

WORTH A TRIP

KOSMAČ FORTRESS

High up in the hills midway between Budva and Cetinje, this artfully abandoned 19th-century fortress looms over some spectacular high-altitude scenery. Once the southernmost fortress in the Austro-Hungarian Empire, the large, formerly three-storey limestone complex was the scene of two bloody rebellions in the late 1800s, and was garrisoned by Italian troops in WWII. Now roofless and ruined, Kosmač (Tvrdjava Kosmač) is nevertheless a fascinating and haunting place to explore, though curious adventurers do so at their own risk; the fortress in not staffed or maintained, and large chunks of stone have a habit of toppling without notice.

Kosmač is near the village of Brajići on the Budva–Cetinje road. Park near the signpost, then walk just over a kilometre through the village to get to the fortress itself. It's also reachable via a three-hour hike from Kamenovo, near Pržno on the coast.

Lake Skadar National Park

Dolphin-shaped Lake Skadar (Скадарско Језеро), the Balkans' largest, has its tail and two-thirds of its body in Montenegro and its nose in Albania. On the Montenegrin side, an area of 400 sq km has been protected by a national park since 1983; today, Skadar is renowned as one of Europe's top bird habitats. It's a blissfully pretty area encompassing steep mountains, island monasteries, clear waters, and floating meadows of water lilies. The main – albeit tiny – towns here are Virpazar and Vranjina, though if you've got wheels, you can easily explore the handful of timeless villages sprinkled along the shore. Lake Skadar is a popular escape for nature lovers, outdoor-activity aficionados and locals fleeing the heat of Podgorica. Legend has it that the lake was created by the tears of a pixie; that may be fanciful, but after one look at magical Skadar, you may find yourself believing in fairy tales too.

🛏 Sleeping

Plavnica Eco Resort   RESORT €€€
(☑ 020-443 700; www.web plavnica.me; ste from €130-180; 🅿 ❄ 🛜 🏊) Day trippers from Podgorica escape the summer heat at this upmarket resort, where there's an impressive pool (day-use €10) set within an amphitheatre that's sometimes used for live performances. The resort has a suitably glam boat that's used for lake tours, and you can hire catamarans (small/large €5/70 per hour), canoes (€4), kayaks (€3) and pedal boats (€6).

It may have all the ambience of a reception hall, but the cavernous restaurant (mains €6 to €20) is an excellent place to try the local *krap* (relax, it's the Montenegrin word for carp). Upstairs are four lavishly furnished suites, each sleeping two adults and potentially a small child.

To get here, head towards Podgorica from the National Park Visitors Centre. After 11km, turn right at the large white war memorial in Golubovci and head back down in the direction of the lake for 6km. The resort's at the end of the road.

Rijeka Crnojevića
☑ 041 / POP 215
The northwestern end of Lake Skadar thins into the serpentine loops of the Rijeka Crnojevića (Ријека Црнојевића; Crnojević River)

and terminates near the pretty village of the same name. It's a charming, tucked-away kind of place.

When Montenegro was ruled from Cetinje, this is where the royals came to escape the Black Mountain's winter. The relatively modest house of Vladika Petar I Petrović (St Peter of Cetinje) still stands; you'll recognise it by its ground-floor arches and upper rooms jutting out over the road.

Construction of the €90 million Porto Skadar Lake ecoresort (www.portoskadar lake.com) near the mouth of the river is set to commence in 2017; it's due to open in 2019. Some locals and tour operators have expressed concerns that the development – which includes plans for a large-scale hotel, villas, shopping centre and a marina – will have a disastrous impact on the region's native bird and marine life.

⊙ Sights & Activities

During the tourist season there are usually small boats lined up on the river, offering cruises for around €25 per hour.

Danilo's Bridge   BRIDGE
(Danilov Most) This arched limestone bridge is the telegenic trademark of Rijeka Crnojevića. It was built in 1853 by Prince Danilo.

Walking Track   WALKING
The village is the starting point of a two-hour, 7.6km circular walking track that passes through the ruins of **Obod**, the site of the region's first printing press, and on to **Obod Cave** (Obodska Pećina) at the source of the river.

🍴 Eating

⭐ Stari Most   SEAFOOD €€
(Old Bridge; ☑ 041-239 505; mains €7-22) Perhaps surprisingly – given its sleepy-village location – Stari Most is one of Montenegro's best resturants. It's well located on the marble riverside promenade, looking to the old bridge from which it derives its name. Fish (particularly eel, trout and carp) is the speciality here and the fish soup alone is enough to justify a drive from Podgorica.

ℹ Getting There & Away

A car is a must if you want to visit. The two closest towns of note are Cetinje (16km) and Podgorica (26km); the village is accessed by side roads that lead off the highway.

Virpazar

⚡ 020 / POP 300

This tiny town, gathered around a square and a river blanketed with water lilies, serves as the main gateway to Lake Skadar National Park.

Virpazar (Вирпазар) may be a small speck on the map now, but it was once considered so strategically important that the occupying Turks built a large fortress on the hill looming above the village. After their downfall, Virpazar became an important trading town (*pazar* means marketplace) with a lively port; in the early 1900s, it was connected to Bar by Montenegro's first narrow-gauge railway. It was also the site of one of the country's first significant uprisings against Axis invaders in WWII. Two reminders of its bloody past still stand in – and over – the town.

If you're interested in sampling local wines, you'll find family-run vineyards and tasting cellars in and around Virpazar.

⊙ Sights

Besac Fortress   FORTRESS
(Tvrđava Besac; admission €1) Looking out over Virpazar, this recently reconstructed fortress was built by the Turks in 1478, and was the scene of many a bloody battle; it was also used as a prison by the occupying Italians in WWII. These days, it's an easy uphill stroll from Virpazar and offers splendid views of the village and its surrounds.

The path leading to Besac is signposted from the road to Murići about 400m after the post office.

�î Activities & Tours

You'll find plenty of boats (and their operators will definitely find you) doing one- to two-hour lake cruises from Virpazar's small marina. Trips generally cost about €25 to €35 per hour. Many of the operators can also organise fishing and birdwatching tours.

★**Undiscovered Montenegro**   ADVENTURE
(⚡069-402 374; www.lake-skadar.com; ⊙Apr-Nov) This excellent agency run by a charming British couple specialises in week-long (or more), lake-based itineraries (per person from €810 including accommodation at Villa Miela; it also runs accommodation booking services and day tours. Their long list of offerings includes guided hikes (from €30), kayaking (from €35), boat tours (from €30), wine tours

(from €30), 'wine-dining' (from €40) and birdwatching (per trip €250).

Zabes Holidays   BOATING
(⚡069-998 737; www.zabesholidays.me) Run by experienced, multilingual locals, Zabes runs a range of boat tours (from €10 per person) that take in tons of different sights along Skadar. They also organise birdwatching, kayaking, fishing and gastronomic tours; contact them for details. Those after the full Skadar experience can rent out their beautifully furnished holiday home (from €50 per night) or pitch a tent at their campground (from €3) in the village of Zabes, 2.5km from Virpazar.

Mountain Riders   HORSE RIDING
(⚡067-343 411; www.mountainriders.me; €60; ⊙Apr-Oct) Day-long trail rides (and horse-and-rider swims) through Lake Skadar's fairy-tale-like Orahovštica Valley.

★ Festivals & Events

Festival of Wine & Bleak   FOOD & DRINK
(Festival vina i ukljeve; ⊙mid-Dec) That's 'bleak' as in a type of fish, not Russian theatre. It's a chance to stuff yourself while tapping your toes to traditional music.

⊨ Sleeping

Locals with budget-friendly rooms to rent often linger around the main square in the afternoons. Check out www.lake-skadar.com/accommodation for a good list of hotels, rooms and apartments.

Virski Pub   PUB €
(⚡068-630 036; r per person from €10; ☎) Sink a few then spend the night at this welcoming watering hole. Rooms aren't posh, but they're comfortable enough. There's a shared kitchen for guests' use, or you can stagger next door to the bakery *(pekara)* to load up on cheap, fattening treats.

Jovićević Apartments   APARTMENT €€
(⚡069-091 185; office@outdoorandmore.me; apt from €40; ❄) The Jovićević family rents a couple of atmospheric apartments right in the centre of town. The Cave Apartment (sleeping four) is built into a natural rock wall and has its own ornamental well. A hammock is strung up between the oaks outside, and bikes are available to rent (€10 per day). Better still is the light-filled apartment in an old building right by the monument (sleeping three).

FEATHERS, FINS & FUR: THE WILDLIFE OF LAKE SKADAR

Covering between 370 and 550 sq km (depending on the time of year), Lake Skadar is one of the most important reserves for wetland birds in Europe. The endangered Dalmatian pelican nests here along with 256 other species, including a quarter of the global population of pygmy cormorants. You might spot whiskered terns making their nests on the water lilies.

The average depth of the lake is 5m, with some spots plunging below sea level; these underwater spring holes are called 'eyes', attracting fish – and fisherfolks – by the hundreds. The deepest eye – Radus – sinks at least 60m down. At least 48 species of fish lurk beneath Skadar's smooth surface, the most common of which are carp, bleak and eel. The tourist offices in **Vranjina** (p100) and **Virpazar** sell fishing permits; if you join a tour, these will be provided.

Mammals within the park's confines include otters, foxes, weasels, moles, groundhogs and the occasional wolf.

Eating

★**Konoba Badanj**   MONTENEGRIN €€
(📞 069-508 019; mains €6-15; ⊗ 8am-midnight) A cool stone-walled interior with solid wooden beams, views of the river and interesting art make this an atmospheric eating option. The fish soup comes with big chunks of fish and delicious scone-like homemade bread, or try the eel straight out of Lake Skadar. They have live music on weekends.

ℹ Information

Virpazar Tourist Office (📞 020-711 102; www.visitbar.org; ⊗ 8am-5pm May-Sep, to 4pm Mon-Fri Oct-Apr; 🛜) This office on the main square can assist with arranging anything on the lake, including boat trips, wine tastings and private accommodation. The office serves as a storefront for the region's wine producers. The National Parks office is upstairs, selling park entry tickets (€4) and fishing permits (per day €5).

You'll find an ATM out the front of Hotel Pelikan, but apparently it often runs out of money; bring cash just in case.

ℹ Getting There & Away

Virpazar doesn't have a bus station but buses on the Bar–Podgorica route stop on the highway (near Hotel Pelikan). A bus from Podgorica takes 30 minutes (€2.50); you'll have to tell the driver that you want to get off at Virpazar.

The train station is off the main road, 800m south of town. There are several trains to/from Bar (€2, 23 minutes) and Podgorica (€2.20, 30 minutes) every day.

Murići

📞 085 / POP 110

The southern edge of Lake Skadar is the most dramatic, with the Rumija Mountains rising precipitously from the water. Murići (Мурићи), a cluster of traditional buildings set around a mosque, is home to one of the lake's best swimming spots. The water's clear, if a little weedy, and swarms of little fish follow your feet as you kick up the nutrients beneath.

🛏 Sleeping

Murići Vacation Resort   CAMPGROUND €
(📞 069-688 288; www.nacionalnipark-izletistemurici.com; cabin per person from €20, campsite per person/car/campervan €5/5/10; ⊗ May-Sep) This shady, pleasant place has simple log cabins sharing a decent ablutions block, nestled within an olive grove on the lakeshore. There's also a good outdoor restaurant (mains €4 to €11) but if you're nervous about dogs, this might not be for you.

ℹ Getting There & Away

From Virpazar, there's a wonderful 40-minute drive (or 56km mountain-biking route) following the contours of the lake through the mountains and an enchanting (possibly even enchanted) chestnut forest. The road heads towards the Albanian border before crossing the range and turning back towards Ulcinj. About halfway along the lake, take the steep side road that descends to Murići.

Islands

An archipelago of islands traces the southern edge of Lake Skadar and, in true Montenegrin fashion, many of them shelter monasteries.

Moračnik island's monastery dates from at least the early 15th century. Its small domed stone church dedicated to the Holy Virgin is watched over by a tower-like accommodation block occupied by a friendly monk.

In the early years of the new millennium, an exceedingly welcoming community of nuns revived Beška Monastery after 300 years of abandonment. Fourteenth-century St George's Church is still undergoing slow reconstruction work, but the smaller Church of the Annunciation is in active use. It was built in 1440 and contains traces of once extensive frescoes.

Beška and its neighbour on Starčevo were once famous for producing religious scripts. Starčevo was named somewhat unflatteringly after the hermit who founded the monastery in 1377; it translates as 'Old Man's Monastery'. Revived in the last three decades, Starčevo again has an old man – a monk who would prefer not to be disturbed (entertaining tourists isn't part of the hermit job description).

Grmožur, the closest island to Virpazar, is topped by a Turkish-built fortress (1843). It served as a prison until the early 20th century and was nicknamed 'the Montenegrin Alcatraz'.

In the swampy northwestern reaches of Lake Skadar near Žabljak Crnojevića, the Church of the Dormition (1415) of Kom Monastery (☎ 067- 887 711; www.manastirkom.org) has the best-preserved frescoes of the lake's many churches.

Getting There & Away

Moračnik, Beška and Starčevo are best reached from Murići. Boats are easy to find in summer, but you might need to ask around at other times. Expect to pay about €25 per hour.

Grmožur is a regular stop on boat trips from Virpazar and Vranjina (the boats are considerably cheaper from Virpazar).

Kom is most easily reached by boat from Vranjina. In the height of summer, it can be approached by a path leading through the marshes from near Žabljak Crnojevića.

Vranjina

☎ 020 / POP 220

The twin hills on Vranjina (Врањина) island are nicknamed 'Sofia Loren' by the locals for wink-wink-nudge-nudge reasons that become apparent when they're viewed from afar. The village itself has the slightly improbable nickname 'the Montenegrin Venice'. In centuries past, the island was used as a hideaway for those embroiled in blood feuds.

Some boat tours leave from Vranjina, though they're generally more expensive than those departing from Virpazar.

◉ Sights & Activities

Lesendro Fortress　　　　　　FORTRESS
(Lesendro Tvrđava) The remains of the 19th-century fortress Lesendro lie just along the causeway. The busy highway and railway tracks prevent land access to the site, but you'll get great views on a boat tour.

Vranjina Walking Trail　　　　　HIKING
This 4km hiking trail begins at the visitor centre and winds its way up towards the 13th-century St Nicholas' Monastery (Manastir Sv Nikole). The trail gets steep and rough in parts, but the views from the top are jaw-dropping. Bring plenty of water and wear suitable boots. The visitor centre has maps and information on hand.

✕ Eating

Jezero　　　　　　　　SEAFOOD €€
(☎ 020-879 106; www.plantaze.com; mains €6-18) This restaurant serves up wonderful, fresh *krap* and bleak (easy now; they're freshwater fish); savour it on the lovely lakeside terrace while enjoying a glass of local vino.

❶ Information

National Park Visitor Centre (☎ 020-879 103; www.nparkovi.me; admission €2, free with national park entry ticket; ⊙ 8am-4pm, to 6pm summer) Lake Skadar's main National Park Visitor Centre rests on the opposite side of the causeway leading to Podgorica from Virpazar. This modern facility has excellent displays about all the national parks, not just Lake Skadar, including lots of taxidermied critters and an ethnographic section with folk costumes and tools. You can buy national park entry tickets (€4) and fishing permits (per day summer/winter €10/5) from a kiosk outside.

❶ Getting There & Away

There are frequent trains between Vranjina and Podgorica (€1.20, 25 minutes).

Vranjina is 20km from Podgorica.

Žabljak Crnojevića

For a brief time in the 15th century, between the fall of Skadar (now Shkodra in Albania) and the founding of Cetinje, this was the capital of Zetan ruler Ivan Crnojević. Now the enigmatic ruins stand forlornly on a lonely hillside surrounded by lush green plains with only some rather large snakes and spiders as occupants.

Walking up from the small village at its base, the 14m-high, 2m-thick walls look

THE CIRCUIT AROUND KORITA

If you've got wheels and a desire to get off the beaten track, rev up and head out along Montenegro's first fully signposted panoramic road. Starting off in Podgorica and skirting the Albanian border before looping back down again, the new Circuit Around Korita (Krug oko Korita) offers 65km of winding, wonderful roads that take in stunning vistas up to 1400m, pit stops in out-of-the-way museums, scenic villages and easygoing hikes – the best of which is a two-hour walk to the Grlo Sokolovo (Falcon's Throat) lookout, where you'll be rewarded with jaw-dropping views of the Cijevna Canyon and Prokletije mountains.

The circuit is fully paved and well marked (keep an eye out for the brown signs), though the roads – in typical Montenegrin fashion – are narrow; the drive isn't recommended for caravans and is best driven between May and October. Fill up before you go; there are no petrol stations along the circuit. The **Montenegrin National Tourist Organisation** (p105) and **Tourist Organisation of Podgorica** (p106) offices can help with maps and information.

intimidating, yet even these couldn't withstand the hammering the Ottoman invaders gave them in 1478 when the town was finally abandoned.

The site's a little hard to find but worth the effort. Heading towards Podgorica, turn left at the only traffic lights in Golubovci. After the railway bridge and the one-way bridge, turn left. Continue for about 4.5km until you see a bridge to your left. Cross it and continue to the car park near the village. Take the stone stairs heading up from the path near the river and follow your nose past the village church and along the overgrown path.

Podgorica

🕗 020 / POP 151,000

Given it's undergone five name changes, passed through the hands of everyone from the Romans to the Turks to the Austro-Hungarians, and twice been wiped off the map entirely, it's little wonder that Podgorica (Подгорица) seems permanently gripped by an identity crisis. It can be difficult to pin a label on the city; its streets are a hotchpotch of Ottoman oddments, brutalist blocks and shiny new malls, and it has a fraction of the big-smoke buzz other European capitals can claim. But with some excellent galleries, plenty of parks and a vibrant cafe culture, pint-sized Podgorica is worth a look.

The city sits at the confluence of two rivers. West of the Morača is the business district, while the Ribnica divides the eastern side in two. The south side is Stara Varoš, the old Ottoman town, while north is Nova Varoš, home to a lively mixture of shops and bars. Its heart is Trg Republika, the main square.

◎ Sights

For a city formerly known as Titograd (literally 'Tito-city'), there is an inordinate number of royal sculptures dotted around its many parks. The most imposing is the huge bronze **statue of Petar I Petrović Njegoš** (Map p102) standing on a black marble plinth on the Cetinje edge of town. A large **equestrian statue of Nikola I** (Map p102) struts grandly opposite the parliament at the head of a lovely park with manicured hedges and mature trees. You won't find Tito anywhere but there's a spectacularly cheesy sculpture of Russian singer **Vladimir Visockij** (Map p102) near the **Millennium Bridge** (Map p102), pictured shirtless with a guitar and a skull at his feet.

Podgorica is pleasantly peppered with a surprising number of parks. One of the nicest – **Kraljev Park** (Map p102; Bul Sv Petra Cetinjskog) – has a great (and free) kids' playground.

Podgorica also has plenty of museums and galleries, and it may soon be adding another to the list; at the time of research, dissident Russian punk band Pussy Riot had expressed interest in opening a women-only museum in the city, with the tentative title New Balkan Women's Museum.

★ Stara Varoš   AREA

(Map p102) Podgorica's oldest neighbourhood retains traces of the 400 years in which it was the centre of a bustling Ottoman Turkish town. The blocky **clock tower** (Sahat Kula; Map p102; Trg Bećir-Bega Osmanagića) overlooking the square was useful for signalling Muslim prayer times. In the maze of streets behind it, two mosques remain. You wouldn't know to look at it, but the **Starodoganjska Mosque**

Podgorica

(Map p102; Nemaljića bb) has its origins in the 15th century. More impressive is the 18th-century **Osmanagić Mosque** (Map p102; Spasa Nikolića bb), which Turkish donations have helped to restore.

At the confluence of the two rivers is the ruin of the **Ribnica Fortress** (Tvrđava na Ribnici; Map p102), built by the Ottomans after their conquest in 1474. The best-preserved element is a little arched bridge crossing the Ribnica.

The rocky Morača riverbank serves as Podgorica's main **beach** (Map p102). It's a far cry from the sea beaches Montenegro's famous for – and locals have a bad habit of littering here – but in the middle of a Podgorica heatwave, it's heavenly.

Museums & Galleries of Podgorica MUSEUM
(Muzeji i Galerije Podgorice; Map p102; ☎ 020-242 543; Marka Miljanova 4; €3; ☺ 9am-8pm Tue-Sun) **FREE** Despite Cetinje nabbing most of the national endowment, Podgorica is well served by this collection of art and artefacts.

There's an interesting section on Podgorica's history that includes antiquities exhumed from Doclea, its Roman incarnation, the remains of which are in the northern fringes of the modern city. Look out for Petar Lubarda's large canvas *Titograd* (1956) in the foyer.

Petrović Palace PALACE
(Dvorac Petrovića; Map p102; ☎ 020-243 914; www. csucg.me; Kruševac bb; ☺ 8am-8pm Mon-Fri, 10am-2pm Sat) **FREE** The Contemporary Art Centre operates two galleries in Podgorica. The bottom two floors of this 19th-century palace are given over to high-profile exhibitions, while the top floor has an oddball collection of traditional and modern art (Indonesian batik, a metal palm tree from Iraq, revolutionary-themed paintings from South America) from its days as Yugoslavia's gallery devoted to art from countries belonging to the Non-Aligned Movement.

The leafy grounds contain interesting sculptures, a tiny church and another trip from Podgorica. The falls are at their dramatic best after the spring thaws, but you'll find plenty of locals taking a dip in their somewhat depleted – but supremely swimmable – depths come Podgorica's sizzling summer. There's an excellent traditional restaurant, also called Niagra (mains from €3), beside the falls.

Niagra is a 10-minute drive from Podgorica; you'll need a car as there's no public transport. Take the signposted road to Tuzi, then turn right before passing the bridge over Cijevna River and follow the signs to Kuće Rakića until you reach the restaurant's carpark.

🏃 Activities & Tours

Montenegro
Eco Adventures   ADVENTURE, CULTURAL
(Map p102; ☑069-123 078; www.montenegro-eco.com; Njegoševa 9; day/multiday tours from €40/295) Promoting sustainable 'soft adventure' tours ranging from day trips to countrywide tailored, multi-day expeditions.

Montenegro Adventures   ADVENTURE
(Map p102; ☑020-208 000; www.montenegro-adventures.com; Jovana Tomaševića 35) This well-respected and long-standing agency creates tailor-made adventure tours, countrywide. It can organise mountain guides, cycling logistics, kitesurfing, hiking, cultural activities, accommodation, flights…you name it.

🎉 Festivals & Events

Podgorica Cultural Summer   CULTURAL
(Podgoričko Kulturno Ljeto; ⊙Jun-Aug) Summer-long festival of various cultural happenings in venues across the city.

December Arts Scene (DEUS)   CULTURAL
(Decembarska Umjetnička Scena; ⊙Dec) Month-long celebration of art, music, literature and theatre.

🛏 Sleeping

Montenegro Hostel   HOSTEL €
(Map p102; ☑069-255 501; www.montenegrohostel.com; Radoja Jovanovića 52, Spasa Nikolića, Stara Varoš; dm €13-18, d €20; ❄🤚) Tucked behind an old stone gate in Stara Varoš, this welcoming place feels more like a home than a hostel, with an enticing common room (and flop-worthy purple couches), fully stocked kitchen and cosy private rooms. Dorms are sparse but sparkling. It's not a hedonistic hostel, but it is friendly.

Note that the hostel's new street name is Spasa Nikolića, though taxi drivers will

exhibition space in the former guardhouse (Perjanički Dom). Temporary exhibitions are also staged in the small **Galerija Centar** (Map p102; ☑020-665 409; Njegoševa 2; ⊙9am-2pm & 5-9pm Mon-Fri, 10am-2pm Sat) **FREE**.

Cathedral of Christ's Resurrection   CHURCH
(Saborni Hram Hristovog Vaskrsenja; Map p102; Bul Džordža Vašingtona) The large dome, white stone towers and gold crosses of this immense new Serbian Orthodox cathedral are a striking addition to Podgorica's skyline. When the building was consecrated in 2014, it attracted much controversy for its lavish frescoes, one of which depicts Tito, Karl Marx and Friedrich Engels burning in hell together.

★Niagra Falls   WATERFALL
(Nijagarini vodopadi; Rakića Kuće) They may not be the thundering cascades so beloved by honeymooners across the ditch in North America, but these waterfalls make for a fantastic day

most likely still be using the original Radoja Jovanovića.

★ **Apartments Athos** APARTMENT €€
(Map p102; ☑067-227 595; www.apartments athos.com; Bul Ivana Crnojevića 58; apt €65-110; P✳🛜) Enormous, easy on the eye and close to everything, these apartments are the best of Podgorica's private pads. All are supremely well equipped (think espresso machines, laundries and dishwashers), come with large terraces (some overlooking the cafe below) and have big, comfortable beds. Staff speak English and go out of their way to help guests. There's even a lift, a peculiarity in Podgorica.

★ **Hotel Hemera** BOUTIQUE HOTEL €€
(Map p102; ☑020-221 650; www.hotelhemera.com; Njegoševa 17; d/ste from €95/125) Exceedingly atmospheric and gorgeously designed, the Hemera is a top choice for those who like a bit of chic in their shelter. Rooms and suites are literal masterpieces, with glorious artworks covering the walls and handmade walnut furniture used to fantastic – and fantastical – effect. There's a superb restaurant attached, and a common-use library that gives every impression of having appa-rated straight from a Harry Potter tale.

Seven Hills Bed & Bike B&B €€
(Map p102; ☑068-322 808; www.sevenhills.me; Slobode 64; s/d/ste from €40/50/55; P✳🛜) Geared towards cyclists – but welcoming everyone – this new B&B is professionally run, spotless and very central. Self-caterers will appreciate the well-equipped communal kitchen. As you'd expect, they rent bikes (guests/nonguests €5/10 per day), organise cycling tours and have plenty of bike storage for those travelling by pedal power. In keeping with their athletic ethos, smoking is banned here, a rarity in puff-happy Podgorica.

Aria HOTEL €€
(☑020-872 572; www.hotelaria.me; Mahala bb; d/apt from €88/150; P✳🛜☀) An oasis of green lawns in the scorched field surrounding the airport, this stylish hotel offers better value than its city equivalents and is a great option if you've got a badly timed flight. There's an excellent pool lined with loungers, and a huge kids' playground. Airport transfers included.

Hotel Podgorica   HOTEL €€€

(Map p102; ☑ 020-402 500; www.hotelpodgor ica.co.me; Svetlane Kane Radević 1; s/d/ste from €100/120/140; P❋✿) A wonderful show-case of 1960s Yugoslav architecture, the Podgorica has been luxuriously modernised yet retains its period charm – the river-stone cladding blending into stone the shade of Montenegro's mountains. The best rooms have terraces facing the river.

✖ Eating

Podgorica is home to some top-notch noshing spots, and offers a variety of cuisines you'll be hard-pressed to find elsewhere in the country.

Head to the **little market** (Map p102; Moskovska bb) or the **big market** (Map p102; Bratstva Jedinstva bb) for fresh fruit and vege-tables, and the large **Idea** (Map p102; Slobode bb; ⊘7am-10pm) supermarket (or any of the other chains; you can't miss them) for other cooking supplies.

★ Pod Volat   MONTENEGRIN €

(Map p102; ☑ 069-618 633; Trg Bećira-Bega Os-managića; mains €4-16) The fantastic food on offer here may be kind to the hip pocket, but not so much to the hips themselves; this is gloriously fattening Montenegrin cuisine at its best. The mixed grill is massive, but it's so good you won't mind loosening your belt a notch or two. It's a popular locals' haunt and its Stara Varoš location (beside the clock tower) is awesomely ambient.

Mantra   INDIAN €€

(Map p102; ☑ 020-242 888; www.mantrapodgorica.com; Ivana Milutinovića 21; mains €5-12; ⊘8am-1am; 🖉) In a country where any cuisine from further away than Italy is considered exotic, this opulently decorated Indian restaurant comes as a pleasant surprise – and a welcome relief for vegetarian travellers bored of pizza and pasta, and vegans sick of salad. Their cur-ry omelettes (€3) are a treat for early risers. Ask for 'spicy' if you want any hint of a kick.

Ziya   LEBANESE €€€

(Map p102; ☑ 020-230 690; www.hotelziya.me; Be-ogradska 10; mains €7-23) Attached to the bou-tique hotel of the same name – but welcoming all comers – Ziya serves delectable Lebanese mains and *meze* in equally tasty surrounds. It's a bit more upmarket than your hometown kebabery, so be sure to scrub up.

★ Dali   INTERNATIONAL €€€

(Map p102; ☑ 067-765 300; Bul Džordža Vašing-tona 87; mains €6.50-24.50; 🖉) As stylish and avant-garde as its namesake, Dali is one of the city's hippest and most popular restaurants. The menu is an eclectic mix of everything from locally sourced seafood dishes to Asian classics. Carnivores will delight in gnashing their teeth over the city's best steaks; there's also a long list of meat-free dishes for vege-tarians.

🍷 Drinking & Nightlife

Podgorica's nightlife is centred on Nova Varoš, particularly in the blocks west of Ulica Slo-bode. The hippest strip right now is Ulica Bokeška. Keep an eye out for posters listing live music events and other happenings.

Culture Club Tarantino   BAR

(Map p102; Bokeška 6; ⊘7am-1am) Exemplifying the offbeat flavour of ul Bokeška, this quirky spot promotes local music, art and other al-ternative happenings. It's a good place for a coffee and local-watching by day; at night it throngs with drinking, dancing students, cre-ative types and other hip folk.

Buda Bar   BAR

(Map p102; ☑ 067-410 777; www.facebook.com/ Budabarpg; Stanka Dragojevića 26; ⊘8am-3am) A golden Buddha smiles serenely as you med-itate over your morning coffee or search for the eternal truth at the bottom of a cocktail glass. This is one slick watering hole; the tent-like semi-enclosed terrace is the place to be on balmy summer nights, especially when there's a local starlet performing.

🛍 Shopping

The pedestrian-only sections of Hercegov-ačka and ul Slobode are Podgorica's best window-shopping strips.

There are three huge malls in Podgori-ca: **Delta City** (www.deltacity.me; Cetinjski Put; ⊘9am-10pm Mon-Sat, 9am-8pm Sun), **Mall of Montenegro** (Map p102; www.mallofmonte negro.com; Bul Bratstva i Jedinstva; ⊘9am-10pm Mon-Sat, 9am-8pm Sun) and the new **Capi-tal Plaza** (Map p102; www.thecapitalplaza.me; Cetinjski Put; ⊘9am-10pm), home to luxury boutiques and international brands.

ℹ Information

Accident & Emergency Clinic (Hitna Pomoć; Map p102; ☑ 020-226 081, 124; www.zhmp.org; Vaka Djurovića bb)

Montenegrin National Tourist Organisation (Map p102; ☑ 077-100 001; www.montenegro. travel; Marka Miljanova 17; ⊘8am-4pm)

ŠIPČANIK WINE CELLAR

When it comes to gastronomic grandeur, it doesn't get more curious than the **Šipčanik wine cellar** (020-444 125; www.plantaze.com). Ten minutes out of Podgorica and 30m underground, the enormous cellar – owned by Montenegro's largest wine company, Plantaže – occupies what was once a secret underground aircraft hangar operated by the Yugoslav People's Army. Partially destroyed by NATO bombing in 1999 and abandoned immediately afterwards, the revamped hangar now houses 2 million litres of wine, ageing gently in wooden vats beneath the very vineyard in which the grapes were grown.

Visits to Šipčanik start at €10 per person, and include a tourist-train ride through the vineyard, a cellar tour, a three-wine tasting and Njeguši cheese nibbling. The more expensive tours (€30) throw in an extra two wines and match them with more substantial gourmet fare. It's best to book ahead.

Tourist Organisation of Podgorica (Map p102; 020-667 535; www.podgorica.travel; Slobode 47; 8am-8pm Mon-Fri)

Getting There & Away

AIR

Podgorica Airport (TGD; 020-444 244; www.montenegroairports.com) welcomes flights from across Europe.

BUS

Podgorica's **bus station** (Map p102; 020-620 430; Trg Golootočkih Žrtava 1) has a left-luggage service, a post office, an ATM, a restaurant and regular services to all major towns, including Herceg Novi (€8.50, three hours), Kotor (€7.50, 2¼ hours), Budva (€6.50, 1½ hours), Ulcinj (€6.50, two hours) and Cetinje (€3.50, 30 minutes).

International destinations include Priština (€18, 7½ hours, daily), Sarajevo (€20, 6½ hours, four daily), Dubrovnik (€21, 4½ hours, two daily) and Belgrade (€25, 10 hours, frequent).

The comprehensive www.busticket4.me website has up-to-date prices and timetables for buses to/from Podgorica and all across the country.

CAR

The Sozina tunnel and toll road (one way €3.50) connects Podgorica to the Adriatic coast.

Car-hire agencies with counters at Podgorica Airport include Alamo, Avis, Europcar, Hertz, and Sixt. Local agency **Meridian** (Map p102; 020-234 944; www.meridian-rentacar.com; Bul Džordža Vašingtona 85) also has a city office; one-day hire starts from €35.

TRAIN

From Podgorica's **train station** (020-441 211; www.zpcg.me; Trg Golootočkih Žrtava 13), there are services to Bar (€2.40, one hour, nine daily), Virpazar (€1.40, 30 minutes, nine daily), Nikšić (€2.80, one hour, seven daily), Kolašin (€3.20, 90 minutes, six daily), Bijelo Polje (€5.20, two hours, six daily) and Belgrade (€20, 10 hours, three daily).

The Montenegro Railways website (www.zpcg.me) has fare and timetable information.

Getting Around

TO/FROM THE AIRPORT

Podgorica airport is 9km south of the city. Taxi fares to the city are about €10. Check the set fare before getting in.

BUS

It's not difficult to explore Podgorica on foot, but if you fancy trying a local bus, they cost 80c for a short journey.

TAXI

Alo Taxi (19700; www.halotaxi.me)
City Taxi (19711; www.citytaxi.com)

Danilovgrad

020 / POP 5200

Little Danilovgrad (Даниловград) could've been a contender. Originally conceived by Petar II Petrović Njegoš as a new capital (to replace then-capital Cetinje), all the sophisticated plans for its supremacy were swept away by the 1878 Congress of Berlin, which gave Montenegro possession of the far-grander cities of Nikšić, Podgorica and Bar.

Despite being dumped, Danilovgrad – 18km northwest of Podgorica – is a cheery place, and worth a short stop en route to Ostrog or Nikšić. The town's main street, Ulica Baja Sekulića, runs between two attractive squares. The one nearest the Zeta River is dominated by an impressive socialist realist **monument** featuring two likely lads and a staunch woman topped by a red star.

If you're around on a Saturday, take a trip out to the wonderful nearby **Donkey Farm**

(Farma Magaraca Martinici; ☏ 067-245 006; Gradina Martinićka; ☉10am-1pm Sat) **FREE**, a welcoming sanctuary for abused and neglected donkeys.

✦ Festivals & Events

River Zeta Festival   CULTURAL
(☉late Aug) Three days of fun on the Zeta, featuring wooden raft and kayak races, diving, fishing and beauty contests plus an organic-food festival.

ⓘ Information

Tourist Organisation of Danilovgrad (☏ 020-816 015; www.tod.co.me; Sava Burića 2)

ⓘ Getting There & Away

There are frequent buses running along the Podgorica–Nikšić route that call in at Danilovgrad. It's half an hour and €2 to either city.

There are seven trains per day between Podgorica (€1.20) and Nikšić (€1.60).

Ostrog Monastery

Resting improbably – miraculously? – in a cliff face 900m above the Zeta valley, the gleaming white **Ostrog Monastery** (www.manastirostrog.com) **FREE** is the most important site in Montenegro for Orthodox Christians, attracting up to a million visitors annually. Even with its numerous pilgrims, tourists and souvenir stands, it's a strangely affecting place.

The **Lower Monastery** (Donji manastir) is 2km below the main shrine. Stop here to admire the frescoes in the **Holy Trinity Church** (Crkva Sv Trojice; 1824). Behind it is a spring where you can fill your bottles with deliciously cold, sweet water (and potentially benefit from an internal blessing as you sup it).

From here the faithful, some barefoot, plod up the steep road to the top. Halfway up, the beautiful stone walls of the little domed **Church of St Stanko the Martyr** (Crkva Sv Mučenika Stanka) gleam golden in the sunset. Non-pilgrims and the pure of heart may drive directly to the main car park and limit their penitence to just the final 200m.

The **Upper Monastery** (Gornji manastir; the really impressive one) is dubbed 'Sv Vasilije's miracle', because no one seems to understand how it was built. Constructed in 1665 within two large caves, it gives the impression that it has grown out of the very rock. Sv Vasilije (St Basil), a bishop from Hercegovina, brought his monks here after the Ottomans destroyed Tvrdoš Monastery near Trebinje.

Pilgrims queue to enter the atmospheric shrine where the saint's fabric-wrapped bones are kept. To enter you'll need to be wearing a long skirt or trousers (jeans are fine) and cover your shoulders. Most women also cover their heads with a scarf. It's customary to back out of the doorways and you'll witness much kissing of lintels and making of signs of the cross from the devout. At the very top the monastery is another cave-like chapel with faded frescoes dating from 1667.

The monastery is so firmly entrenched in the country's psyche that many Montenegrins – even non-believers – commonly 'swear to Ostrog' ('*Ostroga mi..*') when promising to do something.

🛏 Sleeping

In summer, sleeping mats are provided for free to pilgrims in front of the Upper Monastery.

Guesthouse   HOSTEL €
(☏ 020-811 133; www.manastirostrog.com; dm €5) This simple guesthouse near Ostrog's Lower Monastery offers tidy single-sex dorm rooms.

ⓘ Getting There & Away

There's no direct public transport to Ostrog, but numerous tour buses (€20 to €30 for a day trip) head here from all of the tourist hot spots. Trains from Podgorica go to Ostrog train station (€1.80, 45 minutes, seven daily) way down at the bottom of the hill; it's about an hour's hike from there to the Lower Monastery.

If you're driving, we strongly recommend that you take the road from Danilovgrad to the monastery. The old road leaves the main Podgorica–Nikšić highway 19km past Danilovgrad. It's extremely narrow, twisting and steep and in a very poor state of repair; in short, it's terrifying.

Nikšić

☏ 040 / POP 57,000

With no show-stopping sights, Montenegro's second-biggest city isn't high on most travellers' must-see lists. But if you fancy a blow-out in a lively student town, Nikšić (Никшић; pronounced '*nik*-shich') has an array of establishments that offer a more genuine (not to mention cheaper) Montenegrin experience than the tourist-populated bars of Budva. What else would you expect in the town that produces Nikšićko Pivo, the nation's favourite beer? Nikšić is also in the grip of a cultural revival; it's one of the best places in Montenegro to check out alternative, avant-garde art.

CENTRAL MONTENEGRO OSTROG MONASTERY

It's not all parties and paintings here: Nikšić is one of Montenegro's main industrial centres, supporting a large steel mill and bauxite mine.

⊙ Sights

Nikšić Heritage Museum　　MUSEUM, PALACE
(Zavičajni muzej Nikšić; Trg Šaka Petrovića, King Nikola's Palace; adult/child €1/50c; ⊙ 9am-1pm & 5-8pm Tue-Sat, 9am-noon Sun) King Nikola must have kept the country's builders busy as there's yet another of his palaces here (adding to those in Cetinje, Podgorica and Bar). Now used as a museum, it's badly in need of renovating.

Start upstairs in the prehistoric section (where there are various flints dating to the 3rd millennium BC) and progress to the lovingly decorated guns, jewel-encrusted armour and embroidered clothes in the ethnographic section. WWII is covered by photographs and memorabilia (no English explanations); the graves of many of the fallen Partisans pictured are in the nearby cemetery.

Bedem Fortress　　FORTRESS
The original Nikšić was built within sturdy walls on a rocky hill to the west of the current town. This was the site of a 4th-century Roman military base that was taken over by the Goths and fortified. Today, the partially restored fortress hosts an annual **music festival** (www.bedemfest.me; ⊙ late Aug-early Sep).

From Ulica Njegoševa, take Ulica Narodnih Heroja to the end, where you'll see the fortress ahead of you. It's near the train station.

St Basil of Ostrog's Cathedral　　CHURCH
(Saborna crkva Svetog Vasilija Ostroškog; Trg Šaka Petrovića) Sitting grandly on top of a pine-covered hill, Nikšić's hefty Serbian Orthodox cathedral was built between 1895 and 1900. A central dome floods the interior with light and massive chandeliers hang from the ceiling. The exquisite iconostasis is painted in the realistic style popular in the early 20th century, as opposed to the Byzantine look of the more recent icons. Look for local saints Peter of Cetinje and Basil of Ostrog on either side of the sanctuary doors.

🏃 Activities & Tours

Anitra Travel Agency　　ADVENTURE
(📞 040-200 598; www.tara-grab.com; Njegoševa 12) Owned by the same company as Kamp Grab (p117), this local agency can arrange all kinds of active expeditions, including rafting, canyoning, hiking, fishing, mountain biking and jeep safaris.

✦✦ Festivals & Events

September Days　　CULTURAL
(Septembarski Dani Kulture; ⊙ Sep) Month-long, city-wide festival packed with artistic, musical, theatrical, folkloric and foodie events.

🛏 Sleeping & Eating

Montenegro Note Hostel　　HOSTEL €
(📞 068-615 491; www.hostelmontenegronote.com; Borislava Pekica 13; dm/r €10/24; 🅿 🛜) Just because it's the only hostel in Nikšić doesn't mean this cosy little place takes its monopoly for granted. It's small but super-friendly, clean and comfortable. Beds in the tidy eight-bed dorm have curtains for privacy; the homey private room has two singles. You'll find the hostel in a rustic house about 10 minutes' walk from Trg Slobode.

PUNKT ROCKS: HOW NIKŠIĆ GOT ITS GROOVE BACK

Think of Nikšić – if you think at all of Nikšić – and 'bohemia' is probably the last thing that springs to mind. But behind the city's industrial landscape lies a vibrant history of art and culture, a heritage that – after centuries in bloom – wilted in sync with the collapse of Yugoslavia in the 1990s. But creativity is once again flowering in Montenegro's second city, all thanks to a visionary collective called PUNKT.

Set up in 2015 by a group of young creatives, PUNKT is putting Nikšić back on the boho map by bombarding the city with the artistic and musical works of hitherto voiceless up-and-coming locals. Their first exhibition – for which they commandeered a dilapidated Yugoslav Army building – featured a wooden orchestra created by chainsaw, a room painted with eyeballs, avant-garde films and punk performances. Since then, they've held well-received exhibitions and concerts at bars, cafes and galleries across town, and have been revitalising – or, in the words of the crew, 'PUNKTing' – the cityscape with public murals. Keep up with them on www.facebook.com/KCPUNKT; if there's a happening when you're in town, it's well worth checking out.

★ **Hotel Trebjesa**   HOTEL **€€**
(☑ 077-200 060; www.hoteltrebjesa.me; Trebjesa bb; d €55-70, apt €95) Overlooking Nikšić from its forested perch in Trebjesa park, this sparkling hotel offers a literal breath of fresh air. All rooms are clean, comfortable and have beautiful mountain and city views; some have jacuzzis. It's an easy five-minute drive up the hill from the centre of town, or you can toodle about on the hotel's free bikes.

★ **Pekara**   INTERNATIONAL **€€**
(☑ 067-267 943; Marka Miljanova bb; mains €3-10; ⊙ 7am-11pm) Its name means 'bakery', but there's more to this wildly popular hangout than bread rolls. While their baked offerings – waffles, cakes and outrageously stacked pancakes – are indeed divine, it's also worth a visit to sample their burgers, grills and local stews served in hearty, edible bowls.

Forest   INTERNATIONAL **€€**
(cnr Ivana Milutinovića & Manastirska; mains €4-15; ⊙ 8am-midnight) The sidewalk seating at this corner cafe-restaurant makes for an excellent people-watching spot. Goggle at passers-by over a bowl of pasta (reputed to be the best in town) and a glass of wine from their long list. They also make tasty coffees and cakes.

🍷 Drinking & Nightlife

Propaganda Bar   BAR, CAFE
(Trg Slobode; ⊙ 8am-midnight) This vibrant cafe-bar is populated by friendly, arty locals nattering over superb coffees by day and even better cocktails by night.

Blues Brothers Bar   BAR
(Njegoševa 9) Fantastic bar that often hosts various cultural events, from music (orchestra, blues, rock, you name it) to alternative art and cinema exhibitions.

ℹ Information

The helpful **Tourist Organisation of Nikšić** (☑ 040-213 262; www.niksic.travel; Ivana Milutinovića 10) is a short stroll south of Trg Slobode.

General Hospital (Opšta bolnica; ☑ 040-231 111; www.bolnica-nk.com; Radoja Dakića bb)

ℹ Getting There & Away

BUS

The **bus station** (☑ 040-213 018; Gojka Garčevića bb) is next to the main roundabout and has toilets, restaurants and a left-luggage counter (€1). Domestic destinations include Kotor (€8, three hours, seven daily), Budva (€8.70, two hours, 10 daily), Podgorica (€3.50, one hour, frequent),

Plužine (€5.50, one hour, six daily) and Žabljak (€6, 2½ hours, six daily). International services include Trebinje (€6.50, two hours, four daily), Sarajevo (€15, five hours, five daily) and Belgrade (€26, 10¾ hours, one daily).

A good road leads south from Nikšić directly down to Risan on the Bay of Kotor; heading north, it will take you to Žabljak.

CAR

A good road leads south from Nikšić directly down to Risan on the Bay of Kotor; heading north, it will take you to Žabljak.

TRAIN

Train Station (☑ 040-211 912; www.zpcg. me; Gojka Garčevića bb) Seven trains a day head to/from Podgorica (€2.80, one hour) via Danilovgrad and Ostrog.

Around Nikšić

Travelling west on the road to Trebinje in Hercegovina, a large sign on the left (3.5km after the roundabout on the edge of town) points to **Most na Moštanici**, a 3rd-century Roman bridge. It's a bit hard to find as there are no other signs once you leave the main road. Coming off the road, turn sharp left and then right. Veer left after about 300m and head alongside the village. After a kilometre you'll see the bridge near a sturdy little church. The bridge's five graceful arches once spanned a flowing river that is today a dry ditch.

Heading in the same direction, a few kilometres past the turn-off to the bridge, you'll see **Lake Slano** (Slansko jezero) on your left. Although it's an artificial structure (there's a dam at one edge), Slano's sparkling blue waters, low-lying islands and green borders make for a beautiful vista. There are a few tiny villages on the shore but there's no straightforward route down to the water; take whatever turn-off you can find and wind your way down. You'll be unlikely to find more than a few people fishing or sunbathing.

More popular is **Lake Krupac** (Krupačko jezero), another dammed lake to the northwest of town that's been given the local nickname 'Nikšić's sea'. It has a small sandy beach, a couple of beach bars, picnic spots and pedal boats, jet skis and kayaks for hire. The **Lake Fest** (www.lakefest.me; ⊙ mid-Aug) music festival is held on its shores.

There are four ski slopes at **Vučje** (☑ 067-319 719; www.vucje.me; day pass adult/child €10/5), 21km northeast of Nikšić on the road to Šavnik.

Northern Mountains

Best Places to Eat

➡ Sočica (p125)

➡ Lupo D'argento (p119)

➡ Vodenica (p114)

➡ Savardak (p113)

➡ Krojet (p123)

Best Places to Sleep

➡ Eko-Oaza Suza Evrope (p118)

➡ Hikers Den (p118)

➡ Bianca Resort & Spa (p113)

➡ Etno Selo Šljeme (p119)

➡ Zvono (p125)

Why Go?

The mountainous north is the beefy brawn to the coast's polished pulchritude. Peaking at 2534m, this is the roof of Montenegro, where profound massifs, otherworldly vistas and a picturesque smattering of old-school villages offer a literal and metaphorical breath of fresh air.

The region's main drawcards are its three national parks. Durmitor is a dizzying combination of soaring peaks and the plunging depths of the Tara River Canyon, making for spectacular skiing in winter and rip-roaring rafting in summer. The remote treks and trails of Prokletije's Accursed Mountains are more heaven than hell for serious alpinists, while the less hard-core can catch their breath in Biogradska Gora's gentle lakes and timeless forests.

There's not much in the way of infrastructure outside of Kolašin and Žabljak, but don't let that stop you. Hire a car, steady your nerves, and let the twisty, turny, white-knuckle roads take you where they will.

When to Go

➡ In January and February, spend your days skiing and your nights feasting in front of an open fire.

➡ July and August have the best hiking weather, with average Durmitor temperatures in the low 20s.

➡ Watch the forest explode in colour in September and October as autumn hits Biogradska Gora.

Climate

It shouldn't surprise anyone that this mountainous region is cooler than the rest of the country. Average high temperatures range from just above freezing in January to the low 20s in August.

🛈 Getting There & Away

The highway between Podgorica and Belgrade cuts through Mojkovac and Bijelo Polje and is served by buses. A major road connects Nikšić to Durmitor; this road leads south to Risan on the Bay of Kotor. You can travel to Kolašin, Mojkovac and Bijelo Polje by train from Serbia in the north or Podgorica and Bar in the south. There are also road connections with Bosnia, Serbia and Kosovo.

Northern Mountains Highlights

① Tara Canyon (p116) Rafting between the kilometre-plus canyon walls in Durmitor National Park.

② Prokletije National Park (p125) Tackling the trails and treks of the Accursed Mountains.

③ Biogradska Gora National Park (p114) Searching for wood nymphs in the primordial forest.

④ Morača Monastery (p112) Time-warping to the 13th century as you step through the gates.

⑤ Rožaje (p121) People-watching as the evening promenade descends on the main street.

⑥ Gusinje (p123) Soaking up the peaceful Eastern vibe between the mosques and mountains.

⑦ Piva Canyon (p123) Taking a white-knuckle ride between the sheer cliffs and green depths.

ⓘ Getting Around

South of Bijelo Polje, the Podgorica–Belgrade highway joins another highway leading through Berane and Rožaje. Buses take both of these routes. The road from Mojkovac to Žabljak is in excellent condition but gets twistier as it leaves the Tara Canyon and climbs into the mountains; this isn't a regular bus route. Plav is the most isolated town but it's reached by a scenic road used by frequent buses to Berane. It's possible to circle the Bjelasica mountains completely in a 136km loop. The most spectacular section is from Kolašin to Andrijevica, but it is prone to landslides in bad weather and avoided by buses.

It's possible to travel between Kolašin, Mojkovac and Bijelo Polje by train.

Morača Canyon

Heading north from Podgorica, it doesn't take long before the scenery becomes breathtaking. The highway – a thrilling, spectacular stretch of road – gets progressively more precarious as it follows the Morača River into a nearly perpendicular canyon, 300m to 400m deep. If you're driving, pull over into one of the viewing areas to enjoy it properly: this is an extremely busy and unforgiving stretch of road.

The river continues after the canyon recedes; you'll find the **Morača Monastery** (Manastir Morača) near its banks. Founded in 1252, this is one of the most important Orthodox monasteries in Montenegro, with some of its most accomplished religious art.

As you enter the walled compound into a garden courtyard where the bees from the monks' hives dance between the hydrangeas and roses, it's like stepping back into the 13th century. To the right, the small **St Nicholas' Church** (Crkva Sv Nikole) has faded frescoes on its facade which were once as vivid as those inside.

The larger **Church of the Dormition** (Crkva Uspenja Bogorodice) has external frescoes by the celebrated master Djordje Mitrofanović, plus beautiful doors inlaid with geometric patterns. The church's treasures include Mitrofanović's *The Virgin Enthroned with Child, Prophets and Hymnographers* (1617). The other master at work here was Kozma, whose icon of *Saints Sava and Simeon* (1645), on the right-hand wall, includes a border showing the construction of the monastery (the latter saint was the founder's grandfather).

This is an active monastery (albeit with only four monks); dress appropriately.

Kolašin

✔ 020 / POP 3000

Sitting 960m above sea level, Kolašin (Колашин; pronounced 'ko-*la*-shin') is Montenegro's main mountain resort. Although the skiing's not as reliable as in Durmitor, Kolašin's much easier to get to (it's just off the main highway, 71km north of Podgorica) and has ritzier accommodation offerings. Like most ski towns, it looks far prettier under a blanket of snow, but even in summer it's a handy base for exploring Biogradska Gora National Park or other parts of the Bjelasica Mountains.

Most things of interest, including banks and a post office, are set around the two central squares (Trg Borca and Trg Vukmana Kruščića) and the short street that connects them (Ulica IV Proleterske).

◉ Sights

Botanic Garden   GARDENS
(Botanička bašta; botanybasta@t-com.me; Put Braće Vujisić) With a huge collection of indigenous mountain flora and medicinal herbs, this fascinating, privately owned garden has attracted botanists from around the world. The garden's founder and keeper, Daniel Vincek, may be getting along in years, but his knowledge – and the infectious way he shares his passion for plants in excellent English – is timeless.

Hours are at Daniel's whim; if you're keen to visit, ask the tourist office to give him a call, or drop him an email yourself.

Heritage Museum   MUSEUM
(Zavičajni muzej; Trg Borca 1; ⊙ 8am-3pm) `FREE`
Trg Borca contains a stirring statue of a young man and woman marching forward, guns and communist flag aloft. They look like they're about to liberate the museum building, which served as a prison during WWII. Inside, the collection consists mainly of photos and there aren't any English explanations, but the idealistic faces of the town's young comrades, many of whom lost their lives fighting the Nazis, are captivating. There's also an ethnographic section and an art gallery.

🏃 Activities

Three marked **hiking paths** start from Trg Borca and head into the Bjelasica Mountains. From the ski centre there's a 16km, five-hour loop route through forest to **Mt Ključ** (1973m) and on to Eco Katun Vranjak before heading back. If you're staying at the *katun* (traditional shepherd's mountain hut) you can take another scenic trail that knocks off **Zekova Glava** (2117m) and passes **Lake Pešić** (Pešićko jezero), skirting beneath Bjelasica's highest peak. On the loop back it visits the spring that is the source of the Biogradska River before heading up **Troglava** (2072m). The 16km path is easy and well marked and should take less than five hours. For detailed descriptions and maps of both trails, pick up a copy of the *Mountains of Bjelasica* booklet available at either of the tourist offices.

A 93km **mountain-biking route** runs through remote countryside from Podgorica to Kolašin. There are plenty of places in Kolašin to hire bikes, so you could pick one up here, catch the train to Podgorica and cycle back over a few days.

Kolašin 1450 Ski Resort SKIING
(☑ 068-041 450; www.kolasin1450.com; day/week ski pass €15/98) Located 10km east of Kolašin, at an elevation of 1450m, this ski centre offers 30km of runs (graded green, blue, red and black) reached by various ski lifts, as well as a cafe and restaurant in attractive wooden chalets. You can hire a full ski or snowboard kit from €13 per day. The ski season lasts roughly from December to mid-April.

In winter, there are shuttle buses from the Bianca and Lipka hotels; they're free if you're a guest or if you purchase your ski pass from the hotels.

★ Jelka Tours ADVENTURE
(☑ 069-400 094; www.jelka.me) Very well-regarded local operators offering all-season tours, activities (rafting, hiking, canyoning, snowmobiling, et al), photo safaris and excellent, engaging village stays at their mountain *katun* village (from €25 per person) right beside Biogradska National Park.

Explorer Tourist Agency ADVENTURE
(☑ 020-864 200; www.explorer.co.me; Mojkovačka bb) Located near the bus station, this agency specialises in action-packed holidays. It can arrange hiking, skiing, rafting, mountain biking, canyoning, caving, mountain climbing, jeep safaris, horse riding, paragliding and fishing expeditions. It also hires out mountain bikes.

🛏 Sleeping

Premium prices are charged during the ski season, with the absolute peak being around New Year. In summer it's possible to stay high in the mountains in a traveller-friendly version of a traditional *katun* (wooden shepherd's hut); enquire at the tourist office or book through one of the adventure travel agencies.

Apartments Life APARTMENT €€
(☑ 068-003 056; www.apartments-life.com; Toška i Jovana bb; apt from €45; P 🖧) Centrally located and very welcoming, this cosy place offers the choice of a one-bedroom apartment, a private cottage or an entire house; all are cosy, clean and great value. During winter, it rents out ski equipment; in the warmer months, guests can socialise around the communal barbecue. It's a top spot for self-caterers; all accommodations have kitchens, and it's just a quick stroll to Kolašin's produce market.

Brile HOTEL €€
(☑ 020-865 021; www.brile.co; Buda Tomovića 2; s/d €35/74; 🖧) On the edge of the main square, this attractive family-run hotel has comfy rooms with polished wooden floors. There's a sauna for an après-ski defrost and a restaurant downstairs serving warming comfort food such as roasts, grilled meat, pizza and pasta. It also rents out bikes and skis.

★ Bianca Resort & Spa RESORT €€€
(☑ 020-863 000; www.biancaresort.com; Mirka Vešovića bb; d/ste from €120/200; P 🖧 ⛄) Take one large angular hotel with quirky hexagonal windows, completely gut it, add a heap of rakish, rustic touches, and voila! You get this atmospheric, idiosyncratic first-rate ski resort. After a hard day on the slopes, you can soothe out any bumps and bruises in the luxury spa, which includes a large indoor pool, sauna, Turkish bath and gym.

🍴 Eating

★ Konoba MONTENEGRIN €€
(☑ 069-609 144; Trg Vukmana Kruščića; mains €6-8; ⊗ 8am-midnight) Sitting on the square that was the heart of the old Turkish town, this rustic eatery is a standard-bearer for Montenegrin mountain cuisine, such as *kačamak* (polenta porridge with mashed potato), *cicvara* (creamy polenta), *popara* (bread-based porridge) and tender roast lamb that falls off the bone.

Savardak MONTENEGRIN €€
(☑ 069-051 264; savardak@t-com.me; mains €8-9) Located 2.8km from Kolašin on the road to the ski centre, Savardak serves traditional food in what appears to be a big haystack

with a chimney attached. Eat in the atmospheric interior or sit at outdoor tables by the stream. Four-person apartments (€40) are available in a thatch-roofed wooden chalet next door.

Vodenica MONTENEGRIN €€
(☏ 069-241 507; Dunje Dokić bb; mains €6-9; ☺ 9am-11pm) Set in a traditional watermill, Vodenica offers a taste of traditional stodgy mountain food designed to warm your belly on cold nights. Ease back and let your arteries clog over a bowl of *cicvara* or *kačamak*.

ℹ Information

Bjelasica & Komovi Regional Tourism Organisation (☏ 020-860 670; www.bjelasica-komovi.me; Trg Borca 2; ☺ 9am-8pm Mon-Fri, 9am-noon & 4-8pm Sat & Sun) When it's open (hours can be hit or miss), this impressive wooden information centre should be your first port of call for information on hiking and mountain-biking routes. It can help arrange all manner of mountain activities and tours, including visits to local honey and cheese producers. It also rents out mountain bikes (per half-day/day €7/10). You'll find it prominently located near the main square.

The organisation is also involved in the Northern Exposure project (www.northernexposure.me), an EU-backed project promoting year-round activities in the mountainous regions of Montenegro and Bosnia. See the website for tons if information on year-round activities in the Bjelasica, Komovi and Prokletije regions.

Kolašin Tourist Office (☏ 020-864 254; www.to-kolasin.me; Mirka Vešovića bb; ☺ 8am-8pm Mon-Fri, 9am-3pm Sat) The town's tourist office is very useful for arranging private accommodation (including *katun* stays) and for information on local activities.

ℹ Getting There & Away

The **bus station** (☏ 020-864 033; Mojkovačka bb) is a wooden shed by a scrappy parking lot on the road leading into town, about 200m north of the centre. Destinations include Pljevlja (€7, 2½ hours, five daily), Podgorica (€5, 1½ hours, frequent), Bar (€6.50, 2½ hours, five daily), Budva (€10, three hours, seven daily) and Kotor (€10.50, 3¾ hours, five daily).

Kolašin's **train station** (☏ 020-441 492; www.zpcg.me) is 1.5km east from the centre, with services to Bijelo Polje (€2.20, 30 minutes, six daily), Podgorica (€3.20, 90 minutes, six daily), Bar (€5.40, 2½ hours, five daily) and Belgrade (€16, 6½ hours, two daily). Buy your tickets on the train.

Biogradska Gora National Park

Nestled within the Bjelasica mountain range, pretty Biogradska Gora (Биоградска Гора) has as its heart 1600 hectares of virgin woodland – one of Europe's last three remaining primeval forests. King Nikola is to thank for its survival; on a visit in 1878 he was so taken by the beauty of **Lake Biogradska** (Biogradsko jezero) that the locals gifted him the land and he ordered it to be preserved.

Many of the trees in the forest are more than half a millennium old, with some soaring to dizzying heights of 60m. The park is also home to five high-altitude (1820m) glacial lakes.

There are many signposted hiking trails within the park, ranging in difficulty from chilled (a 3.4km amble around Lake Biograd) to challenging (35km trek up to Crna Glava and beyond). The **park office** (☏ 020-865 625; www.nparkovi.me; ☺ 7.30am-8.30pm) has information on hikes and trails; if you're not keen to go it alone, ask about their expert mountain guides (four/eight hours €60/80). The office also rents rowboats (€8 per hour) and kayaks (from €3 per hour).

🛏 Sleeping & Eating

Bring your own picnic or try the lakeside **Restoran Biogradsko Jezero** (mains €5-10), much beloved by tour groups and hungry hikers.

National Park Accommodation CAMPGROUND, BUNGALOWS €
(☏ 020-865 625; www.nparkovi.me; campsites per small tent/large tent/caravan €3/5/10, cabins per person €10) Near the park office, there's a campsite and a cluster of 12 small log cabins, each with two or three single beds. The ablutions block for the cabins is much nicer than the campsite's basic squat toilets.

ℹ Getting There & Away

The main entrance to the park is between Kolašin and Mojkovac on the Podgorica–Belgrade highway. After paying a €3 entry fee, you can drive the further 4km to Lake Biograd.

Getting here via public transport (plus a bit of hoofing it) is also possible. Buses to/from Kolašin and Mojkovac stop (on request) at Kraljevo Kolo, the entrance to the park. From there it's about an hour's walk to the lake.

THE BJELASICA MASSIF

The Bjelasica massif dominates northeastern Montenegro with 10 grand peaks higher than 2000m. The unfortunately named Crna Glava (Black Head) is the highest at 2139m.

Any preconception you may have of Montenegro's mountains as grey and barren will be shattered as the snows recede and reveal virgin forest (within the protected Biogradska Gora National Park) and meadows teeming with wildflowers. In the higher pastures you'll find *katuns*, round thatched structures that have been used for centuries by seminomadic shepherds when they bring their flocks here in summer. It's a much more forgiving environment than the Orjen, Lovćen or Durmitor ranges, and therefore easier to explore.

Trails are accessed from the towns that encircle the mountain: Kolašin, Mojkovac, Bijelo Polje, Berane and Andrijevica. The best times for hiking are at the end of summer and in autumn when the forests are a mash of colours. Be prepared for sudden drops in temperature and storms. Local tourist offices should be able to provide you with maps, information, advice, and contacts for guides. Otherwise, talk to one of the agencies specialising in adventure holidays. The excellent website www.northernexposure.me has loads of useful information on year-round activities in and around the Bjelasica region.

The nearest train station (Štitarička Rijeka) is a 90-minute walk away.

Mojkovac

🕿 050 / POP 4000

Despite being on the doorstep of two national parks, Mojkovac (Мојковац; pronounced '*moy*-ko-vats') hasn't cashed in on its potential – at least not yet. Over recent years there's been a concerted effort to clean up the toxic legacy of centuries of silver, lead and zinc mining. Now that the task has been largely completed, the United Nations Development Programme has turned its attention to encouraging adventure tourism and organic farming – watch this space. In the meantime, don't drink the water.

The centre of town is triangular Trg Ljubomira Bakoča, encompassing a pretty little park and a large pompous statue of Janko Vukotić, who led Montenegrin forces to a bloody, underdog victory against Austria-Hungary in the WWI Battle of Mojkovac.

A steep hiking path leads from the centre to a 17km (six-hour) loop through the surrounding mountains; take trail 310 and return on 319 and then 301. Mojkovac's railway station is the starting point of a 309km, six- to seven-day mountain-biking loop (Top Biking Trail 3: Eastern Enchantment) which takes in Biogradska Gora National Park, Gusinje, Plav and Rožaje. The **Mojkovac Tourism Organisation** (www. mojkovac.travel; Serdara Janka Vukotića bb) can help with trail and trek information.

🛏 Sleeping & Eating

Hotel & Resort Gacka   B&B €€€
(🕿 050-474 720; www.imanjerakocevic.me; tw/d €95/110, 1-/2-bedroom chalets from €120/200; ⊡ 🏊) Less than 5km from Mojkovac's centre but a million miles from its (relative) bustle, this lovely spot is dotted with pristine wooden cabins enjoying picture-perfect mountain views. The 'luxury' cottages have saunas, though all guests can use the spa's indoor pool. There's an excellent on-site restaurant dishing up fattening local fare, which goes a long way towards soaking up their homemade wines and *rakija* (fruit brandy).

❶ Getting There & Away

Mojkovac's large **bus station** (🕿 050-472 247; Podgorica-Belgrade Hwy) is a major stop on the Podgorica–Belgrade route. Destinations include Podgorica (€6, two hours, frequent), Kolašin (€2.50, 35 minutes, frequent), Pljevlja (€6, two hours, two daily) and Belgrade (€17, 9½ hours, six daily). The station is 200m north of the main square.

The train station is on the southern outskirts of town. Trains head from here to Bar (€6.20, 2¾ hours, five daily), Podgorica (€4.40, two hours, six daily) and Bijelo Polje (€1.20, 20 minutes, six daily).

Durmitor National Park

The impossibly rugged and dramatic Durmitor (Дурмитор) is one of Montenegro's – and Mother Nature's – showpieces. Carved out by glaciers and underground streams, Durmitor stuns with dizzying canyons, glittering glacial lakes and nearly 50 limestone peaks soaring to over 2000m; the highest, **Bobotov Kuk**, hits 2523m. From December to March, Durmitor is a major ski resort, while in summer it's popular for hiking, rafting and other active pursuits.

The national park covers the Durmitor mountain range and a narrow branch heading east along the Tara River towards Mojkovac. West of the park, the mighty Tara marks the border with Bosnia and joins the Piva River near Šćepan Polje.

Durmitor is home to 163 bird species, about 50 types of mammals and purportedly the greatest variety of butterflies in Europe. It's very unlikely you'll spot bears and wolves, which is either a good or bad thing depending on your perspective.

All roads (and ski runs and bumpy trails) lead to **Žabljak**, regional capital and – at 1450m – one of the highest towns in the Balkans. Quaintly ramshackle – though slowly smartening up – it's the gateway to Durmitor's mountain adventures. You'll find restaurants, hotels and a supermarket gathered around the car park that masquerades as Žabljak's main square.

◎ Sights

★ Tara Canyon   CANYON

Slicing through the mountains at the northern edge of the national park, the Tara River forms one of the world's deepest canyons (1300m; the Grand Canyon plummets a mere 200m deeper).

The best views are from the water, and rafting (p117) along the river is one of the country's most popular tourist activities. If you'd rather admire the canyon from afar, head to the top of **Mt Ćurevac** (1625m) – although even this view is restricted by the canyon walls.

ⓘ PARK FEES

The road to Black Lake is blocked off just past the National Park Visitors Centre and an entry fee is charged (per person per day €3, free for children under seven). If you're planning on staying in the area, it's worth purchasing a three-day (€6) or weekly ticket (€12). Drivers will need to park outside the gates (€2) and walk the remaining 500m to the lake. Keep hold of your ticket, in case you bump into a ranger.

The viewpoint isn't well signposted and can be difficult to find. From Žabljak's central square, take the main road east and before you leave the town, turn left at a sign reading 'Restoran Momčilov Grad'. Shortly after, turn right and follow this road as it climbs the hill. Where there are any forks, chose the road that loops up and follow any signs that say 'Tepca'. Eventually there are some small wooden signs pointing to Ćurevac or *vidikovac* (viewpoint). Stop at the grassy parking spot with the national park information boards and clamber up the small track behind.

Tara Bridge   BRIDGE

The elegant spans of the 150m-high Tara Bridge were completed just as WWII was starting. At the time it was the largest concrete arched vehicular bridge in Europe. Its 365m length is carried on five sweeping arches, the largest of which is 116m wide.

In May 1942, with large numbers of Italian and German troops stationed in Žabljak, the Partisan command gave the order to blow up the bridge. The honour went to one of its engineers, Lazar Jauković, who planted the bomb that destroyed his beautiful creation. Jauković was captured by the Italians and executed on the remains of his bridge. When it was rebuilt in 1946, Jauković's bravery was acknowledged by a plaque that still stands by the bridge today.

Black Lake   LAKE

(Crno jezero) Eighteen glittering glacial lakes known as *gorske oči* (mountain eyes) dot the Durmitor range. The spectacular Black Lake, a pleasant 3km walk from Žabljak, is the largest and most visited part of the national park. The rounded mass of **Međed** (the Bear; 2287m) rears up behind it, casting an inky shadow into the pine-walled waters. An easy 3.6km walking track circles the lake.

Stećci   CEMETERY

Stećci – mysterious carved stone monuments dating between the 12th and 16th centuries – are found across northern Montenegro. There are two extremely significant *stećci* sites in Durmitor National Park (both were added to Unesco's World Heritage list in 2016): Bare Žugića necropolis and Grčko groblje ('Greek graveyard'). Around 5km south from Žabljak, turn left towards Vražje Jezero (Devil's Lake); Bare Žugića necropolis is beside Bare Žugića village. Grčko groblje is nearby, 200m northwest of Riblje Jezero (Fish Lake) in Novakovići village.

Bare Žugića is dotted with 300 *stećci* while Grčko groblje has 49; many of the stones, slabs and tombstones at both sites are intricately decorated. Though neither site is signposted or staffed, they're easy to visit if you've got wheels.

Dobrilovina Monastery   CHRISTIAN MONASTERY
Near the eastern boundary of the national park, 28km from Mojkovac, this monastery has an idyllic setting in lush fields hemmed in by the mountains and the Tara River.

If you knock at the accommodation wing, a black-robed nun will unlock the church, but only if she's satisfied that you're appropriately attired. Dedicated to St George (Sv Đorđe), the frescoes that remain inside the church are faded but very beautiful.

🏃 Activities
Rafting
A rafting expedition along the Tara is the best way to revel in glorious river scenery that's impossible to catch from land. Trips are suitable for everyone from the white-water novice to experienced foam-hounds. Though it's not the world's most white-knuckled ride, there are a few rapids; if you're after speed, visit in April and May, when the last of the melting snow revs up the flow. Various operators run trips between April and October.

The 82km section that is raftable starts from Splavište, south of the Tara Bridge, and ends at Šćepan Polje on the Bosnian border. The classic two-day trip heads through the deepest part of the canyon on the first day, stopping overnight at Radovan Luka. Summit Travel Agency (p118) offers a range of rafting trips out of Žabljak (half-/one-/two-day tour €45/110/200).

Most of the day tours from the coast traverse only the last 18km from Brstanovica – this is outside the national park and hence avoids hefty fees. You'll miss out on the canyon's depths, but it's still a beautiful stretch, including most of the rapids. The buses follow a spectacular road along the Piva River, giving you a double dose of canyon action.

It's important to use a reputable operator; in 2010 two people died in one day on a trip with inexperienced guides. At a minimum make sure you're given a helmet and life jacket – wear them and do them up. Some noteworthy operators are **Kamp Grab** (📋 040-200 598; www.tara-grab.com; half-day incl lunch €44, 2-day all-inclusive rafting trip €180), **Tara·Tour** (📋 069-086 106; www.tara-tour.com) and **Rafting Centre Waterfall** (📋 069-310

848; www.raftingmontenegro.com; half-/full day rafting ex-Žabljak €45/110). Many of the rafting groups also offer other activities, including horse riding, canyoning and jeep safaris. If you've got your own wheels you can save a few bucks and avoid a lengthy coach tour by heading directly to Šćepan Polje and hooking up with the rafting tours there.

Hiking
Durmitor is one of the best-marked mountain ranges in Europe, with 25 marked trails making up a total of 150km. Some suggest it's a little *too* well labelled, encouraging novices to wander around seriously high-altitude paths which are prone to fog and summer thunderstorms. Ask the staff at the National Park Visitors Centre about tracks that suit your level of experience and fitness.

One rewarding route is the hike to the two **Škrčka Lakes** (Škrčka jezera), in the centre of a tectonic valley, where you can enjoy magnificent scenery and stay overnight in a mountain hut. Another popular hike is from Black Lake to the **ice cave** (ledina pećina) – home in cooler months to stalactite- and stalagmite-like shapes made of ice – on Obla Glava. It's a six- to seven-hour return hike.

If you're considering an assault on Bobotov Kuk or a serious winter expedition, you're best to arrange a local guide.

In any case, check the weather forecast before you set out, stick to the tracks, and prepare for rain and sudden drops in temperature. A compass could be a lifesaver. *Durmitor and the Tara Canyon* by Branislav Cerović (€15 from the visitors centre) is a great resource for mountaineers and serious hikers. The **Mountaineering Association of Montenegro** (www.pscg.me) has contacts and info on the peaks and paths of Durmitor.

The Montenegrin part of the 1930km **Via Dinarica** (www.viadinarica.com) 'mega-trail' – which traverses Slovenia, Serbia, Croatia, BiH, Montenegro, Albania, Kosovo and Macedonia – connects Durmitor with BiH's Sutjeska National Park. See the website for details, or contact Black Mountain (p38) to organise hiking tours.

Skiing
With 120 days of snow cover, Durmitor offers the most reliable – and cheapest – skiing in Montenegro.

Around Žabljak, **Savin Kuk Ski Centar** (📋 052-361 144; 1-day/2-day/weekly pass €10/17/60) and **Javorovača Ski Centar** (📋 067-800 971; adult/child day pass €8/5, weekly pass €48/30) both rent out equipment and offer lessons. See www.skiresortmontenegro.com (in Montenegrin) for more information on Durmitor's ski centres.

Free-riding snowboarders and skiers should check out www.riders.me for off-piste adventure ideas.

Canyoning

Just south of the national park, near Šavnik, is the remarkable 2.7km-long **Nevidio Canyon**. Cut by the Komarnica River, at points it is only metres wide, hence the name (*nevidio* means 'invisible'). It's extremely beautiful but equally dangerous. Canyoning expeditions generally take about three to four hours and participants should be able to swim and have a high level of fitness.

July and August are the safest months to explore, and then only in the company of professional guides. **Montenegro Canyoning** (☑ 069-565 311; www.montenegro-canyoning.com; trip without/with lunch per person €90/100) is a highly recommended group that focuses solely on expeditions to Nevidio. Otherwise, Anitra (p108) organises expeditions out of Nikšić (price on application), and Summit Travel Agency and Durmitor Adventure do so out of Žabljak (€120 per person including lunch, minimum two people).

Ziplining

Get a bird's-eye view of Durmitor's delights with a zoom on a zipline. Two outfits have set up shop here: **Red Rock Zipline** (☑ 069-440 290; www.redrockzipline.com; adult €10; ⏰ 10am-7pm May-Oct) and **Avanturistički Park** (☑ 069-214 110; www.avanturistickipark.me; Black Lake; adults/kids 8-14/kids under 7 €9/8/6; ⏰ 10am-7pm daily Jul & Aug, 10am-6pm Sat & Sun Jun & Sep) for those who prefer mild over wild.

Rock Climbing

Two rock walls have been prepared on the side of the mountain at **Pirlitor**, but you'll need your own ropes.

To get to Pirlitor from Žabljak, head towards the Tara Bridge, turn left at Vrela and follow the signs. The access road is very rough and is best attempted with a four-wheel drive.

The easier eastern wall has six lines graded 3+ to 4+ on the French scale, reaching to about 10m. There are 14 routes on the 30m-high western wall, graded from 5b to 7b+.

Jeep Safaris

Simply driving Durmitor is a delight – if a spine-chilling/twisting one – of its own. If you haven't got your own wheels – or are rightfully nervous about braving the precipitous, twisty-turny roads on your own – a jeep safari is an excellent and easy way to take in the region's magnificent, oft-eerie scenery. Safaris generally include village visits, traditional lunches and off-road bushwhacks.

The National Park Visitors Centre (p119) can arrange jeep safaris from €20; otherwise, almost all hotels and adventure operators offer their own tours.

Tours

Durmitor Adventure   ADVENTURE
(☑ 069-629 516; www.durmitoradventure.com) This well-regarded group offers canyoning expeditions (€120; prices per person decrease with larger groups) to Nevido and a range of guided mountain hikes, including treks to Bobotov kuk (€70) and the ice cave (€60).

Summit Travel Agency   ADVENTURE
(☑ 069-016 502; www.summit.co.me; Njegoševa 12, Žabljak; half-/1-/2-day rafting trip €45/110/200) As well as rafting trips, this long-standing agency can arrange jeep tours, mountain-bike hire and canyoning expeditions. It also has accommodation in the form of cabins (€70) and a guesthouse (from €15) in Žabljak.

🛏 Sleeping

Campgrounds and Žabljak's lone hostel are generally open from April to October.

⭐**Hikers Den**   HOSTEL €
(☑ 067-854 433; www.hostelzabljak.com; Božidara Žugića bb, Žabljak; dm €13-15, s/d €22/35; 📶) Split between three neighbouring houses, this laid-back and sociable place is by far the best hostel in the north. If you're keen on a rafting or canyoning trip, the charming English-speaking hosts will happily make the arrangements.

⭐**Eko-Oaza**
Suza Evrope   CABINS, CAMPGROUND €
(☑ 069-444 590; ekooazatara@gmail.com; Dobrilovina; campsites per tent/person/campervan €5/1/10, cabins €50; ⏰ Apr-Oct) Consisting of four comfortable wooden cottages (each sleeping five people) and a fine stretch of lawn above the river, this magical, family-run 'eco oasis' offers a genuine experience of

Montenegrin hospitality. Home-cooked meals are provided on request, and rafting trips and jeep safaris can be arranged.

Autokamp Mlinski Potok CAMPGROUND €
(☑ 069-497 625; www.facebook.com/camp.durmitor. mlinskipotok; campsites per person/car €3.50/1.50, r €10; ℗) With a fabulously hospitable host (there's no escaping the *rakija* shots), this private campsite above the visitors centre is a sociable option. It's a fairly basic set-up but there are hot-water showers and clean sit-down toilets. Private rooms are also available.

★**Etno Selo Šljeme** CABIN €€
(☑ 063-229 294; www.etnoselosljeme.com; Smrčevo brdo bb, Žabljak; cabin €90; ℗ 🛜) With majestic mountain views and lashings of local cuisine on offer, a stay here is a wonderful way to soak up the scenic splendour of Durmitor. The five gorgeous two-bedroom cabins are more swish than some of the other 'etno' offerings in the vicinity; there's also a playground and bikes for hire. It's close to the ski centres and Žabljak town, but isolated enough to get a feel for the northern wilderness.

Polar Star HOTEL €€
(☑ 067-609 444; www.polarstar.me; Borje; d/apt €80/110; ℗ 🛜) A quick 4km drive from Žabljak, this recently renovated hotel is a clean, comfy and comradely option for those who want to be near town but not in it. Apartments have full kitchens and dishwashers; all guests have access to the free sauna. The hotel can organise various excursions (including quad-bike tours through the national park); during winter, guests can rent snowmobiles (€70, with guide).

✖ Eating

Zlatni Papagaj PIZZA €
(Vuka Karadžića 5, Žabljak; mains €3.50-12; 🛜) The 'Golden Parrot' has the feel of a pirate lair, with wine-barrel tables, a wooden ceiling hung with chandeliers and a thick fug of cigarette smoke (though there is a non-smoking section, a rarity round these parts). The menu offers a crowd-pleasing selection of pizza, creamy pastas and steaks.

★**Lupo D'argento** ITALIAN, STEAK €€
(☑ 069-111 555; Vuka Karadžića bb, Žabljak; mains €4-15; ⊙ 8am-1am) This shiny, modern place is undoubtedly Žabljak's hippest restaurant; so hip, in fact, that you may wonder why it's here at all. Don't question, just enjoy. The menu covers all the Italian classics, and they do wonderful things with steak. Portions are

> **🛈 PEDAL OFF THE METAL**
>
> The gloriously swooping, zigzaggy roads around the Durmitor area seem to inspire reckless racing-car driver fantasies in many locals, but whatever you do, don't follow their lead. Not only are these roads incredibly dangerous, they're heavily patrolled by the traffic police. We've had reports of people being pulled over for even the most minor infractions, so play it straight and watch your speed.

big, the espressos are strong, and if you just can't tear yourself away, the place morphs into a trendy nightclub after 9pm.

🛈 Information

Durmitor National Park Visitors Centre (☑ 052-360 228; www.nparkovi.me; ⊙ 7am-5pm Mon-Fri, 10am-5pm Sat & Sun Jan & Jun–mid-Sep, 7am-3pm Mon-Fri mid-Sep–Dec & Feb-May)

Žabljak Tourist Office (☑ 052-361 802; www.tozabljak.com; Trg Durmitorskih ratnika, Žabljak; ⊙ 7am-10pm mid-Jun–Sep, 8am-8pm Oct–mid-Jun)

🛈 Getting There & Away

All of the approaches to Durmitor are spectacular. The most reliable road to Žabljak follows the Tara River west from Mojkovac. In summer this 70km drive takes about 90 minutes. If you're coming from Podgorica, the quickest way is through Nikšić and Šavnik. The main highway north from Nikšić follows the dramatic Piva Canyon to Šćepan Polje. There's a wonderful back road through the mountains leaving the highway near Plužine, but it's impassable as soon as the snows fall.

The bus station is at the southern edge of Žabljak, on the Šavnik road. Buses head to Nikšić (€5.50, six daily), Podgorica (€8.50, four daily), Pljevlja (€4.30, three daily) and Belgrade (€22, nine hours, two daily).

Pljevlja

☑ 052 / POP 19,500

The road over the vertigo-inducing Tara Bridge, 23km east of Žabljak, heads north to Montenegro's third-largest city. Although it has a long and fascinating history – excavations have revealed life in the town dating back 20,000 years, and the Romans also had a long stint here – Pljevlja (Пљевља) today doesn't quite live up to its previous glories. It's an industrial town, with a large coalmine and thermal powerplant. That said, Pljevlja is not without its charms: Montenegro's most impressive mosque is found here, there's a pleasant park to idle in, and much of the surrounding countryside is extremely pretty.

Despite its prominent mosques, Pljevlja is predominantly an Orthodox town (73%) and nearly half of the population identifies their ethnicity as Serbian, no surprise given the Serbian border is less than 10km away.

⊙ Sights

Hussein Pasha Mosque MOSQUE
(Husein Pašina Džamija; ☑ 052-323 509; Vuka Kneževića bb) Built in 1569 and boasting the highest minaret in the Balkans (42m), this is the most beautiful mosque in Montenegro. Its interiors are unusual as they're painted with elaborate frescoes featuring geometric patterns and floral motifs. If it's locked (as it often is), you'll get a taste from the paintings around the entrance.

Holy Trinity Monastery CHRISTIAN MONASTERY
(Manastir Sv Trojice) Dating from 1537, this impressive monastery occupies a sublimely peaceful nook tucked into the hills, 1km north of the town. Ottoman-style buildings hung with flowerboxes form a backdrop to a solid church with a sumptuously painted interior and gilded iconostasis. Behind the church, a small waterfall tumbles into a pond.

Pljevlja Heritage Museum MUSEUM
(Zavičajni muzej; ☑ 052-322 002; www.muzej pljevlja.com; Trg 13 Jula bb; ⊙ 8am-4pm Mon-Fri) FREE Though crammed into a small space in a dreary building, this little museum is home to some truly exceptional collections including ancient jewellery, rare costumes and prehistoric art discovered nearby. Its star attraction is an exquisite glass 'cage cup' from the 4th century BC. The cup is available for viewing if you make an appointment beforehand.

✦ Festivals & Events

Days of Pljevlja Cheese FOOD & DRINK
(⊙late Oct) Three delicious days devoted to Pljevlja's famous cheese and other local dairy delights.

🛏 Sleeping & Eating

Hotel Pljevlja HOTEL
(☑ 052-323 140; hotelpljevlja@gmail.com; Kralja Petra bb; r/ste €30/60; P ❋ 🛜) This old state-run hotel may not be posh, but it's smack bang in the middle of town, and you won't find cheaper. All rooms have balconies, and there's a decent restaurant on-site. You'll find it above a Maxi supermarket.

Tri Šešira MONTENEGRIN €
(☑ 052-352 005; Njegoševa 26; mains €4-9) Locals love this little place. The meals are huge, simple and hearty, and if you're looking to have a few drinks and meet the natives, this is a top place to do it.

❶ Information

Tourist Office (☑ 052-300 148; www.pljevlja. travel; Kralja Petra 43; ⊙8am-4pm Mon-Fri)

❶ Getting There & Away

From the **bus station** (cnr Miloša Tošica & III Sandžačke; 🛜) buses head to Žabljak (€3.50, 1¼ hours, three daily), Mojkovac (€6, two hours, five daily), Kolašin (€7, 2½ hours, five daily), Podgorica (€7.50, four hours, eight daily) and Budva (€14, 5½ hours, two daily). International destinations include Belgrade (€19, seven hours, three daily) and Sarajevo (€10, five hours, daily).

Bijelo Polje

☑ 050 / POP 15,900

Montenegro's fourth-largest city, Bijelo Polje (Бијело Поље; pronounced 'bi-*ye*-lo po-lye') was once part of the evocatively named Sandžak of Novi Pazar, the Ottoman-controlled region that separated Montenegro from Serbia until 1912. Today almost 54% of the town's population identify as Orthodox and 45% as Muslim, with mosque minarets and church bell towers sprouting in nearly equal profusion. It's one of the most diverse cities of Montenegro.

'Bijelo Polje' means 'white field', a reference to centuries past when the area was supposedly covered in white flowers. Alas, it's not quite as picturesque today, but still, it's far from being derelict. The broad Lim River skirts the town centre, where you'll find lots of cafe-bars, pizzerias, banks and the post office.

🛏 Sleeping & Eating

Hotel Franca HOTEL €€
(☑ 050-433-442; www.francahotels.me/bijelopol je.html; Munib Kučevića bb; s/d/apt €40/60/100; P ❋ 🛜) This clean, modern hotel is right in the middle of town. Rooms are spacious, staff are helpful and there's a very good restaurant attached. It's the best option in Bijelo Polje.

ℹ Information

Bijelo Polje Tourist Office (☑ 050-484 795; www.tobijelopolje.me; Nedeljka Merdovića bb)

ℹ Getting There & Away

The bus station is on the highway, near the town centre. Services head in both directions on the Podgorica–Belgrade highway. There are frequent buses to Podgorica (€5.50, 2¼ hours), Mojkovac (€2, 40 minutes) and Belgrade (€15, seven hours).

There's a large train station further along the highway, 2.5km north of town, with services to Bar (€7.20, 3¼ hours, five daily), Podgorica (€5.20, two hours, six daily), Kolašin (€2.20, 30 minutes, six daily), Mojkovac (€1.20, 15 minutes, six daily) and Belgrade (€15, eight hours, two daily).

Rožaje

☑ 051 / POP 9500

Rožaje (Рожаје) is Montenegro's most easterly town, nestled within the mountainous folds bordering Serbia and Kosovo. Almost 95% of its population are Muslim, and the song of muezzins can be heard echoing from its minarets at prayer times. It's fascinating to sit by the main square and watch the evening promenade. While this social ritual is common to every town in Montenegro, here you'll spot plenty of men strolling together arm in arm and some women wearing hijabs (head coverings).

With a backdrop of rocky cliffs and plenty of old wooden houses achieving a look bordering on designer decrepitude, Rožaje could be very pretty indeed. The main thing preventing that happening is the scandalous state of the Ibar River, which seems to be used as the main waste disposal. Plastic bags full of household refuse line its banks as it gurgles through town.

⊙ Sights

Ganića Kula   TOWER

(Trg IX Crnogorske Brigade bb; ⊙ 8am-4pm Mon-Fri) **FREE** Residential towers of this sort were once common throughout eastern Montenegro, Kosovo and Albania. Not just a defence against invaders, a *kula* was particularly useful for protecting the menfolk during interfamily blood feuds. There's a revamped ethnographic **museum** inside the tower, with a well-presented collection of costumes, crafts and artefacts. The tower is a two-minute walk north from the main square.

🛏 Sleeping & Eating

Hotel Rožaje   HOTEL €€

(☑ 051-240 000; www.facebook.com/hotelrozaje; Maršala Tita bb; s/d €45/85; ❄ @ ⚹ ⚹) This wonky, mirrored M-shaped hotel is one of the most distinctive buildings in town. Only limited services are offered, but the rooms are excellent, with opulently draped curtains, thickly embroidered bedspreads and attractive en suites. The central location is handy, and its restaurant is very popular.

ℹ Information

Tourist Office (☑ 051-270 158; www.to.rozaje. me; 13 Juli bb; ⊙ 8am-4pm)

ℹ Getting There & Away

From Rožaje, the main highway continues into Serbia, 22km to the northeast. Montenegro's only border crossing with Kosovo is on a winding road heading southeast.

The **bus station** (☑ 051-271 115) is on the highway above the town centre, with services to Herceg Novi (€18, 7¼ hours, four daily), Bar (€10.50, five hours, daily), Ulcinj (€12, 5¾ hours, daily), Podgorica (€9.50, four hours, four daily) and Berane (€2.50, 40 minutes) for onward services to Plav and Gusinje. International destinations include Peć (€6.50, 1½ to three hours, daily), Priština (€11.50, four hours, daily) and Belgrade (€14, six hours, four daily).

Plav

☑ 051 / POP 3800

Heading from Andrijevica, the road to Plav (Плав) follows the Lim River through lush fields, and the imposing Prokletije Mountains (Montenegro's highest) begin to reveal themselves.

As if knowing that such beauty demands a mirror, Lake Plav (Plavsko jezero) has positioned itself to provide it. Devastatingly pretty, it swarms with tiny fish swimming between the reeds and water lilies, and a chorus of birds and frogs sing their contentment to call it home. The human occupants seem rather less appreciative, judging by the amount of rubbish washing into it from the township. The lakeside road passes a crop of massive turreted houses that either take their inspiration from fairy tales or nightmares, take your pick.

Plav is a predominantly Muslim town, with 80% of locals identifying their ethnicity as Bosniak or Muslim and a further 9% as Albanian.

Plav and nearby Gusinje are the best towns to access Prokletije National Park.

Plav is one of those towns that doesn't believe in street names, so you'll have to either ask for directions or wander through the twisting laneways of its hilly *čaršija* (old market area). The post office has an ATM attached and is near the main roundabout leading down to the *čaršija*. The area around the bus station is called Racina.

◉ Sights & Activities

Mosques   MOSQUE
The minarets of multiple mosques are the most prominent feature of Plav's centre. The most imposing is Sultana Mosque (Džamija Sultanija; 1909) near the main roundabout, capped by a set of large and small domes. Nearby is the Old Mosque (Stara Džamija; 1471), easily identified by its decorated wooden minaret.

Continue to the main street, turn right and head up the hill to reach Redžepagić Mosque (Redžepagića Džamija; 1774), with its slender minaret made of geometrically arranged wood panels.

Redžepagića Kula   TOWER
(Redžepagića tower) This defensive tower, slightly up the hill from the Redžepagić Mosque, officially dates to 1671, although it's possibly 16th century. The bottom two floors have stone walls over a metre thick, capped by a wooden storey with lovely jutting balconies.

Brezojevica Monastery   CHRISTIAN MONASTERY
Three kilometres north of Plav, Brezojevica Monastery is a study in rural tranquillity. Meadows of yellow and purple flowers line the riverbank broken by the occasional abandoned stone building.

A stone gate, topped by a golden Orthodox cross, leads from the highway. Inside the Holy Trinity Church (Crkva Sv Trojice) are the faded remains of original frescoes, although the only subject that's easy to discern is the Dormition of the Mother of God over the door. The present structure of Holy Trinity Church was built in the 16th century on 13th-century foundations, but was damaged during WWII and left to decay, used only by the local Orthodox community for funerals. It's a testimony to the religious revival of recent years that the monastery is (very slowly) being restored.

Ask at the Plav Tourist Organisation if someone can let you in, or try your luck at the monastery; there's often someone about.

Lake Plav   SWIMMING
(Plavsko jezero) The pier extending over the lake is a good spot to swim from, or you can hire paddle boats (€2 per hour) or kayaks (€1.50 per hour) nearby.

🛏 Sleeping & Eating

Aqua   BUNGALOW €
(☑ 069-889 759; visitaqua@gmail.com; Brezojevica bb; r/cabin €35; P 🛜) Hugging Lake Plav's western shore near the beginning of the road to Gusinje, this complex has simple free-standing bungalows (sleeping up to four people) and a handful of rooms with three single beds. It's a simple set-up but reasonably comfortable. Upstairs, the restaurant (mains €4-12) offers lake views to accompany pizza, pasta, salad, fish and gigantic meat dishes.

Komnenovo Etno-Selo   HOTEL €€
(☑ 067-638 311; www.kuladamjanova.com; Vojno Selo bb; s/d/ste from €40/55/70; P 🛜) Located on the south shore of the lake (reached by the back road from Plav), this large complex conjures up an 'ethno' ambience with its wood and stone construction. The theme continues with the traditional specialities served in the restaurant (breakfast is included in the room rates). Activities on offer include fishing, horse riding and guided mountain expeditions.

★Restoran Abas   MONTENEGRIN €€
(☑ 069-611 503; www.facebook.com/restaurant. abas; mains €5-17; ⊗ 7am-11pm) Don't be put off by the alarming intergalactic-castle exterior; this is possibly the best restaurant in Montenegro's north. Inside, its elegant decor sets the tone for a superb dining experience, with excellent fresh lake fish, mouth-watering grills and a handful of vegetarian offers all crafted with flair and local, organic ingredients. The owners have extensive overseas restaurant experience, and it shows.

Abas is a three-minute drive from Plav's centre, just before the Lake Views campground. They also have some rooms (€20) available upstairs if you want to stick around for breakfast the next morning.

ℹ Information

Plav Tourist Office (☑ 051-250 151; www. toplav.me; Racina bb; ⊗ 8am-4pm Mon-Fri, 9am-3pm Sat) They don't speak much English but the staff here are friendly and surprisingly helpful, considering. They stock the *Prokletije*

Hiking & Biking map (€5, scale 1:50,000), which outlines 10 bike paths and 15 hiking tracks.

Police Station (Jezerska bb) In theory at least, the Plav police should be able to help with organising cross-border permits for those taking on the Peaks of the Balkans trans-national hiking trail.

Gusinje

051 / POP 1700

Along with its big sister Plav, 10km away, Gusinje (Гусиње; pronounced '*gu*-si-nye') is the main gateway to the Prokletije National Park. It's a tidy, laid-back place with an idyllic setting, surrounded by verdant farmland and hemmed in by the rugged majesty of the Prokletije Mountains. You could easily lose a day exploring the back roads and villages by bicycle or car.

While the 1700-strong community is overwhelmingly Muslim, the town's two mosques coexist comfortably with both an Orthodox and a Catholic church. The most architecturally impressive is the 1626 **Vizier's Mosque** (Vezirova Džamija), a stone structure with a wooden porch and minaret similar to – but better preserved than – the mosques in Plav.

In the centre of Gusinje you'll find a post office, an ATM, cafes and plenty of options for pizza or *burek* (meat or cheese pastry).

Sights

Ali Paša Springs SPRING
(Ali Pašini izvori) In a beautiful, bucolic setting at the foothills of the Prokletije mountains, these karst springs are an ideal spot for a picnic. Locals extol the health benefits of drinking the springs' water, purportedly rich in therapeutic minerals. The springs are a five-minute drive – or an easy 25-minute hike – south of Gusinje.

Sleeping & Eating

Hotel Rosi HOTEL €
(069-610 999; Gusinje bb; d/tr €35/50; P) On top of a supermarket and right by the bus stop, the family-run Rosi isn't big on glamour, but it is convenient, clean and comfortable. Its good restaurant will fatten you up nicely.

The family also offers village accommodation (from €25) in Vusanje, 5km south of Gusinje on the border with Albania.

Krojet MONTENEGRIN €
(068-432 587; mains €4-9.50) At the Ali Paša Springs, this excellent restaurant and

attached campground (sites €5) enjoy a beautiful, bucolic location. The atmospheric restaurant was once a watermill, and its rustic charm – not to mention the heaped dishes of local specialities – makes a meal here a memorable one.

Information

The Prokletije **National Park Visitors Centre** (www.nparkovi.me; 9am-5pm daily summer, 8am-4pm Mon-Fri rest of yr) is at the southern end of town, en route to Ali Pasha springs. They can help with organising and recommending park activities, mountain guides and accommodation; the attached shop sells books, guides and all manner of locally made souvenirs. It also rents snowshoes (€4 per day) and hiking sticks (€3 per day).

Getting There & Away

Buses to and from Plav (€2, four daily) stop here. Four buses a day go to Podgorica (€11.50). To access other bus routes, you'll need to go to Berane (€4.50, 1½ hours).

Piva Canyon

The highway north from Nikšić meets the Piva River after passing through 40km of farmland. It then tangos with the river until both reach the border at Šćepan Polje. The river was blocked in 1975 by the building of the 220m-high hydroelectric Mratinje Dam (Brana Mratinje), flooding part of the Piva Canyon (Кањон Пива) to create the tremendously turquoise Lake Piva (Pivsko Jezero), which plummets to depths of more than 180m.

The road alongside the river is a feat of engineering in itself, clinging to the cliffs and passing through 56 small tunnels carved out of the stone. The narrow but equally spectacular route through the mountains from Žabljak joins this road near Plužine, the Piva region's unofficial capital. Heading north from here the route gets even more dramatic, with the steep walls of the canyon reflecting in the toothpaste-blue waters below.

Sights & Activities

Piva Monastery CHRISTIAN MONASTERY
(Manastir Piva) Small Piva Monastery has an intriguing history: originally constructed between 1573 and 1586, it was the only Serbian Orthodox monastery to be built during the Ottoman occupation (the Grand Vizier was a relative of Piva's founder; connections

PEAKS OF THE BALKANS HIKING TRAIL

Winding 192km through the Accursed Mountains of Prokletije, the border-hopping **Peaks of the Balkans** (PoB; www.peaksofthebalkans.com) hiking trail is the epitome of epic. The signposted circuit, which runs through Montenegro, northern Albania and eastern Kosovo, follows shepherds' paths and alpine trails through verdant valleys, remote villages and up (literally) breathtaking mountains; the highest point of the trail is 2300m. While there are other transnational hiking paths in Europe, this one is extra impressive, not only for its otherwise inaccessible, utterly astonishing scenery, but the fact that it exists at all, given the centuries of bad blood between the countries and previously rigorously guarded borders.

Being a circular route, the trail has multiple entry points. In Montenegro, the main gateway is Plav, though you can begin in the Grbaja Valley if you want to keep mountain paths, rather than pavement, under your feet (the standard PoB circuit does involve the odd bit of bitumen here and there). Though the full hike takes between 10 and 13 days to complete, you can easily tailor your own trek; there are almost limitless shorter or alternative hikes to choose from, and it's easy to hop on and off to visit nearby historical sites, clamber up off-trail peaks or simply take a breather in relative civilisation.

A popular 10-hour hike that stays within Montenegro's boundaries runs from Plav to the village of Vusanje, taking in 27km of fresh springs, lakes, forests, shepherd communities and a climb up the Bor peak (2106m), offering staggering views of the craggy Karanfil Mountains, nicknamed – with good reason – the 'Dolomites of Montenegro'. Those keen – and equipped with the proper paperwork – to cross the border can overnight at Vusanje and continue on a 21km route to Theth in Albania; the route is particularly fascinating for its Communist-era remnants, including an abandoned military post and bunker.

Apart from wild camping, village guesthouses and homestays are the only accommodation options along the trail; the cultural immersion and traditional hospitality you'll receive are as magical as the mountains themselves. It's best to arrange your digs ahead of time; if you're not on an organised trek, local tourist offices and the PoB website can help.

Don't be lulled by its marketable name, the flash website and the fact that it's (mostly) signposted; the Peaks of the Balkans is not a journey to be undertaken lightly. Hikers should be fit and come equipped with proper equipment, including sturdy hiking boots, torches, GPS, phone (don't count on reception), first-aid kit, sleeping bag, tent and waterproof clothing. June to October is the best time to make the trek, though inclement weather can strike at any time.

The trail meanders through some incredibly isolated areas: tackling it on your own is not recommended. If you don't want to join an agency-organised group trek, at the very least go with two or more friends; better yet, hire a local guide. Those listed on the PoB website have been trained by the DAV (Deutscher Alpen Verein, German Alpine Club). The website also has a long list of recommended adventure travel agencies that can customise and organise your entire PoB adventure, including sorting out accommodation and all bureaucratic requirements. If you're the masochistic type, you can attempt to arrange your own cross-border permits (required from each country you plan to cross in or out of), but be warned: this is not a process for the faint of heart. Try your luck at the Plav police station or download an application form at www.balkanspeacepark.org; forms must be submitted at least 15 days before you begin your hike.

have always been everything in Montenegro). It hulked by the Piva River until the late 1960s when plans for the Mratinje Dam forced it to be moved – brick by brick, fresco fragment by fresco fragment – over 12 years to its current location near Gorankso village.

Piva Lake Cruises BOATING
During summer, boats ply Lake Piva offering cruises and expeditions to secret swimming spots. The **tourist centre** (040-270 068; www.pluzine.travel; Baja Pivljanina bb, Plužine) in Plužine can give you the heads up on the season's offerings, or you could go direct to Zvono (p125), where the English-speaking owner runs excellent trips around the lake's coves and caves, with breaks for hikes, beers and swims. It also has a four-seater canoe available for lake jaunts.

🍽 Sleeping & Eating

In addition to private rooms and apartments in town, accommodation is available at the rafting camps around Šćepan Polje and in various *etno sela* ('ethno villages' offering traditional digs) scattered around Plužine and the back road to Žabljak.

The Plužine Tourism Organisation (p124) website lists loads of hotels and village accommodation in the Piva region.

Zvono   GUESTHOUSE €

(☏ 069-471 893; www.zvono.me; ul Baja Pivljanina bb, Plužine; s/d from €20/35; 🅿 🛜) Plužine's surprisingly cosmopolitan Zvono ('Bell') offers characterful cottage accommodation, fresh trout lunches and homemade *medovina* (honey wine), best sipped in the cosy, cluttered restaurant with Zvono's jazz-cat owner. It also runs some of Plužine's best boat cruises and offers canoe hire.

★ Sočica   MONTENEGRIN

(Baja Pivljanina bb, Plužine) This gorgeous old cottage is worth a stop even if you're not staying in Plužine. The traditionally dressed waiters may take their time getting the delectable local specialities (think lamb, just-caught trout and *cicvara*, akin to a creamy polenta dish) to your table, but if you've got a glass of their homemade *kruška rakija* (pear brandy), you won't care one bit.

ℹ Information

Opening hours are seemingly decided on a daily whim, but if they're open, drop into the **Plužine Tourism Organisation** (p124) for maps and information on activities, accommodation and more in and around Plužine.

ℹ Getting There & Away

Plužine's tatty bus stop is on the highway at the entrance to town. There are four buses a day to Nikšić (€5.30, two hours). If you want to get to Šćepan Polje (€2, 30 minutes), hop on a bus bound for Sarajevo (€9.50, four hours). A hideously timed 1am bus leaves nightly for Herceg Novi (€15, five hours).

Prokletije National Park

The Prokletije Mountains (Проклетије) are a huge, hulking expanse of wilderness forming the border with Albania and Kosovo. They're the southernmost – and highest – part of the Dinaric Alps. Surreally scenic and eerily remote, this magnificent area may well rate as one of Europe's least explored. In 2009, a 160-sq-km chunk of the Montenegrin side of the range was declared the country's fifth national park. Ambitious plans are afoot for the entire range to be declared a cross-border Balkans Peace Park; follow the progress at www.balkanspeacepark.org.

The epic Peaks of the Balkans (p124) hiking trail is a 192km circuit that crosses through all three countries.

Both the Montenegrin and the Albanian (Bjeshkët e Namuna) names for the range translate to the rather ominous-sounding 'Accursed Mountains'. Leave your hoodoo at home; this is a reference to the harsh environment of these sky-punching, jagged peaks rather than any high-altitude jinx.

🍽 Sleeping & Eating

Plav and Gusinje are good bases if you need access to facilities. Otherwise, the gorgeous Grbaja Valley, 8km from Gusinje and in the shadows of the range has mountain huts and other basic accommodation.

Wild camping is possible in the mountains, as are homestays (from €20) in shepherds' huts; see www.peaksofthebalkans.com or Gusinje's National Park Visitors Centre (p123). Book ahead for all accommodation.

If you're heading up the mountains, you'll need to take all of your own supplies, including water.

Eko Katun Grebaje   CABIN €

(☏ 069-044 572; Grbaja Valley; per bed €10; ☉ summer) This collection of rustic, charming cabins is as flash as it gets out here. It's comfortable and quaint, the owner is a font of local knowledge, and its setting at the foot of the mountains can't be beaten. There's a restaurant attached, serving hearty regional dishes.

ℹ Getting There & Away

From both Gusinje and Plav – the gateways to the park – yellow signs point to various walking tracks and give both the distance and estimated time required for each. Within a few hours, you can reach glacial lakes and mountain springs. Many trails run to and from the Grbaja Valley (*Dolina Grbaje*), 8km from Gusinje and 20km from Plav. There is no public transport out here, but you can catch a taxi to Grbaja from Plav or Gusinje.

Dubrovnik (Croatia)

POP 28,500

Best Places to Eat

➡ Pantarul (p133)

➡ Restaurant 360° (p136)

➡ Nishta (p134)

➡ Shizuku (p133)

➡ Amfora (p136)

Best Places to Sleep

➡ Karmen Apartments (p132)

➡ Villa Klaić (p133)

➡ Hotel Kompas (p133)

➡ Villa Dubrovnik (p132)

➡ Hostel Angelina (p132)

Why Go?

Why have we included a Croatian city in a book on Montenegro? The first reason is practical: many travellers to Montenegro fly into Dubrovnik airport, which is, after all, only 17km from the border. More importantly, it seems inconceivable that you'd come this close and not visit one of the most beautiful cities in the entire Mediterranean, if not the world. Its proximity to the Bay of Kotor makes at least a day trip practically obligatory.

Dubrovnik is simply unique; its beauty is bewitching, its setting sublime. Regardless of whether you are visiting Dubrovnik for the first time or the hundredth, the sense of awe when you set eyes on the remarkable old town, ringed by its mighty defensive walls, never fades. Indeed it's hard to imagine anyone becoming jaded by the city's marble streets, baroque buildings and the endless shimmer of the Adriatic.

When to Go

➡ May and June offer warm sunny days, without the scorching heat or crowds of midsummer.

➡ Sate your cultural appetite during Dubrovnik's prestigious Summer Festival in July and August.

➡ September and October are still warm enough for swimming and the beaches aren't as crowded.

History

After the Slavs wiped out the Roman city of Epidaurum (site of present-day Cavtat) in the 7th century, survivors fled to the safest place they could find – a rocky islet separated from the mainland by a narrow channel. By the end of the 12th century the city they founded, Ragusa (later called Dubrovnik), had become

an important trading centre on the coast. It came under Venetian authority in 1205, finally breaking away from its control in 1358. Through canny diplomacy, the Republic of Ragusa maintained good relations with everyone – even the Ottoman Empire, to which it began paying tribute in the 16th century.

DUBROVNIK (CROATIA)

Dubrovnik Highlights

1 City Walls & Forts (p128) Revelling in the most fascinating and touristy of activities: seeing Dubrovnik from the vantage point of its venerable walls.

2 Lokrum (p131) Taking the short ferry ride out to the beaches, forest, monastery and gardens of Dubrovnik's island playground.

3 Cable Car (p132) Catching a ride up Mt Srđ for breathtaking views of Dubrovnik from above.

4 War Photo Limited (p128) Visiting this affecting gallery and putting recent Balkan history in perspective.

5 Rector's Palace (p129) Wandering the rarified confines of Dubrovnik's most significant civic building and learning about the unique republic it once served.

6 Lapad (p131) Swimming in the crystal-clear waters of the bays scattered around the peninsula.

Centuries of peace and prosperity allowed art, science and literature to flourish, but most of the Renaissance art and architecture in Dubrovnik was destroyed in the earthquake of 1667, which killed 5000 people and left the city in ruins. The earthquake also marked the beginning of the economic decline of the republic. The final *coup de grâce* was dealt by Napoleon in 1808.

Caught in the war that ravaged former Yugoslavia, Dubrovnik was pummelled with some 2000 shells in 1991 and 1992.

Sights

Old Town

 City Walls & Forts FORT
(Gradske zidine; Map p134; adult/child 120/30KN; ⊙8am-7.30pm Apr-Oct, 9am-3pm Nov-Mar) No visit to Dubrovnik would be complete without a walk around the spectacular city walls, the finest in the world and the city's main claim to fame. From the top, the view over the old town and the shimmering Adriatic is sublime. You can get a good handle on the extent of the shelling damage in the 1990s by gazing over the rooftops: those sporting bright new terracotta suffered damage and had to be replaced.

The first set of walls to enclose the city was built in the 9th century. In the middle of the 14th century the 1.5m-thick defences were fortified with 15 square forts. The threat of attacks from the Turks in the 15th century prompted the city to strengthen the existing forts and add new ones, so that the entire old town was contained within a stone barrier 2km long and up to 25m high. The walls are thicker on the land side – up to 6m – and range from 1.5m to 3m on the sea side.

The round **Minčeta Tower** (Tvrđava Minčeta; Map p134; City Walls) protects the landward edge of the city from attack, the **Bokar Tower** (Tvrđava Bokar; Map p134) and **Fort Lawrence** (Tvrđava Lovrijenac; Map p134; admission 30KN; ⊙8am-7.30pm) look west and out to sea, while **Fort Revelin** (Map p134; Trg Oružja) and **Fort St John** (Tvrđava sv Ivana; Map p134) guard the eastern approach and the Old Harbour.

There are entrances to the walls from near the Pile Gate, the Ploče Gate and the Maritime Museum. The Pile Gate entrance tends to be the busiest, and entering from the Ploče side has the added advantage of getting the steepest climbs out of the way first (you're required to walk in an anticlockwise direction). Don't underestimate how strenuous the wall walk can be, especially on a hot day.

Pile Gate GATE
(Gradska vrata Pile; Map p134) The natural starting point to any visit to Dubrovnik, this fabulous city gate was built in 1537. While crossing the drawbridge, imagine that this was once lifted every evening, the gate closed and the key handed to the rector. Notice the statue of St Blaise, the city's patron saint, set in a niche over the Renaissance arch.

Onofrio Fountain FOUNTAIN
(Velika Onofrijeva fontana; Map p134; Placa bb) One of Dubrovnik's most famous landmarks, this large fountain was built in 1438 as part of a water-supply system that involved bringing water from a well 12km away. Originally the fountain was adorned with sculpture, but it was damaged in the 1667 earthquake and only 16 carved masks remain, with water dribbling from their mouths into a drainage pool.

Franciscan Monastery & Museum CHRISTIAN MONASTERY
(Muzej Franjevačkog samostana; Map p134; Placa 2; adult/child 30/15KN; ⊙9am-6pm) Within this monastery's stone walls is a gorgeous mid-14th-century **cloister**, a historic **pharmacy** and a small **museum** with a collection of relics, paintings, gold jewellery and pharmacy items such as laboratory gear. The remains of artillery that pierced the monastery walls during the 1990s war have been saved, too.

War Photo Limited GALLERY
(Map p134; ☑020-322 166; www.warphotoltd.com; Antuninska 6; adult/child 40/30KN; ⊙10am-10pm daily Jun-Sep, 10am-4pm Wed-Mon May & Oct) An immensely powerful experience, this gallery features exhibitions curated by New Zealand photojournalist Wade Goddard, who worked in the Balkans in the 1990s. Its declared intention is to 'expose the myth of war...to let people see war as it is, raw, venal, frightening, by focusing on how war inflicts injustices on innocents and combatants alike'. There's a permanent exhibition on the upper floor devoted to the wars in Yugoslavia, but the changing exhibitions cover a multitude of conflicts.

Synagogue & Jewish Museum SYNAGOGUE
(Sinagoga i Židovski muzej; Map p134; Žudioska 5; admission 40KN; ⊙9am-9pm May-Oct, to 3pm Nov-Apr) Established in 1352, this is said to be the second-oldest functioning synagogue in the world, and the oldest Sephardic one. Inside a museum with relics and documentation on the local Jewish population, including records relating to their persecution during WWII.

ENTER THE GAME OF THRONES

Dubrovnik is like a fantasy world for most people, but fans of *Game of Thrones* have more reason to indulge in flights of fancy than most, as a large chunk of the popular TV series was filmed here. While Split and Šibenik were also used as locations, Dubrovnik has featured the most prominently, standing in for the cities of King's Landing and Qarth. If you fancy taking your own Walk of Shame through the streets of Westeros, here are some key spots:

Fort Lawrence (p128) King's Landing's famous Red Keep. Cersei farewelled her daughter Myrcella from the little harbour beneath it.

City Walls (p128) Tyrion Lannister commanded the defence of King's Landing from the seaward-facing walls during the Battle of the Blackwater.

Minčeta Tower (p128) The exterior of Qarth's House of Undying.

Uz Jezuite The stairs connecting the **St Ignatius of Loyola Church** (Crkva svetog Ignacija Lojolskoga; Map p134; Uz Jezuite) to **Gundulić Square** (Gundulićeva poljana; Map p134) were the starting point for Cersei Lannister's memorable naked penitential walk. The walk continued down Stradun.

Ethnographic Museum (Etnografski muzej; Map p134; www.dumus.hr; Od Rupa 3; adult/child multimuseum pass 100/25KN; ⊙9am-4pm Wed-Mon) Littlefinger's brothel.

Dominican
Monastery & Museum   CHRISTIAN MONASTERY
(Muzej Dominikanskog samostana; Map p134; Sv Dominika 4; admission 30KN; ⊙9am-5pm) This imposing structure is an architectural highlight, built in a transitional Gothic-Renaissance style, and containing an impressive art collection. Constructed around the same time as the city walls in the 14th century, the stark exterior resembles a fortress more than a religious complex. The interior contains a graceful 15th-century cloister constructed by local artisans after the designs of the Florentine architect Maso di Bartolomeo.

Sponza Palace   PALACE
(Palača Sponza; Map p134; Placa bb) This superb 16th-century palace is a mixture of Gothic and Renaissance styles beginning with an exquisite Renaissance portico resting on six Corinthian columns. The 1st floor has late-Gothic windows and the 2nd-floor windows are in a Renaissance style, with an alcove containing a statue of St Blaise. Sponza Palace was originally a customs house, then a mint, a state treasury and a bank.

St Blaise's Church   CHURCH
(Crkva svetog Vlahe; Map p134; Luža Sq) Dedicated to the city's patron saint, this imposing church was built in 1715 in the ornate baroque style. The interior is notable for its marble altars and a 15th-century silver gilt statue of St Blaise, who is holding a scale model of pre-earthquake Dubrovnik.

★ Rector's Palace   PALACE
(Knežev dvor; Map p134; ☎020-321 422; www.dumus.hr; Pred Dvorom 3; adult/child multimuseum pass 100/25KN; ⊙9am-6pm Apr-Oct, to 4pm Nov-Mar) Built in the late 15th century for the elected rector who governed Dubrovnik, this Gothic-Renaissance palace contains the rector's office, his private chambers, public halls, administrative offices and a dungeon. During his one-month term the rector was unable to leave the building without the permission of the senate. Today the palace has been turned into the **Cultural History Museum**, with restored rooms, portraits, coats of arms and coins, evoking the history of Dubrovnik.

Dulčić Masle Pulitika Gallery   GALLERY
(Map p134; www.ugdubrovnik.hr; Držićeva poljana 1; adult/child multimuseum pass 100/25KN; ⊙9am-8pm Tue-Sun) This small offshoot of the city's main gallery unites three friends beyond the grave: local artists Ivo Dulčić, Antun Masle and Đuro Pulitika, who all came to the fore in the 1950s and 1960s. There's a permanent collection featuring the trio's work on the lower floor, while the upper gallery is given over to temporary exhibitions by current artists.

Cathedral of the Assumption   CATHEDRAL
(Stolna Crkva Velike Gospe; Map p134; Držićeva poljana; ⊙8am-5pm Mon-Sat, 11am-5pm Sun) Built on the site of a 7th-century basilica, Dubrovnik's original cathedral was enlarged in the 12th century, supposedly funded by a gift from England's King Richard I, the Lionheart, who was saved from a shipwreck on the nearby

DUBROVNIK (CROATIA) SIGHTS

Dubrovnik

DUBROVNIK (CROATIA) SIGHTS

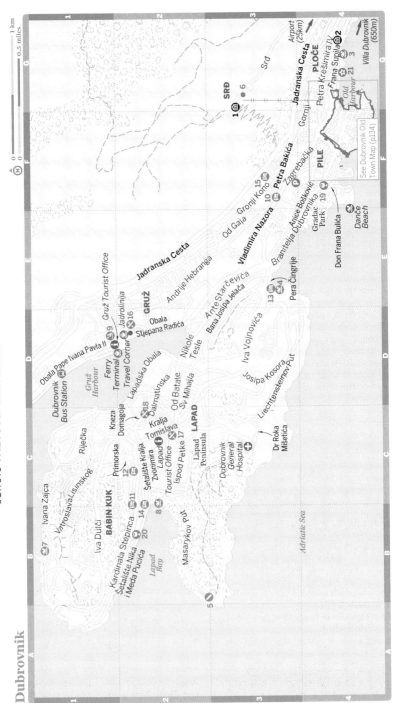

1 km
0.5 miles

Airport (25km)

PLOČE

Villa Dubrovnik (650m)

Jadranska Cesta

Petra Krešimira IV

Frana Supila 2

3

21

Old Harbour

SRD

1

6

Srđ

Gornji

See Dubrovnik Old Town Map (p134)

PILE

Petra Bakića

Zagrebačka

Gronji Kono 15

10

Vladimira Nazora

Od Gaja

Anice Bošković

Gradac Park 19

Braniteljia Dubrovnika

Don Frana Bulića

Dance Beach

Jadranska Cesta

Andrije Hebranga

Ante Starčevića

Bana Josipa Jelačia

Pera Čingrije

13 4

Iva Vojnovića

Josipa Kosora

Liechtensteinov Put

GRUŽ

Obala Stjepana Radića

Jadrolinija

Gruž Tourist Office 9

16

Obala Pape Ivana Pavla II

Dubrovnik Bus Station

Gruž Harbour

Ferry Terminal

Travel Corner

Lapadska Obala

Kneza Domagoja

Nikole Tesle

18

Od Batale

Sv Mihajla

Kralja Tomislava 17

LAPAD

Dalmatinska

Dr Roka Mišetića

Dubrovnik General Hospital

Lapad Peninsula

Masarykov Put

Adriatic Sea

Rječka

Primorska

12

Šetalište Kralja Zvonimira

Lapad Tourist Office

Ispod Petke

11

14

20

8

BABIN KUK

Ivana Zajca

Vatroslava Lisinskog

Kardinala Stepinca

Šetalište Nika i Meda Pucića

Iva Dulči

Lapad Bay

7

5

Dubrovnik

island of Lokrum. Soon after the first cathedral was destroyed in the 1667 earthquake, work began on this, its baroque replacement, which was finished in 1713.

⊙ Surrounds

★ Lokrum ISLAND
(www.lokrum.hr; adult/child incl boat 100/20KN; ⊙Apr-Nov) Lush Lokrum is a beautiful, forested island full of oaks, ash, pines and olive trees, and an ideal escape from Dubrovnik. It's a popular swimming spot, although the beaches are rocky. To reach the nudist beach, head left from the ferry and follow the signs marked FKK; the rocks at the end are Dubrovnik's de facto gay beach. Also popular is the small saltwater lake, the **Dead Sea**.

Dubrovnik During
the Homeland War MUSEUM
(Dubrovnik u domovinskom ratu; Map p130; Fort Imperial, Srđ; adult/child 30/15KN; ⊙8am-10pm) Set inside a Napoleonic fort near the cable-car

terminus, this permanent exhibition is dedicated to the siege of Dubrovnik during the 'Homeland War', as the 1990s war is dubbed in Croatia. If the displays are understandably one-sided, they still provide in-depth coverage of the events, including lots of video footage.

Museum of Modern &
Contemporary Art MUSEUM
(Umjetnička galerija; Map p130; ☑020-426 590; www.ugdubrovnik.hr; Frana Supila 23; adult/child multimuseum pass 100/25KN; ⊙9am-8pm Tue-Sun) Spread over three floors of a significant modernist building east of the old town, this excellent gallery showcases Croatian artists, particularly painter Vlaho Bukovac from nearby Cavtat. Head up to the sculpture terrace for excellent views.

⚔ Activities
Swimming
Banje Beach SWIMMING
(Map p130; www.banjebeach.eu; Frana Supila 10) Banje Beach is the closest beach to the old town, just beyond the 17th-century Lazareti (a former quarantine station) outside Ploče Gate. Although many people rent lounge chairs and parasols from the beach club, there's no problem with just flinging a towel on the beach if you can find a space.

Bellevue Beach SWIMMING
(Map p130) The nicest beach within an easy walk of the old town is below the Hotel Bellevue. This pebbly cove is sheltered by high cliffs, which provide a platform for cliff divers but also cast a shadow over the beach by late afternoon – a boon on scorching days. Access is via a steep staircase off Kotorska street.

Lapad Bay SWIMMING
(Map p130; Masarykov put bb) Dubrovnik's second-most popular beach after Banje sits at the apex of the Lapad horseshoe. There are plenty of diversions here, both in and out of the water, including a floating inflatable playground, slides and lots of cafes and bars.

Copacabana Beach SWIMMING
(Map p130; Ivana Zajca bb) On the northern coast of Babin Kuk, this pebbly strip has lots of facilities including showers, loungers, an inflatable floating playground, a restaurant, masseurs, and kayaks and jet skis for hire.

Kayaking
Adriatic Kayak Tours KAYAKING, CYCLING
(Map p134; ☑020-312 770; www.adriatickayaktours.com; Zrinsko Frankopanska 6; half-day from 280KN)

Offers sea-kayak excursions (from a half-day paddle to a weeklong trip), hiking and cycling tours, and Montenegro getaways (including rafting).

Outdoor Croatia   KAYAKING
(Map p130; ☑020-418 282; www.outdoorcroatia. com; Sv Križa 3; day trip 400KN) Rents kayaks and offers day trips around the Elafiti Islands, along with multiday excursions and kayaking-cycling combos.

Other Activities

★**Cable Car**   CABLE CAR
(Žičara; Map p134; ☑020-414 355; www.dubrovnikcablecar.com; Petra Krešimira IV bb; return adult/child 120/50KN; ☺9am-5pm Nov-Mar, to 9pm Apr, May, Sep & Oct, to midnight Jun-Aug) Dubrovnik's cable car whisks you from just north of the city walls to Mt Srđ in under four minutes. At the end of the line there's a stupendous perspective of the city from a lofty 405m, taking in the terracotta rooftops of the old town and the island of Lokrum, with the Adriatic and Elafiti Islands filling the horizon.

Blue Planet Diving   DIVING
(Map p130; ☑091 89 90 973; www.blueplanetdiving.com; Dubrovnik Palace Hotel, Masarykov put 20; introductory dive €65, 2-dive boat trip €65, PADI Open Water course €345) There's great diving around Dubrovnik, including at the wreck of the *Taranto*, an 1899 merchant ship that hit a mine during WWII. Blue Planet's experienced crew offers recreational dives and courses.

Buggy Safari Dubrovnik   ADVENTURE
(Map p130; ☑098 16 69 730; www.buggydubrovnik. com; cable-car terminus, Mt Srđ; 45min trip 240KN; ☺9am-7pm) Take a trip in a souped-up quad bike through the mountainous nether regions of Mt Srđ, visiting forts and a farm. Expect to come back caked in mud and dust.

🎊 Festivals & Events

Feast of St Blaise   CULTURAL
(☺3 Feb) A city-wide bash marked by pageants and processions.

Carnival   CARNIVAL
(☺Feb) Venetian-style masked high jinks, held in the lead-up to Lent (usually February).

Dubrovnik Summer Festival   CULTURAL
(Dubrovačke ljetne Igre; ☑020-326 100; www. dubrovnik-festival.hr; ☺Jul-Aug) From 10 July to 25 August, Croatia's most prestigious summer festival presents a program of theatre, opera, concerts and dance on open-air stages throughout the city. Tickets are available

online, from the festival office on Placa, and on site one hour before each performance.

🛌 Sleeping

Dubrovnik is the most expensive city in Croatia. You should book well in advance, especially in summer. There's limited accommodation in the compact old town itself. If you want to combine a beach holiday with your city stay, consider the leafy Lapad peninsula, 4km west of the centre.

Old Town

Hostel Angelina   HOSTEL €
(Map p134; ☑091 89 39 089; www.hostelangelina oldtowndubrovnik.com; Plovani skalini 17a; dm 208KN; ☀🛜) Hidden away in a quiet nook of the old town, this cute little hostel offers bunk rooms, a small guest kitchen and a bougainvillea-shaded terrace with memorable views over the rooftops.

★**Karmen Apartments**   APARTMENT €€
(Map p134; ☑098 619 282; www.karmendu.com; Bandureva 1; apt from €95; ☀🛜) These four inviting apartments enjoy a great location a stone's throw from Ploče harbour. All have plenty of character with art, splashes of colour, tasteful furnishings and books to browse. Apartment 2 has a little balcony while apartment 1 enjoys sublime port views. Book well ahead.

City Walls Hostel   HOSTEL €€
(Map p134; ☑091 79 92 086; www.citywallshostel. com; Sv Šimuna 15; dm/r from 303/536KN; ☀@🛜) Tucked away by the city walls, this classic backpackers is warm and welcoming with a lively atmosphere. Downstairs there's a small kitchen and a space for socialising. Upstairs you'll find clean and simple dorms and a cosy double with a sea view.

Rooms Vicelić   GUESTHOUSE €€
(Map p134; ☑095 52 78 933; www.rooms-vicelic. com; Antuninska 10; r from €100; ☀🛜) Situated on one of the steeply stepped old-town streets, this friendly, family-run place has four atmospheric stone-walled rooms with private bathrooms. Guests have use of a shared kitchenette with a microwave and a kettle.

Viktorija

★**Villa Dubrovnik**   HOTEL €€€
(☑020-500 300; www.villa-dubrovnik.hr; Vlaha Bukovca 6; r from €581; P☀🛜🏊) Gazing endlessly at the old town and Lokrum from its prime waterfront position, this elegant low-slung boutique hotel gleams white against a back-

DUBROVNIK (CROATIA) EATING

ⓘ DUBROVNIK CARD

If you want to get through all the essentials of Dubrovnik in one day, it's worth buying the Dubrovnik Card (150KN). If you were already planning on walking the city walls (120KN) and buying a museum pass (100KN), the 150KN card makes a lot of sense. Plus it scores you free rides on buses and discounts at various restaurants and shops. The card is available from tourist offices, hotels and museums.

drop of honey-coloured stone. The windows retract completely to bring the indoor pool into the outdoors, but sunseekers can laze on a lounger by the sea or commandeer a day bed in the rooftop prosciutto-and-wine bar.

🏠 Pile

Apartments & Rooms Biličić GUESTHOUSE €

(Map p130; ☎ 098 802 111; www.dubrovnik-online.net/apartments_bilicic; Privežna 2; r/apt from €50/100; ❋ 🞉) A highly atmospheric place to stay, partly due to the green fingers of the friendly host, whose subtropical garden is a delight. Rooms are bright, clean and pleasant, though bathrooms are not en suite. There's a guest kitchen on the terrace.

★ Villa Klaić B&B €€

(Map p130; ☎ 091 73 84 673; www.villaklaic-dubrovnik.com; Šumetska 9; s/d from €70/90; ☊❋🞉) Just off the main coast road, high above the old town, this outstanding guesthouse offers modern rooms and wonderful hospitality courtesy of the owner, Milo Klaić. Extras include a small swimming pool, continental breakfast, free pick-ups and free beer!

MirÓ Studio Apartments APARTMENT €€€

(Map p134; ☎ 099 42 42 442; www.mirostudioapartmentsdubrovnik.com; Sv Đurđa 16; apt €140; ❋🞉) Located in a residential nook only metres from the sea, hidden between the town walls and Fort Lawrence, this complex is an absolute gem. The decor marries stone walls and whitewashed ceiling beams with design features such as uplighting, contemporary bathrooms and sliding glass partitions.

🏠 Lapad

Apartments Silva GUESTHOUSE €€

(Map p130; ☎ 098 244 639; silva.dubrovnik@yahoo.com; Kardinala Stepinca 62; r/apt from €90/120; ☊❋🞉) Lush Mediterranean foliage lines the terraces of this hillside complex, a short hop

up from the beach at Lapad. The rooms are comfortable and well priced, but best of all is the top-floor apartment (sleeping five).

Begović Boarding House GUESTHOUSE €€

(Map p130; ☎ 020-435 191; www.begovic-boarding-house.com; Primorska 17; dm/r 256/527KN; ☊❋@🞉) This welcoming long-standing family-run place has simple, tidy rooms and a communal terrace with amazing views. The apartments have kitchenettes and the other rooms have use of a guest kitchen.

★ Hotel Kompas HOTEL €€€

(Map p130; ☎ 020-299 000; www.adriaticluxuryhotels.com; Kardinala Stepinca 21; r/ste from €210/542; ☊❋🞉🏊) By the beach at Lapad, this big hotel has more personality that you'd expect, due in large part to interesting art, design and charming staff. The breakfast buffet is excellent and the outdoor pool is pleasantly cool on a scorching day (the indoor one's warmer).

Hotel Bellevue HOTEL €€€

(Map p130; ☎ 020-330 000; www.hotel-bellevue.hr; Pera Čingrije 7; r from €342; ☊❋@🞉🏊) Positioned on a cliff near the very beginning of the Lapad peninsula (a 20-minute walk west of Pile Gate), this classy hotel has modern decor (despite its dated smoky-glass facade), excellent facilities and a top-notch restaurant. Best of all is the lift access to the cove below.

🍴 Eating

Oliva Pizzeria PIZZA €

(Map p134; ☎ 020-324 594; www.pizza-oliva.com; Lučarica 5; mains 41-86KN; ⏱10am-midnight) There are a few pasta dishes on the menu, but this attractive little place is really all about pizza. And the pizza is worthy of the attention. Grab a seat on the street and tuck in.

★ Pantarul MODERN EUROPEAN €€

(Map p130; ☎ 020-333 486; www.pantarul.com; Kralja Tomislava 1; mains 70-128KN; ⏱noon-4pm & 6pm-midnight) This breezy bistro serves exceptional homemade bread, pasta and risotto, alongside the likes of pork belly, steaks, ox cheeks, burgers and a variety of fish dishes. There's a fresh modern touch to most dishes but chef Ana-Marija Bujić knows her way around traditional Dalmatian cuisine too – she's got her own cookbook to prove it.

★ Shizuku JAPANESE €€

(Map p130; ☎ 020-311 493; www.facebook.com/ShizukuDubrovnik; Kneza Domagoja 1f; mains 65-99KN; ⏱noon-midnight Tue-Sun; 🞉) Tucked away in a residential area between the harbour and Lapad Bay, this charming little restaurant has an appealing front terrace and an interior decorated with silky draperies, paper lampshades and colourful umbrellas. The Japanese owners will be in the kitchen, preparing authentic sushi, sashimi, udon and gyoza. Wash it all down with Japanese beer or sake.

★ Nishta   VEGETARIAN €€
(Map p134; ☑ 020-322 088; www.nishtarestaurant. com; Prijeko 29; mains 77-85KN; ☺ 11.30am-11.30pm;

DUBROVNIK (CROATIA) EATING

) The popularity of this tiny old-town eatery (expect to queue) is testament not just to the paucity of options for vegetarians and vegans in Croatia but to the excellent food within. Alongside curries, pastas and vege burgers, the menu delivers more unusual delicious options such as eggplant tartare, 'tempehritos' and pasta-free zucchini 'spaghetti'.

Taj Mahal BOSNIAN €€
(Map p134; ☎020-323 221; www.tajmahal-dubrovnik.com; Nikole Gučetićeva 2; mains 80-

Dubrovnik Old Town

165KN; ⊙10am-2am) This tiny restaurant is loaded with Ottoman decorations. Order the *džingis kan* (dried beef, sausage, peppers and spring onions with curdled milk) for a taste of everything Bosnian, or feast on spicy *sudžukice* (beef sausage).

Konoba Ribar   DALMATIAN €€
(Map p134; ☑020-323 194; Kneza Damjana Jude bb; mains 77-122KN; ⊙10am-midnight; 🔊) Serving local food the way locals like it, at more or less local prices, this family-run eatery is a blissfully untouristy choice. They don't attempt anything fancy or clever, just big serves of favourites such as risotto and stuffed squid. It's set in a lane pressed hard up against the city walls.

★Restaurant 360°   MODERN EUROPEAN €€€
(Map p134; ☑020-322 222; www.360dubrovnik.com; Sv Dominika bb; mains 240-290KN, 5-course degustation 780KN; ⊙6.30-11pm) Dubrovnik's glitziest restaurant offers fine dining at its finest, with flavoursome, beautifully presented, creative cuisine, and slick, professional service.

The setting is unrivalled, on top of the city walls with tables positioned so you can peer through the battlements over the harbour.

★Amfora   INTERNATIONAL €€€
(Map p130; ☑020-419 419; www.amforadubrovnik.com; Obala Stjepana Radića 26; mains 145-185KN; ⊙noon-4pm & 7-11pm) From the street, Amfora looks like just another local cafe-bar, but the real magic happens at the six-table restaurant at the rear. Dalmatian favourites such as *pašticada* (stew with gnocchi) and black risotto sit alongside fusion dishes like swordfish sashimi, veal kofte, and miso fish soup.

Restaurant Dubrovnik   EUROPEAN €€€
(Map p134; ☑020-324 810; www.restorandubrovnik.com; Marojice Kaboge 5; mains 105-210KN; ⊙noon-midnight) One of Dubrovnik's most up-market restaurants has a wonderful setting, occupying a rooftop terrace hidden among the old town's stone buildings. A French influence pervades the menu full of decadent and rich dishes, such as confit duck and Adriatic lobster tail served on homemade pasta.

DUBROVNIK (CROATIA) EATING

🍷 Drinking & Entertainment

★ Bard
BAR

(Map p134; off Ilije Sarake; ☺9am-3am) The more upmarket and slick of two cliff bars pressed up against the seaward side of the city walls, this one is lower on the rocks and has a shaded terrace where you can happily lose a day, mesmerised by the Adriatic vistas. At night the surrounding stone is lit in colours.

Buža
BAR

(Map p134; off Od Margarite; ☺8am-2am) Finding this ramshackle bar-on-a-cliff feels like a real discovery as you dive around the city walls and finally see the entrance tunnel. However, Buža's no secret – it gets insanely busy, especially around sunset. Wait for a space on one of the concrete platforms, grab a cool drink and enjoy the vibe and views.

Cave Bar More
BAR

(Map p130; www.hotel-more.hr; Hotel More, Šetalište Nika i Meda Pucića; ☺10am-midnight) This little beach bar serves coffee, snacks and cocktails to bathers reclining by the dazzling waters of Lapad Bay, but that's not the half of it – the main bar is set in a cave. Cool off beneath the stalactites in the side chamber, where a glass floor exposes a water-filled cavern.

Art
BAR

(Map p130; Branitelja Dubrovnika 25; ☺9am-midnight Mon-Thu, to 2am Fri-Sun) Dubrovnik's most bohemian cafe-bar has seats constructed from bathtubs, tables made from washing-machine agitators, funky music (James Brown when we last visited) and terraces front and rear.

D'vino
WINE BAR

(Map p134; ☎020-321 130; www.dvino.net; Palmotićeva 4a; ☺10am-late; 📶) If you're interested in sampling top-notch Croatian wine, this upmarket little bar is the place to go. As well as a large and varied wine list, it offers themed tasting flights (multiple wine tastings; three wines for 50KN) accompanied by a thorough description by the knowledgable staff.

Buzz Bar
BAR

(Map p134; ☎020-321 025; www.thebuzzbar.wixsite. com/buzz; Prijeko 21; ☺8am-2am) Appropriately named, this buzzy little bar is rocky and relaxed, with craft beer and cocktails being the main poisons.

Troubadour
BAR

(Map p134; ☎020-323 796; Bunićeva poljana 2; ☺7.30am-2am; 📶) Tucked into a corner behind the cathedral, Troubadour looks pretty nondescript during the day. That all changes

on summer nights, when jazz musicians set up outside and quickly draw the crowds.

Revelin
CLUB

(Map p134; www.clubrevelin.com; Sv Dominika 3; ☺11pm-6am daily Jun-Sep, Fri & Sat Oct-May) Housed within the vaulted chambers of Fort Revelin, this is Dubrovnik's best club space, with international DJs playing in summer.

Lazareti
ARTS CENTRE

(Map p130; www.lazareti.com; Frana Supila 8) A former quarantine centre, Lazareti hosts cinema and club nights, live music, art exhibitions and pretty much all the best things in town.

🛍 Shopping

★ Portrait
FASHION & ACCESSORIES

(Map p134; www.portrait.hr; Od Puča; ☺10am-10pm) The phrase 'cool souvenir T-shirt' would seem to be an oxymoron, yet this upmarket boutique nails it with their range of Dubrovnik-themed tees by Croatian designer Matija Čop, whose work has featured in a Lady Gaga video.

Gundulić Square Market
MARKET

(Map p134; Gundulićeva poljana; ☺6am-1pm Mon-Sat) Stallholders sell produce, local artisanal products and craft at this open-air market.

Uje
FOOD & DRINKS

(Map p134; www.uje.hr; Placa 5; ☺9am-11pm) Uje specialises in olive oils – among the best is Brachia, from the island of Brač – along with a wide range of other locally produced epicurean delights, including some excellent jams (the lemon spread is divine), pickled capers, local herbs and spices, honey, figs in honey, chocolate, wine and *rakija* (grappa).

ℹ Information

Dubrovnik's tourist board has offices in **Pile** (Map p134; ☎020-312 011; www.tzdubrovnik.hr; Brsalje 5; ☺8am-9pm Jun-Sep, 8am-7pm Mon-Sat, 9am-3pm Sun Oct-May), **Gruž** (Map p130; ☎020-417 983; Obala Pape Ivana Pavla II 1; ☺8am-9pm Jun-Sep, to 3pm Mon-Sat Oct-May) and **Lapad** (Map p130; ☎020-437 460; Kralja Tomislava 7;

ℹ GETTING TO MONTENEGRO

Airport Transfer

There are no buses from Dubrovnik Airport to Montenegro, but you should be able to pre-arrange a transfer through a Herceg Novi travel agent or accommodation provider for about €40.

Bus

Up to six buses head to Kotor (124KN, 2½ hours) from Dubrovnik bus station daily, stopping in Herceg Novi on the way. The trip's duration depends entirely on how busy the border is.

Car

The distance between the old towns of Herceg Novi and Dubrovnik is only 47km but the border crossing can cause major delays, particularly on the Croatian side; to be safe, allow an hour for the crossing during the peak season. There's a smaller, lesser-known border crossing on the tip of the Preklava peninsula. We have been told that it's only supposed to be for locals, but we've never had a problem crossing there.

⊙ 8am-8pm Mon-Fri, 9am-noon & 5-8pm Sat & Sun Jun-Sep) that dispense maps, information and advice.

Dubrovnik General Hospital (Opća bolnica Dubrovnik; Map p130; ☑ 020-431 777; www. bolnica-du.hr; Dr Roka Mišetića 2; ⊙ emergency department 24hr) On the southern edge of the Lapad peninsula.

Post Office (Map p134; www.posta.hr; Široka 8; ⊙ 8am-9pm Mon-Sat May-Oct, 8am-7pm Mon-Fri, to noon Sat Nov-Apr)

Travel Corner (Map p130; ☑ 020-492 313; Obala Stjepana Radića 40; internet per hr 25KN, left luggage 2hr 10KN then per hr 4KN, per day 40KN; ⊙ 9am-8pm Mon-Sat, 9am-4.30pm Sun) This shop has a luggage service and internet terminals, dispenses tourist information, books excursions and sells Kapetan Luka ferry tickets.

ℹ Getting There & Away

AIR

Dubrovnik Airport (p173) is in Čilipi, 19km southeast of Dubrovnik. Both Croatia Airlines and British Airways fly to Dubrovnik all year round. In summer they're joined by dozens of other airlines flying seasonal routes and charter flights.

BOAT

The **ferry terminal** (Map p130; Obala Pape Ivana Pavla II 1) is in Gruž, 3km northwest of the old town. Ferries for Lokrum and Cavtat depart from the Old Harbour.

Local ferries head to Croatian islands and coastal towns. From April to October, **Jadrolinija** (Map p130; ☑ 020-418 000; www.jadrolinija.hr; Obala Stjepana Radića 40) has two to six car ferries per week travelling between Dubrovnik and Bari, Italy (passenger/car from €44/59, 10 hours).

BUS

Buses from **Dubrovnik Bus Station** (Map p130; ☑ 060 305 070; Obala Pape Ivana Pavla II 44a;

🛜) can be crowded, so book tickets in advance in summer. The station has toilets and a *garderoba* for storing luggage (5KN for the first hour then 1.50KN per hour).

Destinations include Split (130KN, 4½ hours, 21 daily), Zagreb (219KN, 9¼ to 11¾ hours, 10 daily), Sarajevo in Bosnia (175KN, 6½ hours, two daily), Ljubljana in Slovenia (300KN, 13 hours, two daily) and Trieste in Italy (459KN, 14¾ hours, daily).

Departure times are detailed at www.libertas dubrovnik.hr.

ℹ Getting Around

TO/FROM THE AIRPORT

Atlas runs the airport bus service (40KN, 30 minutes), timed to run around flights. Buses to Dubrovnik stop at the Pile Gate and the bus station; buses to the airport pick up from the bus station and from the bus stop near the cable car.

City buses 11, 27 and 38 also stop at the airport but are less frequent and take longer (28KN, four daily, no Sunday service).

Allow up to 280KN for a taxi to Dubrovnik.

CAR

The entire old town is a pedestrian area. Cars with Montenegrin plates are targets for vandals if they're left on the street, so you're best to park in a monitored car park. The **Ilijina Glavica Car Park** (Map p130; ☑ 091 23 00 366; Zagrebačka bb; per hr/day/week 35/420/2100KN; ⊙ 24hr) is a 10-minute walk above the Pile Gate.

PUBLIC TRANSPORT

Dubrovnik has a superb bus service; buses run frequently and generally on time. The key tourist routes run until after 2am in summer. The fare is 15KN if you buy from the driver, and 12KN if you buy a ticket at a *tisak* (news-stand). Timetables are available at www.libertasdubrovnik.hr.

Understand Montenegro

Montenegro Today

When Montenegro chose to part ways from Serbia in 2006, it was a brave move, especially given its tiny population. But toughing it out is something these gutsy people have had plenty of experience in. Montenegro's national identity is built around resisting the Ottoman Empire for hundreds of years in a mountainous enclave much smaller than the nation's current borders. Today, fierce little Montenegro has its sights set on joining an entirely different kind of union: the EU.

Best on Film

Casino Royale (2006) James Bond plays poker in a casino in Montenegro; suspend your disbelief, as the Montenegro scenes were actually filmed in Italy and the Czech Republic.

The Battle of Neretva (1969) Featuring a stellar cast including Yul Brynner and Orson Welles, this movie garnered an Academy Award nomination. It's set and filmed across the border in Bosnia, but director Veljko Bulajić was born in (what is now) Montenegro.

Best in Print

The Son (Andrej Nikolaidis; 2011) Set in Ulcinj over the course of a single night, this novel won a European Union Prize for Literature.

Realm of the Black Mountain (Elizabeth Roberts; 2007) An interesting and detailed dissection of Montenegro's convoluted history.

Montenegro: A Novel (Starling Lawrence; 1997) An entertaining tale of politics, bloodshed and romance set at the dawn of the 20th century.

Black Lamb and Grey Falcon (Rebecca West; 1941) One of the classics of travel literature.

The Never-Changing Government

Montenegro's 2016 general election was a hugely contentious affair, marked by protests, scandal and intrigue. But for all of the kerfuffle, the results remained the same as they have since 1990, with the Democratic Party of Socialists (DPS) holding tight to the reins once again. Considering that the DPS was born out of Montenegro's Communist Party, one could argue that it's been in power continuously since 1945 in one form or other. However, today's DPS is a long way from communist, having embarked on an enthusiastic and often controversial campaign of privatisations since the demise of Yugoslavia.

Much of the party's successes – and many controversies – boil down to one man: Milo Djukanović. A charismatic, handsome man with alleged mafia ties, Djukanović has been the president of the DPS since 1997, and – apart from a few scattered years of 'retirement' – has been either the prime minister or president of Montenegro since 1991. Following the 2016 election, Djukanović handed over the prime minister's position to Duško Marković (formerly deputy PM), though there's little doubt that he will remain the chief mover and shaker in Montenegrin politics; he's said to be eyeing the presidency in 2017. It's a situation redolent of Vladimir Putin and his many power swaps and perennial string-pulling, but don't tell Djukanović that: Russia is one of the reasons he's stepping down (for now).

Djukanović has alleged that Russia – with a little help from Serbia – was behind a coup plot to derail the elections because of the DPS' pro-NATO and EU stance. The Montenegrin prosecutor claimed the suspected would-be coup members – 20 of whom were arrested on election day – planned to incite violence on election night and have Djukanović assassinated. Djukanović also accused his opposition – the Democratic Front Alliance (DF), a coalition composed mostly of pro-Russian and pro-Serbian groups – of being funded by Russia, a charge the party has denied. The DF – which won 20% of the vote – accused the DPS of faking the attempted coup to improve their vote count; they and all other opposition parties have refused to accept the election results.

The Big Issues

In the early 2000s, Djukanović was investigated by an Italian anti-mafia unit and charged for his alleged role in a billion-dollar cigarette-smuggling operation; the charges were later dropped. He was named Person of the Year (2015) by the Organized Crime and Corruption Reporting Project for his work in 'promoting crime, corruption and uncivil society'; the OCCRP also called Djukanović's Montenegro 'one of the most dedicated kleptocracies and organized crime havens in the world'. It's a claim that echoes the 2012 billing of Montenegro as a 'mafia state' by *Foreign Affairs* magazine. The European Commission noted in its 2015 Montenegro Progress Report that 'corruption remains prevalent in many areas and continues to be a serious problem', noting the country's track record on pursuing high-level corruption cases 'remains limited'.

In October 2015, widespread anti-government protests climaxed in riots in Podgorica, during which demonstrators were tear-gassed by police. The protests – which demanded fair elections, transitional government and the resignation of Djukanović – were organised by the Democratic Front, an opposition alliance made up of seven parties. In May 2016, members of the coalition disrupted a speech Djukanović was giving in parliament, calling him a 'thief' amid general mayhem. Protests continued during and after the mayhem of the 2016 election.

NATO & the EU

Shortly after independence in 2006, Montenegro applied to join both the North Atlantic Treaty Organisation (NATO) and the European Union (EU); it opened formal accession negotiations with the latter in June 2012.

In December 2015, Montenegro was formally invited to join NATO, and at the time of research it was expected to be ratified as the 29th member in spring 2017. Joining the organisation is a contentious issue in Montenegro; memories of the NATO bombing of Serbia during the Kosovo conflict are still fresh in many people's minds. (Montenegro wasn't entirely spared either, with bombs dropped on and around Podgorica.) Anti-NATO protests erupted in Podgorica in late 2015, followed by a split in the ruling coalition in early 2016. The accession to NATO has also upset the historically close relationship between Russia and Montenegro. Some have theorised that Montenegro's NATO membership would be a symbolic slap in the face to Russia, proving to them that the organisation's expansion cannot be halted.

POPULATION: **676,870**

AREA: **13,812 SQ KM**

GDP: **€3.78 BILLION**

AVERAGE MONTHLY WAGE: **€500**

UNEMPLOYMENT: **18%**

if Montenegro were 100 people

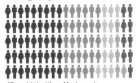

45 would identify as Montenegrin
29 would identify as Serb
12 would identify as Bosniak/Muslim
5 would identify as Albanian
9 are undeclared or another ethnicity

belief systems
(% of population)

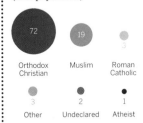

Orthodox Christian 72
Muslim 19
Roman Catholic 3
Other 3
Undeclared 2
Atheist 1

population per sq km

Montenegro

UK

USA

≈ 1 person

History

Nothing about Balkan history is straightforward. In this part of the world, events that are centuries old factor heavily in the national consciousness and in the (occasionally heated) public discourse. State boundaries have changed continuously down the ages – since WWI alone, Montenegro has gone through seven incarnations – and each ethnic and religious group has their own tales to tell, making this a complex country with many distinct histories.

The Illyrians & the Romans

The Illyrians were the first known people to inhabit the region, arriving during the late Iron Age. By 1000 BC a common Illyrian language and culture had spread across much of the Balkans. Interaction among groups was not always friendly – hill forts were the most common form of settlement – but distinctive Illyrian art forms such as amber and bronze jewellery evolved. In time the Illyrians established a loose federation of tribes centred in what is now Macedonia and northern Albania.

Maritime Greeks created coastal colonies on the sites of some Illyrian settlements around 400 BC. Thereafter Hellenic culture gradually spread out from Greek centres, particularly from Bouthoe (Budva). The Romans eventually followed, initially at the behest of the Greeks who sought protection from the Illyrian Queen Teuta. The Illyrians continued to resist the Romans until 168 BC, when the last Illyrian king, Gentius, was defeated. The Romans fully absorbed the Balkans into their provinces and established networks of forts, roads and trade routes from the Danube to the Aegean. However, outside the towns, Illyrian culture remained dominant.

The Romans established the province of Dalmatia, which included what is now Montenegro. The most important Roman town in this region was Doclea (present-day Podgorica), founded around AD 100. Archaeological finds indicate that it was a hub in an extensive trade network.

Over the centuries, the Roman Empire gradually declined. Invaders from the north and west began encroaching on Roman territory and

The Romans took advantage of the beautiful Adriatic coastline to build lavish seaside villas complete with mosaic floors, the remains of which are displayed in both Risan and Petrovac. Other Roman ruins can be seen at the site of Doclea, on the northern edge of Podgorica.

TIMELINE	300 BC	231–228 BC	AD 100
	Illyrian tribes achieve supremacy in the Balkans, founding city states (including one at Lake Skadar near the modern Montenegro–Albania border) and establishing themselves as maritime powers in the Adriatic.	Illyrian Queen Teuta establishes her base at Risan and pirates under her command roam the Adriatic, harrying the Romans, among others. Eventually the Romans bring her reign to an end.	Doclea (present-day Podgorica), a settlement established by the Illyrians, grows to become a significant city under Roman rule. It is home to up to 10,000 people.

in 395 the empire was formally split, the western half retaining Rome as capital and the eastern half (which eventually became the Byzantine Empire) choosing Constantinople (present-day Istanbul). What is now Montenegro lay on the fault line between these two entities.

In the 6th century, the Byzantine Emperor Justinian took control of the previously Roman-ruled parts of the Balkans, pushing out the Ostrogoths who had bowled through the region. He brought Christianity with him.

The Slavs Arrive

In around the early 6th century, a new group, the Slavs, began moving south from the broad plains north of the Danube. It is thought that they moved in the wake of a nomadic Central Asian people, the Avars, who were noted for their ferocity. The Avars tangled with the Byzantines, razing Doclea while roaring through the Balkans. They had too much momentum, however, rolling on and besieging the mighty Byzantine capital at Constantinople in 626. The Byzantines duly crushed them and the Avars faded into history.

Controversy remains as to the role the Slavs played in the demise of the Avars. Some claim that Byzantium called on the Slavs to help stave off the Avar onslaught, while others think that the Slavs merely filled the void left when the Avars disappeared. Whatever the case, the Slavs spread rapidly through the Balkans, reaching the Adriatic by the early 7th century.

Two closely related Slavic groups settled along the Adriatic coast and its hinterland: the Croats and the Serbs. Byzantine culture lingered on in the towns of the interior, thus fostering the spread of Christianity among the Slavs.

First Slavic Kingdoms

In the 7th century, the Bulgarians created the first Slavic state in the Balkans. By the 9th century, the Bulgarian Prince Boris was advocating that the Slavonic language be used for the church liturgy. The subsequent spread of Cyrillic script allowed various other Slavic kingdoms to grow as entities separate from Byzantium.

One such polity was Raška, a group of Serbian tribes that came together near Novi Pazar (in modern Serbia) to shake off Bulgarian control. This kingdom was short-lived, being snuffed out by Bulgarian Tsar Simeon around 927, but not before Raška recognised the Byzantine emperor as sovereign, further speeding the spread of Christianity in the region.

Soon another Serbian state, Duklja, sprang up on the site of the Roman town of Doclea. Under its leader Vladimir, Duklja swiftly expanded its territory to take in Dubrovnik and what remained of Raška. By 1040 Duklja was confident enough to rebel against Byzantine control, expand

It seems that the Byzantines' first impressions of the Slavs weren't entirely positive. The Byzantine historian John of Ephesus remarked that they were 'rude savages'.

HISTORY THE SLAVS ARRIVE

The legacy of the Raška state can be seen in the Church of the Dormition in Reževići Monastery, founded by Stefan Nemanja, and Morača Monastery, founded by his grandson. Raškan royals feature in church frescoes throughout the country.

395	614	800s	869
The Roman Empire is divided into two. Present-day Croatia and Bosnia land in the western half and Serbia in the eastern Byzantine Empire, while Montenegro sits on the dividing line.	The Avars sack the Roman cities of Salona (Split) and Epidaurum (Cavtat). The Slavic tribes follow in their wake, either as invited defenders or as opportunistic vacuum-fillers.	The first Serbian entity, Raška, arises near what is now the Serbian city of Novi Pazar. It is squeezed between the Byzantine and Bulgarian Empires.	At the behest of Byzantium, Macedonian monks Methodius and Cyril create the Glagolitic alphabet, precursor of the Cyrillic alphabet, to help speed the spread of Christianity among the Slavic peoples.

its territory along the Dalmatian coast and establish a capital at Skadar (modern Shkodra in Albania). Around 1080 Duklja achieved its greatest extent, absorbing present-day Bosnia. Civil wars and various intrigues led to Duklja's downfall and power shifted back to Raška during the 12th century.

The Nemanjići & the Golden Age

Stefan Nemanja (born near present-day Podgorica) was to establish the dynasty that saw Raška (which came to be known as Serbia) reach its greatest territorial extent. By 1190 he had regained Raška's independence from Byzantium, also claiming present-day Kosovo and Macedonia for his kingdom. Nemanja later retired as a monk to Mt Athos in Greece, while his sons conquered further territory. After his death he was canonised by the Orthodox Church and became St Simeon.

Meanwhile, the Fourth Crusade in 1204 had hobbled the Byzantines, and Venetian influence began spreading through the Adriatic. In 1219, Sava, one of Nemanja's sons, made an agreement with a weakened Byzantium that the Serbian church should be autocephalous (self-ruling), and appointed himself its first archbishop; he too was eventually canonised.

Around 1331 Dušan was proclaimed the 'young king'. He was to prove a towering figure in Serbian history, both physically (he was around 2m tall) and historically. He swiftly confirmed he was in control by chasing the Bulgarians out of Macedonia and capturing territory from the Byzantines. In expanding so rapidly under Dušan, Serbia became an 'empire', its territory doubling as it took in Serbs, Albanians, Bulgarians and Greeks. More than just an aggressive campaigner, Dušan also

THE BATTLE OF KOSOVO POLJE

In 1386, the Ottoman Turks took the Serbian stronghold at Niš, then in 1389 at Kosovo Polje, the amassed armies of Serbian Prince Lazar and Ottoman Sultan Murat met. This proved to be one of the most pivotal events in Balkan history. Both leaders were killed and while neither side could conclusively claim victory, the Serbian empire was emphatically brought to an end and the Ottomans were free to continue their march into central Europe. Lazar's widow accepted Ottoman suzerainty and the battle entered Serbian legend, portrayed as a noble and ultimately hopeless act of Serbian bravery in the face of overwhelming odds.

The battle remains a defining part of Serbian identity to this day and partly explains Serb hostility to the notion of an independent, Albanian-dominated Kosovo. You'll see 'Kosovo je Srbija' (Kosovo is Serbia) graffiti throughout Serbia and the Serb-identified parts of Montenegro, often accompanied by '1389', the date of the battle.

1015	1054	1166	1208
With the decline of the Bulgarian Empire, following the death of Tsar Samuil, Duklja arises as a Serb-controlled principality in the place of the recently departed Raška.	The Great Schism irrevocably splits Christianity into (eastern) Orthodox and (western) Catholic strands. Modern-day Montenegro lies on the fault line between the two.	Stefan Nemanja establishes the Nemanjić dynasty, a Serbian line which is to reign for more than 200 years. He is later recognised as an Orthodox saint.	Sava returns to the Balkans from the Orthodox monasteries at Mt Athos and begins to organise the Serbian Orthodox Church as a distinct ecclesiastical entity.

codified the Serbian law (known as the *Zakonik*) and established the Serbian Patriarchate. In linking the Orthodox Church with the Serbian royal line, Dušan also created a sense of cohesion among previously fractious Serbian tribes.

Nonetheless, throughout this period Zeta (as Duklja was now called) remained distinct from Serbia. Zetan nobles displayed a reluctance to submit to the Raškan rulers of Serbia, while the Raškan rulers generally appointed their sons to oversee Zeta, further indicating the separation of the two entities. As Raška became Serbia, so Duklja/Zeta is seen as the antecedent of Montenegro.

Enter the Venetians and Turks

During the reign of Dušan's son, Uroš, various factions tussled for power and the Balšić family rose to prominence in Zeta. The Balšići established a base near Skadar and began claiming territory along the Adriatic coast. In the north the Venetians reappeared, taking control of Kotor by 1420. By the time Uroš died, Serbian barons were busy squabbling among themselves, oblivious to a greater threat that was steadily advancing through the Balkans: the Ottoman Turks.

By 1441 the Ottomans had rolled through Serbia and in the late 1470s they lunged at the previously unbowed region of Zeta. Ivan Crnojević led a beleaguered group of Zetan survivors to the easily defensible and inaccessible heights near Mt Lovćen and in 1482 established a court and a monastery at what was to become Cetinje. Venetian sailors began calling Mt Lovćen the 'Monte Negro' (meaning 'black mountain'). Meanwhile, the Ottomans continued assailing Cetinje and succeeded in overrunning it in 1514.

Sites related to Ivan Crnojević include the ruins of his abandoned fortress, Žabljak Crnojevića, and Cetinje Monastery, which he founded.

Ottoman Control of the Balkans

Despite taking Cetinje, the Ottomans withdrew. This remote corner was inhospitable and barren, and in any case the Turks were more intent on controlling the Adriatic. Under Süleyman the Magnificent, the Turks took Belgrade in 1521, putting beyond doubt their dominance of the Balkans. That one rocky eyrie, Mt Lovćen, and its environs became the last bastion of Serbian Orthodox culture holding out against the Ottomans.

Despite being barely known in the rest of Europe, the Montenegrins retained a degree of autonomy. Innately warlike and uncontrollable, their behaviour was such that the Ottomans opted for pragmatism and largely left them to their own devices. With the Venetians extending their control in the Adriatic, taking Kotor and Budva, the Montenegrins found themselves at the fault line between the Turkish and Venetian empires.

Through the 17th century a series of wars in Europe exposed weaknesses in the previously invincible Ottoman war machine. At one stage,

1331	1389	1420	1482
Allegedly the tallest man alive at the time, Dušan assumes the leadership and raises Serbia to be one of the largest kingdoms in Europe.	At the battle of Kosovo Polje, much of the Serbian nobility is killed by the invading Ottoman Turks. In time the Ottomans regroup and expand further into the Balkans.	Kotor begins 377 years under Venetian rule.	After a series of Ottoman attacks against Zeta during the late 1470s, Ivan Crnojević leads the remaining nobility to Cetinje, which will become the kernel of the Montenegrin state.

the Ottomans became determined to remove the concessions that the Montenegrins had long enjoyed and that they now considered rightfully theirs. Montenegrin resistance to the Turkish attempt to enforce a tax regime was violent and the Turkish retribution horrific. As Turkish reactions grew more violent, the bonds between previously unruly Montenegrin clans became stronger.

During the 1690s the Ottomans took Cetinje several times, but each time they were forced to retreat due to persistent harrying from Montenegrin tribesmen. At the conclusion of the Morean War in 1699, the Ottomans sued for peace for the first time ever, ceding territory at Risan and Herceg Novi to Venice. The Montenegrins' enthusiastic and effective participation in the war had brought them – and their martial virtues – to the attention of the Habsburgs and the Russians, while also furthering a sense of common purpose among the previously squabbling tribes.

It was then that the Ottomans finally realised they would not be able to control Montenegro; nonetheless they were clearly reluctant to give up their claim. To encircle it, they built a string of fort towns that attracted the Muslim population of the region. The Orthodox tribes and peasants remained in the countryside, developing a sense of solidarity and separateness from the relatively well-off town populations. For the locals, identity was tied to the notion of tribe and the Serbian Orthodox Church, rather than Serbia or Montenegro. Nonetheless, distinct Serbian and Montenegrin identities were evolving: the Serbs were directly ruled by the Ottomans, while the Montenegrins retained a degree of autonomy in their mountain fastness and had managed to avoid being entirely weighed down by the Ottoman 'yoke'.

The Vladikas

In 1696, Danilo Petrović-Njegoš was elected *vladika,* the equivalent of a bishop within the Orthodox Church hierarchy. Ambitious and warlike, he declared himself 'Vladika of Cetinje and Warlord of all the Serb lands'. In so doing, Danilo presumed a role as the leader of the Serbs, perhaps a reflection of Montenegrins dubbing themselves 'the best of the Serbs' during their years of battles against the Turks. Beyond this, Danilo succeeded in elevating the *vladika* role into that of a hereditary 'prince-bishop' – a political (and military) leader as well as a church leader – and founded the Petrović dynasty, which would rule Montenegro until WWI.

In 1766 the Ottomans established the Ecumenical Patriarchate in Constantinople responsible for all of the Orthodox churches in the Ottoman domain. The Serbs later set up their own patriarchate in Habsburg territory, beyond the reach of Ottoman authorities. These moves effectively led to the creation of separate Montenegrin and Serbian Orthodox churches and, while the Montenegrins retained some sense of community with the

1521	1593–1606	1667	1697
The Ottomans take Belgrade, thereby confirming their control of Serbia. The Venetians have been expanding along the Adriatic coast for more than a century and now control most of it.	During the Austrian-Ottoman wars, the pope attempts to incite the Montenegrins, as fellow Christians, to fight against the Ottomans, but with limited success. The Ottomans have control of Bar and Ulcinj.	A devastating earthquake hits the Adriatic coast, destroying much of Kotor, which is under Venetian control. The city has also recently endured an outbreak of plague.	Danilo becomes *vladika* (prince-bishop) and establishes the Petrović dynasty. He mediates disputes between tribes and clans and within 15 years begins the fight back against the Ottomans.

Serbs, this was another factor in the divergent experience and the evolution of a separate national consciousness among the Montenegrins.

Dealing with the Great Powers

Napoleon appeared in 1797 claiming Venice's Adriatic territories, thus removing Montenegro's main rival for power in the Adriatic. The years to come saw Napoleon tangling with the Montenegrins, British and Austrians in the Adriatic. The Montenegrins operated with military support from the Russians and briefly captured Herceg Novi, a long-hoped-for Adriatic coastal town, but in the aftermath they were forced to abandon it due to diplomatic horse-trading.

In 1830 Petar II Petrović Njegoš became *vladika* upon the death of his uncle. Two metres tall, Njegoš fulfilled the requirement that the *vladika* be striking, handsome and dashing. Njegoš made further unsuccessful attempts to gain access to the sea, but in other aspects of nation-building he was more successful. He increased the role of government and developed a system of taxation for Montenegro. He also canonised his predecessor Petar I, thus bringing a saintly aspect to the role of *vladika*, in emulation of the saintly kings of medieval Serbia.

> Petar I was not only a social and ecclesiastical leader; he is also credited with introducing the potato to Montenegro.

Njegoš made the now-traditional trip to St Petersburg in search of military and monetary support from the Russian tsars and set about modernising his nation, which was primitive and undeveloped. Succeeding Petrović rulers continued the process of modernisation, albeit gradually. Danilo came to power in 1851 and promptly declared himself prince, thus bringing an end to the ecclesiastical position of *vladika* as leader of the Montenegrins. In 1855 he won a great victory over the Ottomans at Grahovo and he skilfully steered a course between the interests of the Great Powers – Austria-Hungary, Russia, France and Britain – all of whom had designs on Montenegro and the broader Balkan region.

Nikola, who became prince after Danilo, pressed on with a road-building program and introduced the telegraph to Montenegro. He was also responsible for founding a school for girls in Cetinje, the first-ever such institution in Montenegro. During the 1860s Nikola established contact with Mihailo Obrenović, ruler of the Serbian principality (by then de facto independent from the Ottoman rule). The two leaders signed an agreement to liberate their peoples and create a single state. Most significantly, Nikola reorganised the Montenegrin army into a modern fighting force.

Freedom from the Ottomans

A rebellion against Ottoman control broke out in Bosnia and Hercegovina (BiH) in 1875. Both Serbs and Montenegrins joined the insurgency, Montenegrins (under Nikola) again excelling themselves and making

1784	1797–1815	1800s	1830
Petar I is consecrated as *vladika*, eventually becoming an enduring military and spiritual hero. In 1796 he defeats the Ottoman renegade Kara Mahmud and expands Montenegrin territory considerably.	Napoleon brings the Venetian Republic to an end; Venetian dominions are initially given to the Habsburgs, but in 1806 Napoleon gains the Adriatic coast, which he dubs the Illyrian Provinces.	Petar I courts Russia in the hope of military and financial support in the struggle against the Ottomans. Russia's interest waxes and wanes in the wake of other diplomatic priorities.	Petar II Petrović Njegoš rules as the last *vladika* and becomes one of the nation's most acclaimed leaders. His epic poem *The Mountain Wreath* is regarded as Montenegro's greatest literary work.

significant territorial gains. In the wake of the struggle for Bosnia, the Congress of Berlin in 1878 saw Montenegro and Serbia officially achieve independence from the Ottomans. Montenegro won control of upland territories in Nikšić, Podgorica and Žabljak and territory around Lake Skadar and the port of Bar, effectively tripling in size. The expansionist Austrians annexed BiH, thus stymying any further Montenegrin expansion to the north. The Montenegrins, however, managed to take control of the Ulcinj region of the Adriatic coast.

After 1878 Montenegro enjoyed a period of ongoing peace. Nikola's rule, however, became increasingly autocratic. His most popular move during these years was marrying off several of his daughters to European royalty, including two Russian monarchs. In 1910, on his 50th jubilee, Nikola raised himself from the role of prince to king.

In the early years of the 20th century, there were increasing calls for union with Serbia and rising political opposition to Nikola's rule. The Serbian King Petar Karađorđević (whose late wife was one of Nikola's daughters) was suspected of being involved in attempts to overthrow King Nikola, and Montenegrin-Serbian relations reached their historical low point.

The Balkan Wars of 1912–13 saw the Montenegrins patching things up with the Serbs to join the Greeks and Bulgarians in an effort to throw the Ottoman Turks out of Europe once and for all. During the wars, the Montenegrins gained Bijelo Polje, Berane and Plav and in so doing bordered Serbia for the first time in more than 500 years. The idea of a Serbian-Montenegrin union gained more currency, and in the elections of 1914 many voters opted for union. King Nikola pragmatically supported the idea on the stipulation that both the Serbian and Montenegrin royal houses be retained.

WWI & the First Yugoslavia

Before the union could be realised, WWI intervened. Montenegro entered the war on the side of Serbia and the Allies. Austria-Hungary invaded shortly afterwards and swiftly captured Cetinje, sending King Nikola into exile in France. In 1918, the Serbian army entered Montenegro and the French, keen to implement the Serbian-Montenegrin union, refused to allow Nikola to leave France, formally bringing an end to the Petrović dynasty. The same year, Montenegro ceased to exist after being subsumed into the newly created Kingdom of Serbs, Croats and Slovenes – the first Yugoslavia.

Throughout the 1920s some Montenegrins, peeved at their 'little brother to Serbia' status, as well as the loss of their sovereignty and distinct identity, put up spirited resistance to the union with Serbia. This resentment increased after the abolition of the Montenegrin

In 1904, the country was allied with Russia in the Russo-Japanese War, with Montenegrin volunteers fighting alongside their Slavic brethren in Manchuria. When peace was declared in 1905, Montenegro wasn't included in the treaty. It wasn't until 2006 – 101 years later – that a separate peace treaty was signed and the 'war' between Japan and Montenegro was formally over.

1851	1876–78	1910	1918
Njegoš' nephew Danilo becomes the country's first secular leader, taking the title 'prince'. He is assassinated in 1860, a victim of a blood feud with a rival Montenegrin clan.	Wars of independence see Serbia, Bulgaria and Montenegro finally win their freedom from the rapidly shrinking Ottoman Empire. Montenegro triples in size, gaining Nikšić, Podgorica, Žabljak and Bar.	Prince Nikola takes the title of 'king', raising eyebrows across Europe that such a diminutive and impoverished territory, home to only 200,000 souls, could really qualify as a kingdom.	The Kingdom of Serbs, Croats and Slovenes is created in the aftermath of WWI. Serbia's King Petar I Karađorđević assumes the monarchy. Montenegro is included within his domains.

church, which was subsumed into the Serbian Orthodox Patriarchate in Belgrade. Taking advantage of fears of a Serb-Croat civil war, on 6 January 1929, King Aleksandar proclaimed a royal dictatorship, abolished political parties and suspended parliamentary government, thus ending any hope of democratic change. In 1934, while on a state visit in Marseilles, King Aleksandar was assassinated by the fascist-inspired Croatian Ustaše.

Meanwhile, during the mid-1920s, the Yugoslav Communist Party arose; Josip Broz Tito was to become leader in 1937. The high level of membership of the Communist Party among Montenegrins was perhaps a reflection of their displeasure with the status of Montenegro within Yugoslavia.

WWII & the Second Yugoslavia

During WWII the Nazis invaded Yugoslavia on multiple fronts. The Italians followed on their coat-tails. After routing the Yugoslav army, Germany and Italy divided the country into a patchwork of areas of control. The Italians controlled Montenegro and parts of neighbouring Dalmatia. Some anti-union Montenegrins collaborated with the Italians in the hope that the Petrović dynasty would be reinstated. Meanwhile, Tito's Partisans and the Serbian Četniks (royalists) engaged the Italians, sometimes lapsing into fighting each other. The most effective antifascist struggle was conducted by Partisan units led by Tito. With their roots in the outlawed Yugoslav Communist Party, the Partisans attracted long-suffering intellectuals and antifascists of all kinds. They gained wide popular support with an early manifesto which, although vague, appeared to envision a postwar Yugoslavia based on a loose federation.

Although the Allies initially backed the Serbian Četniks, it became apparent that the Partisans were waging a far more focused and determined fight against the Nazis. With the diplomatic and military support of Churchill and other Allied powers, the Partisans controlled much of Yugoslavia by 1943. The Partisans established functioning local governments in

WAS TITO TITO?

Across the former Yugoslavia, the identity – and actual existence – of Tito has sparked many a debate. While the official records state that he was born into a peasant family, naysayers have cited everything from his unusual accent, playboy proclivities and – gasp! – ability to play Chopin on the piano as proof that he was not who he claimed to be. Was he a Russian plant? An undeclared aristocrat? A body double of the 'real' Tito who 'died' in 1915? While historians and linguists dismiss the claims, it's hard to keep a good conspiracy theory down (especially in the Balkans).

1941	1943	1945–48	1960s
Hitler invades Yugoslavia and divides it into areas of German and Italian control. Mussolini occupies Montenegro with plans to absorb it as an Italian protectorate.	Tito's communist Partisans achieve military victories and build a popular antifascist front. They reclaim territory from retreating Italian brigades. The Partisans eventually take control of Yugoslavia.	The Federal People's Republic of Yugoslavia is founded. In time, Tito breaks with Stalin and steers a careful course between Eastern and Western blocs, including establishing the nonaligned movement.	Tourism takes off in Yugoslavia, with a particular focus on the Adriatic coast. Hot spots such as Sveti Stefan attract the international jet set right up until the Yugoslav wars.

the territory they seized, which later eased their transition to power. Hitler made several concerted attempts to kill Tito and wipe out the Partisans, but was unsuccessful. As the tide of the war turned, the Italians surrendered to the Allies and, with the Partisans harassing them, the Germans withdrew. On 20 October 1944, Tito entered Belgrade with the Red Army and was made prime minister.

The communist federation of Yugoslavia was established. Tito was determined to create a state in which no ethnic group dominated the political landscape. Montenegro became one of six republics – along with Macedonia, Serbia, Croatia, BiH and Slovenia – in a tightly configured union. Tito effected this delicate balance by creating a one-party state and rigorously stamping out all opposition whether nationalist, royalist or religious. The border of the modern state was set: Montenegro won Kotor, but lost some areas of Kosovo in the horse-trading that Tito undertook in order to establish a balance between the various Yugoslav republics.

In 1948 Tito fell out with Stalin and broke off contacts with the USSR. This caused some consternation in Montenegro, given its historical links with Russia. Of all the Yugoslav republics, Montenegro had the highest per capita membership of the Communist Party, and it was highly represented in the army.

During the 1960s, the concentration of power in Belgrade became an increasingly testy issue as it became apparent that money from the more prosperous republics of Slovenia and Croatia was being distributed to the other republics, and not always fairly. Unrest reached a crescendo in 1971 when reformers called for greater economic autonomy and the loosening of ties within the Yugoslav federation, but nationalistic elements manifested themselves as well. Tito's 1974 constitution afforded the republics more autonomy, but the stage was set for the rise of nationalism and the wars of the 1990s.

Tito left a shaky Yugoslavia upon his death in May 1980. A presidency rotating among the six republics could not compensate for the loss of his steadying hand at the helm. The authority of the central government sank with the economy, and long-suppressed mistrust among Yugoslavia's ethnic groups resurfaced.

In 1946 the Montenegrin capital was moved from Cetinje to Podgorica and renamed Titograd. In 1992 Titograd was changed back to Podgorica, which remains the capital.

Union with Serbia, then Independence

As communism collapsed throughout Eastern Europe, Slobodan Milošević used the issue of Kosovo to ride to power in Serbia on a wave of nationalism. Montenegrins largely supported their Orthodox co-religionists.

In 1991 Slovenia and Croatia declared independence from the federation and the Yugoslav wars commenced. There was no fighting in Montenegro, but Montenegrin paramilitary groups, in conjunction with

1979	1980	1991	1997
An earthquake registering 7.1 on the Richter scale causes large-scale devastation across the country; countless historic buildings collapse, rail lines are cut and 101 people die.	The death of President Tito prompts a genuine outpouring of grief. Tributes flow, but Yugoslavia is beset by inflation, unemployment and foreign debt, setting the scene for the difficulties to come.	Yugoslavia splits. As Slovenia, Croatia, BiH and Macedonia seek their independence, the question of Montenegrin independence is raised, but a year later Montenegrins vote to remain in Yugoslavia.	Milo Đukanović wins a further election victory. Montenegro adopts a pro-Western stance and distances itself from the Serbian position during the NATO raids in defence of Kosovo in 1999.

the Serb-dominated Yugoslav army, were responsible for the shelling of Dubrovnik and parts of the Dalmatian littoral. These acts appeared to serve no strategic purpose and were roundly criticised in the international press. In 1992, by which point BiH and Macedonia had also opted for independence, the Montenegrins voted overwhelmingly to remain in the Yugoslav state with Serbia. Admittedly there was some Montenegrin edginess about their place within 'Greater Serbia', and the autocephalous Montenegrin church was revived in 1993.

As the bloody war in Bosnia wound down with the signing of the Dayton accords in 1995, Montenegrin Prime Minister Milo Đukanović began distancing himself from Milošević. Previously a Milošević ally, Đukanović, who had been elected in 1991, realised that in the face of declining living standards and rising discontent, Montenegro would fare better if it adopted a more pro-Western course. In doing so he became the darling of Western leaders, who were trying to isolate and bring down Milošević. As the Serbian regime became an international pariah, the Montenegrins increasingly moved to re-establish their distinct identity. Political relations with Serbia rapidly cooled, with Đukanović winning further elections in Montenegro despite spirited interference from Belgrade. Nevertheless, Montenegro was bombed (though nowhere near as much as Serbia) during the NATO strikes of 1999, with Podgorica and its airport taking direct hits; eight civilians died. In a sign of solidarity with Serbia – which was bombed for 78 days straight – graffitti appeared in Nikšić reading 'Bomb us too: we're not lepers'.

In 2000 Milošević lost the election in Serbia, and in 2001 he was arrested; he died in prison in The Hague while on trial for war crimes. In 2003 the name Yugoslavia was consigned to the dustbin of history and Montenegro entered into a state union with Serbia. In theory, the union was based on equality between the two members but in practice, Serbia was such a dominant partner that the union proved infeasible from the outset. Again, this rankled, given the Montenegrins' historic self-opinion as the 'best of the Serbs'. In May 2006, a slim majority voted for independence and the modern state of Montenegro was formed.

In 2011, Montenegro adopted a law that recognised the official role of the Petrović-Njegoš dynasty. Though said role is largely limited to promoting the country and its culture, some have criticised the move, saying it's the beginning of a process to have the monarchy reinstated.

At the time of writing, Montenegro was a candidate for EU membership and it was expected that the country would become a member of NATO by mid-2017.

2003	2006	2011	2015
Yugoslavia expires and is replaced by the state union of Serbia and Montenegro. The union is intended to be an equal partnership but it rapidly proves unworkable.	In May Montenegrins vote in a referendum for independence from Serbia. With a slim majority (55%) voting in the affirmative, Montenegro declares independence in June.	Parliament grants French citizen Prince Nikola II Petrović Njegoš, King Nikola's great-grandson, dual Montenegrin citizenship and allows him to represent the country in certain non-political duties.	Montenegro is formally invited to join NATO, sparking nationwide protests and political discord.

Montenegro's People

In this part of the world, questions of ethnicity are so thickly embroiled with history, politics and religion that discussions of identity can be a minefield. Yet to an outsider, the more you travel in the Balkans, the more you're struck by the similarities between its various peoples: the warm hospitality, the close family bonds, the social conservatism, the fiery tempers, and the passionate approach to life.

Ethnicity vs Nationality

Throughout the Balkans, people tend to identify more by ethnicity than citizenship. This is hardly surprising; a family that has never left its ancestral village may have had children born in Montenegro, parents born in Yugoslavia, grandparents born in the Kingdom of Serbs, Croats and Slovenes, and great-grandparents born in the Ottoman or Austro-Hungarian Empires. Countries may come and go, but self-identity tends to stick around. It's understandable then that an Albanian, Bosniak (South Slav Muslim), Croat or Serb might not call themselves Montenegrin, even if their family has lived in the area that is now Montenegro for generations.

In the last census (2011), the country's main ethnic groups were Montenegrins (45%), Serbs (29%), Bosniaks (9%) and Albanians (5%). Tellingly, the next major group was 'Does not want to declare' at 5%. To give you an idea of the kind of ethnic knots people tie themselves in, smaller categories represented in the census include Montenegrin Serbs, Serb Montenegrins, Montenegrin Muslims, Muslim Montenegrins, Muslim Bosniaks, Bosniak Muslims, Bosnians and just plain Muslims.

In fact, these myriad ethnic identities have little to do with actual genetic heritage and despite the 29 ethnicities listed in the census, around 88% of the population could reasonably be labelled as some flavour of South Slav, with Albanians (5%) and Roma (1%) being the largest non-Slavic minorities. Scratch a little further and its even more complicated, as numerous armies have raped and pillaged their way through these lands over the millennia.

Montenegrins are in the majority in most of the country, while Albanians dominate in the southeast (Ulcinj), Bosniaks in the far east (Rožaje and Plav), and Serbs in Herceg Novi (due to a large influx caused by the Yugoslav wars) and parts of the north and east (Plužine, Pljevlja, Bijelo Polje, Berane and Andrijevica).

Religion and ethnicity broadly go together in these parts. More than 72% of the population is Orthodox (mainly Montenegrins and Serbs), 19% Muslim (mainly Bosniaks and Albanians), 3% Roman Catholic (mainly Albanians and Croats) and only 1% atheist.

A popular self-belief is that Montenegro has a better tolerance of ethnic and religious minorities than many of its neighbours. This is possibly true, although you may still hear some mutterings from locals about the threat of a Greater Serbia/Albania/Croatia.

Montenegro's stirring national anthem – 'Oh, Bright Dawn of May' – celebrates its citizens' fierce independence and passion for the craggy country itself with lines like 'We love you, the rocky hills/And your awesome gorges/That never came to know/The chains of shameful slavery'.

The Warrior Spirit

It's no surprise that the areas where people most strongly identify as Montenegrin are those that were part of Montenegro before the dawn of the 20th century, especially in the old heartland around Cetinje. This is where the archetype of the noble Montenegrin warrior, fierce in battle and devoted to freedom and the Orthodox Church, has its origins.

A staple feature of nearly every museum in Montenegro is a display of weapons. These aren't any old guns and swords. Inlaid with mother-of-pearl and set with precious jewels, these are finely crafted objects that have been handled with obvious love and care. The period architecture was solid and perfunctory and the paintings largely devotional, but when it came to making guns, the Montenegrins were happy to indulge themselves. Men weren't properly dressed without a pair of fancy pistols protruding from their waistbands; one can only imagine what kind of accidental injuries were sustained.

One of the most famous Montenegrin warrior stories (and there are many) is about Aleksandar Lekso Saičić, a volunteer in the Russian army in the Russo-Japanese War of 1904–1905. The oft-told tale – immortalised also in song – goes that the Russian commander asked for a volunteer to duel to the death with a legendary and hitherto invincible samurai. The cowardly Russian troops shuffled their feet, but the Montenegrin villager put his hand up and – in a whirl of savage sword clanging – decapitated the Japanese samurai, paid tribute to the body and gained instant *junak* (hero) status for life (and beyond).

The warrior spirit may traditionally have been at the heart of Montenegrin society, but today most people are keen to get on with their lives and put the turbulence of the last 25 years behind them. Gunshots can still be heard here but only in celebration. It's the traditional accompaniment to weddings and other festivities, as a flight from Ljubljana

Football (soccer), basketball, water polo and handball are the national sporting obsessions. Given the national tendancy towards tallness, it's little wonder you'll find Montenegrins playing in America's NBA. Current players include Orlando Magic's Nikola Vučević (2.13m), Nikola Mirotić (2.08m) of the Chicago Bulls, and Minnesota Timberwolves' Nikola Peković (2.11m). Nikola is clearly a name of great stature.

MONTENEGRIN VS SERB

The issue of identity is particularly thorny with regard to current Montenegrin-Serb relations. For centuries, Montenegrins considered themselves 'the best of the Serbs', keeping the flame of independent Serbian culture alive while their brethren elsewhere were under the Ottoman yoke. Pro-Serbian graffiti covers the country and while most Montenegrins feel a strong kinship to their closest siblings, this is usually coupled with a determination to maintain their distinct identity.

The main unifying factor has traditionally been the Serbian Orthodox Church (SOC), but even that was shaken with the formation of a new Montenegrin Orthodox Church (MOC) in 1993, claiming to revive the self-governing church of Montenegro's *vladikas* (prince-bishops) which was dissolved in 1920. Furthermore, they claim that all church property dating prior to 1920, and any churches built with state funds since, should be returned to it. The SOC doesn't recognise the MOC and neither do the other major Orthodox churches. The SOC still controls most of the country's churches and monasteries. Relations between the two churches has been acrimonious, to the say the least.

On a temporal level, things have been equally tense. After negotiating a reasonably amicable divorce from the unhappy state union with Serbia in 2006, relations took a turn for the worse. In 2008 Serbia expelled Montenegro's ambassador after Montenegro officially recognised the former Serbian province of Kosovo as an independent country, joining around 50 other nations who had already done so. Serbia has vowed never to recognise Kosovo, which many Serbs view as their spiritual heartland.

Diplomatic relations between Montenegro and Serbia have since improved. After his election in 2012, Serbian president Tomislav Nikolić, regarded as a nationalist, stated, 'I recognise Montenegrin independence, but I don't recognise any difference between Serbs and Montenegrins, because it doesn't exist.'

to Podgorica discovered when it took an accidental hit during celebrations for Orthodox Christmas Eve in 2008. There were no casualties.

Tied in with the warrior culture is the importance of *čojstvo i junaštvo*, which roughly translates as 'humanity and bravery' – in other words, chivalry. In the past, it inspired soldiers to fight to the death rather than abandon their mates to the enemy or face the shame of being captured. While it might not have exactly the same practical application today, don't expect a Montenegrin to back down from a fight, especially if the honour of their loved ones is at stake. Luckily Montenegro doesn't (yet) attract stag-party groups – it doesn't take much to imagine the sort of reception that drunken louts would receive if they were stupid enough to be disrespectful to the local women.

The fictional Nero Wolfe – of Rex Stout's famously hard-boiled detective stories – was a Montenegrin by birth. Stout chose Montenegro for Nero because he'd read that Montenegrin men were romantic, loyal, proud, brave and stubborn, traits that fit his intense character perfectly.

Montenegrin Life

On a warm summer's evening, the main street of every town fills up, as they do throughout the Balkans, with a constant parade of tall, beautiful, well-dressed people of all ages, socialising with their friends, checking each other out and simply enjoying life. In summer, life is lived on the streets and in the cafes.

The enduring stereotype of Montenegrins is that they are lazy, an accusation that they themselves sometimes revel in. Certainly the cafes and bars are always full, but perhaps no more so than in the neighbouring countries. As a popular local joke goes, 'Man is born tired and lives to rest'. This accusation of indolence probably derived from the era when occupations other than fighting and raiding the neighbouring Turks were seen to be beneath a man's dignity. It's certainly not true of Montenegrin women, to whom all the actual heavy labour fell.

Montenegrin society has traditionally been rigidly patriarchal and women were expected to kiss a man's hand as a sign of respect. In 1855 Prince Danilo caused a scandal by publicly kissing the hand of his beloved fiancée; one of his officials berated him, saying: 'I would never kiss the hand of a woman or a Turk'. Despite major advances in education and equality for women during the communist years, distinct gender roles remain. If you're invited to a Montenegrin home for dinner, for example, it's likely that women will do all the cooking, serving of the meal and cleaning up, and it's quite possible that an older hostess may not sit down and eat with you but spend her whole time in the kitchen.

These days you'll see plenty of younger women out and about in cafes and bars. Literacy and employment levels are relatively equal, and basic rights are enshrined in law including (since 1945) the right to vote.

Montenegrin society has traditionally been tribal, with much emphasis placed on extended family-based clans. This can create the potential for nepotism; accusations that major employers and public officials favour family, friends or business associates are commonplace. Family ties are strong and people generally live with their parents until they are married. This makes life particularly difficult for gays and lesbians or anyone wanting a taste of independence. Many young people get a degree of this by travelling to study in a different town.

Although people have drifted away from the more remote villages, Montenegro isn't particularly urbanised, with about half of the populace living in communities of fewer than 10,000 people. Roughly a third of the population live in the two cities that have more than 20,000 people (Podgorica and Nikšić).

Art & Architecture

Montenegro's historic preoccupation with religion and war focussed its earliest artistic endeavours on sumptuously painted churches, beautifully crafted weapons and epic poetry. The modern stereotype of the bed-wetting poet whimpering on about romantic failures or fields of daffodils had no place in macho Montenegrin society; traditionally the role of the warrior and the poet went hand in hand. Peacetime in Communist Yugoslavia saw a flourishing of divergent artistic expression, particularly in the fields of painting, sculpture, cinema and architecture.

Literature

Towering over Montenegrin literature is Petar II Petrović Njegoš (1813–51); towering so much, in fact, that his mausoleum overlooks the country from the top of the black mountain itself. This poet and prince-bishop produced the country's most enduring work of literature, *Gorski vijenac* (The Mountain Wreath; 1847), a verse play romanticising the struggle for freedom from the Ottomans. It's not without controversy, as the story glorifies the massacre of Muslims on Orthodox Christmas Eve in 1702, known as the Montenegrin Vespers. It's not certain whether it actually happened, but according to the story, Vladika Danilo, Njegoš's great-granduncle, ordered the leaders of the Montenegrin tribes to kill all of their kinspeople (men, women and children) who had converted to Islam. Some commentators have drawn a parallel between this story of ethnic cleansing and the atrocities that took place in Bosnia in the 1990s.

Following in the same epic tradition was Avdo Međedović (1875–1953), a peasant from Bijelo Polje who was hailed as the most important *guslar* (singer/composer of epic poetry accompanied by the *gusle,* a one-stringed folk instrument) of his time. If you think that 'Stairway to Heaven' is too long, it's lucky you didn't attend the marathon performance over several days where Međedović is said to have recited a 13,331-line epic.

He may have been born a Bosnian Croat, but Ivo Andrić (1892–1975), Yugoslavia's greatest writer, had a home in Herceg Novi. Andrić was awarded the Nobel Prize in 1961 for his brilliant *Bridge over the Drina* (1945). While you're rafting along the Tara River, it's worth remembering that the Tara becomes the Drina just over the Bosnian border.

Miodrag Bulatović (1930–91) was known for his black humour and graphic portrayals of dark subjects. His most famous books including *Hero on a Donkey* (1967), *The Red Rooster Flies Heavenward* (1959) and *The Four-Fingered People* (1975) are available in English.

Danilo Kiš (1935–89) was an acclaimed author of the Yugoslav period who had several novels translated into English, including *Hourglass* (1972) and *A Tomb for Boris Davidovich* (1976). He was born in what is now Serbia but moved to Cetinje with his Montenegrin mother after his Hungarian Jewish father was killed in the Holocaust.

Montenegrin-born Borislav Pekić (1930–92) was another significant name in Yugoslav literature. His huge opus includes novels, dramas, science fiction, film scripts, essays and political memoirs. His work has been translated into many languages, but at present only the early novels

Northern Montenegro and other parts of the Western Balkans are a treasure trove of carved medieval tombstones known as *stećci*. Their origins and symbolism continue to puzzle archaeologists. A collection of *stećci* in Cetinje and the northern mountains were added to the Unesco World Heritage list in 2016.

The Montenegrin language lends itself to poetry and it was once commonplace to frame formal language in verse. A British diplomat from the time of King Nikola reported that a government minister once delivered an entire budget in verse.

The Time of Miracles (1965), *The Houses of Belgrade* (1970) and *How to Quiet a Vampire* (1977) are available in English.

A popular modern author is Andrej Nikolaidis, whose novel *Sin* (The Son; 2011) won the European Union Prize for Literature and has been translated into English, alongside *Dolazak* (The Coming; 2009). Another one to watch is Ognjen Spahić, whose *Hansenova djeca* (Hansen's Children; 2004) – available in English – won a regional award.

Visual Arts

Montenegro's fine-arts legacy can be divided into two broad strands: religious iconography and Yugoslav-era painting and sculpture.

The nation's churches are full of wonderful frescoes and painted iconostases (the screen that separates the congregation from the sanctuary in Orthodox churches). A huge number were produced by members of the Dimitrijević-Rafailović clan from Risan in the Bay of Kotor, who turned out 11 painters between the 17th and 19th centuries.

Earlier Serbian masters (pre-dating Montenegro) include Longin, a monk from 16th-century Peć (in present-day Kosovo), whose unique approach to colour created otherworldly scenes of saints and Serbian royalty backed by blue mountains and golden skies. You'll find his work at Piva Monastery. Following him half a century later was Đorđe Mitrofanović from Hilandar (now in northern Greece), whose accomplished icons and frescoes feature in the Morača and Pljevlja monasteries. A talented contemporary of his was Kozma, who also worked at Morača.

Yugoslavia proved to be something of a golden age for the arts. Among the modern painters, an early great was Petar Lubarda (1907–74) whose stylised oil paintings included themes from Montenegrin history. Miodrag (Dado) Đurić (1933–2010) was known for his accomplished surrealist paintings and drawings, but he also produced engravings, sculpture and, in later years, digital work. In 2012 an offshoot of the Montenegrin Art Gallery devoted to 20th-century and contemporary art was opened in Cetinje and named in his honour.

Other names to look out for include Milo Milunović (1897–1967), Jovan Zonjić (1907–61), Vojo Stanić (born 1924), Filip Janković (born 1935), Dimitrije Popović (born 1951) and sculptor Risto Stijović (1894–1974). The best places to see the works of these and others are at Cetinje's Montenegrin Art Gallery and the museums and galleries of Podgorica.

MUSIC, SACRED & PROFANE

Archbishop Jovan of Duklja was producing religious chants in the 10th century, making him the earliest known composer in the region. Traditional instruments include the flute and the one-stringed *gusle*, which is used to accompany epic poetry.

The most famous Montenegrin musician of the moment is 30-year-old classical guitarist Miloš Karadaglić, who won the Breakthrough Artist prize at the 2012 Classical BRIT Awards and has been touring the world on the back of number-one recordings on the US, UK and Australian classical charts.

In the 1990s, the excruciatingly named Monteniggers carried the torch for home-grown hip hop. Continuing on the unfortunate name theme, Rambo Amadeus is Montenegro's answer to Frank Zappa. He's been releasing albums since the late 1980s, flirting with styles as diverse as turbofolk, hip hop and drum and bass – all with a large serving of laughs. In 2012 he created one of the more memorable Eurovision Song Contest moments, performing his song 'Euro Neuro' backed by a wooden 'Trojan donkey' and breakdancers.

If anyone doubts the relevance of Eurovision, they should travel through Montenegro. Montenegrins love their local pop, particularly if it's a gut-wrenching power ballad or a cheesy ditty played loud and accompanied by a thumping techno beat.

Of the contemporary crop, one to watch is Jelena Tomašević, whose paintings and video installations have been exhibited in New York, Berlin, Milan and Venice. Born in Belgrade to Montenegrin parents, performance artist Marina Abramović won the Golden Lion in the Venice Biennale in 1997. One of her most well-known pieces was *The Artist Is Present,* where she sat immobile in a chair in New York's Museum of Modern Art for 75 days while museum visitors took turns to sit opposite her.

Cinema

In the decade since independence, Montenegrin cinema has yet to set the world alight. Someone that's working hard to change that is Marija Perović, who is credited with being the country's first female film and TV director. She followed up her 2004 debut *Opet pakujemo majmune* (Packing the Monkeys, Again!) with *Gledaj me* (Look at Me) in 2008.

Montenegro-born Veljko Bulajić has been directing movies since the 1950s, with his most recent being *Libertas* in 2006. His *Vlak bez voznog reda* (Train Without a Timetable) was nominated for the Golden Palm at Cannes in 1959, while *Rat* (War) was nominated for the Golden Lion at the 1960 Venice Film Festival. In 1969 he wrote and directed *Bitka na Neretvi* (The Battle of Neretva), which was nominated for the Academy Award for Best Foreign Language Film.

Another noteworthy Yugoslav-era director was Živko Nikolić (1941–2001), who directed 24 features from the 1960s to 1990s.

Montenegro's biggest Hollywood success is cinematographer Bojan Bazelli, whose titles include *King of New York* (1990), *Kalifornia* (1993), *Mr & Mrs Smith* (2005), *Hairspray* (2007) and *Rock of Ages* (2012).

Ironically, the movie that springs to most people's minds when they think of Montenegro is the 2006 Bond flick *Casino Royale;* the Montenegrin scenes were actually shot in the Czech Republic. The Golden Palm-nominated *Montenegro* (1981), directed by Serb Dušan Makavejev, was set in Sweden.

The unusual *oro* is a circle dance accompanied by the singing of the participants as they tease each other and take turns to enter the circle and perform a stylised eagle dance. For a dramatic conclusion, the strapping lads form a two-storey circle, standing on each other's shoulders.

Architecture

Traditional Montenegrin houses are sturdy stone structures with small shuttered windows and terracotta-tiled pitched roofs. In the mountainous regions a stone base is topped with a wooden storey and a steeply pitched cut-gable roof designed to let the snow slide off. The *kula* is a blocky tower-like house built for defence that's common in the country's far eastern reaches. They are usually three to four stories tall, with no windows on the lowest floor, and they sometimes have ornate overhanging balconies in wood or stone on the upper level.

The influence of Venice is keenly felt in the walled towns of the coast, which echo the spirit of Dubrovnik and other Dalmatian towns. Cetinje's streets include late-19th-century mansions and palaces remaining from its days as the royal capital.

It's easy to be dismissive of the utilitarian socialist architecture of the Yugoslav period, yet there are some wonderfully inventive structures dating from that time. James Bond would have been quite at home settling in with a martini beneath the sharp angles and bubbly light fixtures of some of the 1970s hotels. It would be a shame if those that haven't already been bowled over or modernised aren't restored to their period-piece glory.

As for the concrete apartment blocks of the cities, they may look grim but they're hardly the slums you'd expect of similar-looking housing projects in the West. While nobody seems to be charged with the upkeep of the exteriors, inside they're generally comfortable and well looked after.

The Montenegrin Kitchen

Loosen your belt and pack pants one size up: you're in for a treat. Eating in Montenegro is generally an extremely pleasurable experience. By default, most of the food is local, fresh and organic, and hence very seasonal. Despite its small size, Montenegro has at least three distinct regional styles: the food of the old Montenegrin heartland, mountain food and coastal cuisine.

Montenegrin Heartland Specialities

Many people distil their own *rakija* (akin to schnapps or a very strong brandy). The most common variety in Montenegro is *loza,* made out of grapes, but it can be made from just about anything. It's offered as a sign of hospitality, so brace yourself – it typically ranges from 40% to 60% alcohol.

The village of Njeguši on the edge of Lovćen (the black mountain) is famous for its *pršut* (smoke-dried ham) and *sir* (cheese). Anything with 'Njeguški' in its name is going to be a true Montenegrin dish and stuffed with these two goodies; this might be pork chops, veal, steak or spit-roasted meat *(Njeguški ražanj).*

Old Montenegro extended to the Crnojević River and the upper reaches of Lake Skadar, where the cuisine is dominated by three main freshwater fish: eel *(jegulja),* bleak *(ukljeva)* and carp *(krap).*

Mountain Food

In the northern mountains, the food was traditionally more stodgy, meaty and Serb-influenced, providing comfort and sustenance on those long winter nights. A traditional method of cooking is *ispod sača,* where meat and vegetables are roasted under a metal lid covered with hot coals, usually set in a hearth in the middle of the room for warmth. Lamb may also be slowly poached in milk with spices and potato *(brav u mljeku)* in a dish that's particularly popular in the Albanian areas. Beef is cooked with cabbage-like *raštan,* rice and red peppers to make a rich stew called *japraci.* You might eat it with *cicvara* (a cheesy, creamy polenta or buckwheat dish) or *kačamak* (similar but with potato). The best honey *(med)* is also produced in the mountains. The higher up you go, the better the *kajmak,* somewhat similar to a salty clotted cream. Slather it on bread, meat or potatoes, or just guts it straight.

Coastal Cuisine

For most sun-seeking holidaymakers, this is the food they'll mainly encounter – and it's absolutely delicious. The food on the coast is indistinguishable from Dalmatian cuisine: lots of grilled seafood, garlic, olive oil and Italian-style dishes.

Hearty, flavoursome fish soup *(riblja čorba)* is a must-try, as are grilled squid *(lignje na žaru)* – its crispy tentacles coated in garlic and olive oil – and *punjene lignje,* served stuffed with *pršut* (smoke-dried ham) and *sir* (cheese). Nearly 400 years of Venetian rule has left a legacy of excellent risotto and pasta dishes. Black risotto *(crni rižoto)* gets its rich colour and subtle flavour from squid ink and includes pieces of squid meat. Seafood risotto can also be white or red (made with a tomato-based sauce) and served hot or cold.

> ### MONTENEGRIN WINE
> Montenegro's domestic wine is eminently drinkable and usually the cheapest thing on the menu. *Vranac* is the indigenous red grape, producing excellent, full-bodied wines. It's traditionally aged in walnut rather than oak barrels and its history goes back an extremely long way. Illyrian Queen Teuta is said to have been particularly fond of the drop and encouraged its production in the 3rd century BC. Locally produced whites include Chardonnay, Sauvignon Blanc and the native *krstač*.

While all of these dishes make filling mains, at a formal dinner they're just a precursor to the grilled fish. In most fish restaurants, whole fish *(ribe)* are presented to the table for you to choose from and sold by the kilogram according to a quality-based category. A standard portion is around 200g to 250g; ask for a rough price before you choose a fish if you're unsure.

Local varieties tend to be small but tasty; the bigger ones are probably fresh but imported. Fish dishes are flavoured with wild herbs such as laurel and parsley as well as lemon and garlic. The traditional accompaniment is a delicious mixture of silverbeet *(blitva)*, mushy boiled potato, olive oil and garlic, often referred to on English menus as a 'Dalmatian garnish'.

Regional Dishes

Various types of grilled meat are common throughout the former Yugoslavia, including *ćevapčići* (pieces of minced meat shaped into small skinless sausages), *pljeskavica* (spicy hamburger patties) and *ražnjići* (pork or veal kebabs). Grills are often served with fried chips and salad.

For dishes that have more than just meat (although they're by no means vegetarian), try *musaka* (layers of aubergine, potato and minced meat), *sarma* (minced meat and rice rolled in sour-cabbage leaves), *kapama* (stewed lamb, onions and spinach with yoghurt) and *punjene tikvice* or *paprike* (courgettes or capsicum stuffed with minced meat and rice). Other regional dishes include Hungarian goulash *(gulaš)* and Turkish kebabs *(kebap)*.

The cheapest and most ubiquitous Balkan snack is *burek*, a greasy filo-pastry pie made with cheese, meat *(meso)*, potato *(krompir)* or occasionally mushrooms *(pečurke)*, most commonly consumed with yoghurt. Savoury or sweet pancakes *(palačinke)* are served from kiosks in busy areas. Toppings include chopped walnuts and almonds, jam and banana. For a major artery clog, go for a *slane* (salty) *palačinke* – a heart attack disguised as a crumbed, deep-fried, cheese-filled pancake.

The Main Meals

Breakfast *(doručak)* usually consists of fresh bread with slices of cheese and cured meat (salami or *pršut*) or perhaps a sweet pastry. Locals often skip breakfast and grab something like *burek* on their way to work. Omelette *(omlet)* is the most common cooked breakfast.

Lunch *(ručak)*, served mid-afternoon, has traditionally been the main family meal, but with Western working hours catching on, this is changing. A family lunch might consist of a soup followed by a salad and a cooked meat or fish dish of some description. Dinner *(večera)* would then be lighter, possibly just bread with cured meats, cheese and olives. However, if you're heading out for a proper sit-down evening meal, you'll probably start late (after 8pm) and eat a similar meal to the typical lunch.

Sweets are eaten at all times of the day, especially with coffee or after dinner. The most typical Montenegrin sweet dish is *priganice* (fritters) served with honey, cheese and jam *(džem)*. Incredibly sweet cakes and tortes are offered with coffee, including delicious baklava. The local ice cream *(sladoled)* is also excellent.

Thanks to the fairly common religious Orthodox habit of not eating meat/animal products on certain holy days, many restaurants will have a *post* (Lent) menu on hand; ask your waiter for *posna hrana* (meatless food). Otherwise, pasta, pizza and salad are the best fallback options; beware of ordering stuffed vegetables as they're likely to be stuffed with meat.

National Parks & Wildlife

'Wild Beauty', crows Montenegro's enduring tourism slogan, and indeed the marketing boffins are right to highlight the nation's extraordinary natural blessings. In the mountainous interior are pockets of virgin forest and large mammals, long since hunted out of existence on most of the continent, still hanging on – just.

Durmitor National Park

Montenegro's first three national parks were declared in 1952: Lovćen, Biogradska Gora and Durmitor. The most interesting and popular of the three is Durmitor, a magnificent place for nature-lovers, blessed with springs of clear mountain water and glacial lakes that mirror the heavens. In 1980 it was recognised by Unesco as a World Heritage Site.

The 39,000-hectare park comprises the Durmitor mountain range and a narrow strip forming an elephant's trunk along the Tara Canyon. The Durmitor range has 48 peaks over 2000m including Bobotov Kuk (2523m), which is often referred to as the country's highest mountain. There's actually a higher peak in the Prokletije Mountains bordering Albania, but Bobotov Kuk is the highest mountain entirely within Montenegro. The Tara River is hidden in the deepest canyon in Europe (1300m at its apogee). It's not the sheer force of the water that has gouged such an impressive rift through the mountains, but rather the carbon dioxide in the water reacting with the hard limestone (calcium carbonate) to form soluble calcium bicarbonate.

Popular activities in the park include rafting (between April and October), skiing (from January to March), hiking, rock climbing and jeep safaris (best in summer). These can all be organised from Žabljak, the park's gateway town.

Lovćen National Park

Montenegro has 500 types of herbs with medicinal properties, many of which are harvested for essential oils and ingredients for natural remedies. Wormwood is an ingredient of absinthe and was once exported to Italy to make the bitter liqueur Amaro Montenegro.

Lovćen National Park's 6220-hectare offering is cultural as well as natural, encompassing the old Montenegrin heartland and the impressive mausoleum of the national hero, Njegoš. Like many of Montenegro's mountains, Lovćen is karstic in nature with craggy grey-white outcrops, sparse vegetation and, below, caves. Water disappears into the rock and bubbles up elsewhere to form springs.

Heading up Mt Lovćen (1749m), the lower slopes are covered in forests of black beech. Once these deciduous trees lose their leaves and their distinctive black trunks are bared, you'll understand why the Venetians named it the 'black mountain'. Higher up, the beech is joined by an endemic pine called munika. Healing and sweet-smelling herbs poke out from the rocky slopes, including sage, rosemary, balm, mint, chamomile and St John's wort.

Cetinje, Montenegro's historic capital, is a great place to base yourself while tackling the park's hiking and mountain-biking trails, although Kotor and Budva are also nearby.

Biogradska Gora National Park

The smallest of the national parks, Biogradska Gora covers a 5650-hectare chunk of the Bjelasica Mountains which includes 1600 hectares of virgin forest – one of the most significant untouched stands remaining in Europe. Here you'll find groves of juniper, wild rose, pine, beech, maple, fir and elm trees, the tallest of which reach 60m.

There are no settlements within this park, but campsites and bungalows are available near the park office. Mojkovac is the nearest town, although Kolašin makes a better base. Hiking is great in summer but autumn is the best time to visit, when the leaves erupt in colour.

Lake Skadar National Park

In 1983, Lake Skadar became the country's fourth national park and the first non-mountainous one. Skadar is the largest lake in southern Europe, stretching between Montenegro and Albania, where it's called Shkodër. It's mainly fed by the Morača River in the northwest and drained into the Adriatic by the Bojana River at its opposite corner. The lake is what is known as a cryptodepression, meaning that the deepest parts are below sea level. The lake's marshy edges are carpeted with white and yellow water lilies, reeds, willows and edible water chestnuts. Rare endemic species of orchids may also be found.

More than half of Montenegro is more than 1000m above sea level and 15% is higher than 1500m.

Lake Skadar National Park protects 40,000 hectares on the Montenegrin side of the lake, but the whole lake is recognised by an international treaty, the Ramsar Convention, as a 'wetland of international importance'. It is home to a quarter of the world's population of pygmy cormorants and 262 other, mainly migratory, species including the great snipe and the great bustard (mind how you read that). Other fabulous flappers include the Dalmatian pelican, the largest of all pelicans, which is the posterbird of the park.

As well as birdwatching, activities include hiking, kayaking, swimming and boat trips to various island monasteries and fortresses. The weather is usually best in August. Virpazar is the main gateway, but other settlements include Murići, Vranjina and Rijeka Crnojevića.

Prokletije National Park

Montenegro's newest national park was declared in 2009, covering 16,000 hectares of the mountainous region on the border with Albania and Kosovo. It contains the country's highest peak, Kolac (2534m); on the Albanian side of the border, the Prokletije mountains soar to 2694m. There has long been talk of declaring the entire range a cross-border Balkan Peace Park, but the politics have yet to be ironed out.

ENVIRONMENTAL ISSUES

Much of the credit for Montenegro's 'wild beauty' lies with the terrain itself. Its rugged contours haven't just hindered foreign invaders, they've limited population spread and the worst excesses of development. The Montenegrin government has realised the value of this by declaring the country the world's first 'ecological state', yet it remains to be seen what this means in a country where hunting is popular, recycling is virtually unknown and people litter as a matter of course. Despite trumpeting the existence of bears, lynx and wolves, no one knows what numbers remain. Hunting (illegal or otherwise) is of real concern.

On the coast, development continues unabated. With most of the Budva Riviera now given over to hulking resort complexes, attention has turn to the previously unspoiled Luština Peninsula.

NATIONAL PARKS & WILDLIFE BIOGRADSKA GORA NATIONAL PARK

Ancient glaciers formed the Plav Valley on the edge of the mountains. Lake Visitor, in the mountain of the same name above Plav, has the unusual quirk of a floating island. Local legends say that it was once a raft used by the ancient shepherds to transport stock. Because it was well fertilised, it developed soil and foliage and now drifts around the lake.

Tourist infrastructure is limited in the gateway towns of Plav and Gusinje, but that is bound to improve. The park's potential for mountain biking, hiking and serious mountaineering has been realised with the establishment of the 192km Peaks of the Balkans transnational trail.

Wildlife

The Bojana River occasionally performs the unusual trick of flowing upstream. This happens in winter when the swollen waters of its Albanian tributary, the Drim, cut across it and the volume of water forces part of the flow back into its source, Lake Skadar.

Many species of animals and birds have managed to find solace in Montenegro's hidden nooks. Precisely because those nooks are so hidden, you're unlikely to see any of the more dramatic mammals.

Birdwatchers are more likely to have their tendencies gratified with plenty of rare wetland birds congregating around Lake Skadar and near Ulcinj, and flashy birds of prey swooping over the mountains. King of them all is the golden eagle. It has a wingspan of up to 240cm and can sometimes supplement its rodent diet with lambs and small goats.

The big mammals (brown bear, grey wolves, Eurasian lynx) tend to keep their heads down so as not to have them blown off. Brown bears like to hang out in the forests at altitudes of 900m and higher. In 2000 there were estimated to be fewer than 130 remaining in Montenegro, concentrated in the northern and eastern mountains. Despite the male bears weighing up to 200kg, they pose little threat to humans unless they're protecting a cub or are startled.

Likewise, grey wolves don't pose much of a threat unless they're rabid or starving. They too fancy forest living, but may venture out into the meadows to make closer acquaintance with the odd bit of livestock. For this reason, there's still a price on their heads in some areas.

Look out for European otters going about their unspeakably cute business around Lake Skadar and the Tara River. Badgers hang out in Durmitor and Biogradska Gora National Parks. Balkan chamois join roe deer in Durmitor, while the latter also wander the Lovćen and Bjelasica Mountains. Golden jackals are known to live around Bar and Ulcinj, with three packs spotted on Ada Bojana. Foxes, weasels, moles, groundhogs, hares, shrews, bats, wild boar, red squirrels and dormice complete the diverse mammalian picture.

If you're wandering the remote trails you'll often catch sight of something reptilian scurrying off the path. Montenegro has an impressive collection of lizards, newts, frogs, turtles and snakes. The isolated glacial lakes of the karstic mountain ranges harbour species such as the serdarski triton, a type of alpine newt that only exists in one small lake in Durmitor. The European pond turtle is listed as near-threatened but can still be spotted in both Lovćen and Lake Skadar National Parks.

Of more interest or concern to most visitors are the snakes. Commonly spotted and often mistaken for a snake is the harmless slow-worm (sometimes called blindworm), a 50cm-long brown legless lizard. Rather less harmless is the horned viper. Reaching up to 95cm, this is the largest and most venomous snake in Europe. It likes rocky habitats (which doesn't rule out much in Montenegro) and has a zigzag stripe on its body and a distinctive scaly 'horn' on its nose. If you're close enough to spot the horn, you're probably a little too close. The good news is that this guy isn't at all aggressive and will only bite with extreme provocation, so mind where you tread.

Survival Guide

Directory A–Z

Accommodation

Montenegro offers a great variety of accommodation. Booking ahead in the summer – especially on the coast – is essential.

➡ **Hotels** Range from slick seaside offerings to off-the-beaten-track Yugoslavian-style digs. Prices range accordingly.

➡ **Hostels** Popping up in popular destinations but thin on the ground elsewhere.

➡ **Campgrounds** Usually offer million-dollar views for penny-pinching prices. Facilities vary wildly.

➡ **Private accommodation** Almost every town and village offers private rooms (*sobe*) and/or apartments (*apartmani*).

➡ **Eco villages** Old-school cabins in the countryside.

Camping & Caravan Parks

Facilities at camping grounds tend to be basic, often with squat toilets and limited water. Some national parks have cabin-style accommodation but most camping grounds don't. Charges are a combination of a nightly rate per vehicle, size of tent, number (and age) of guests and whether you require power or not. Camping grounds are most common along the coast (including the Bay of Kotor) and near Žabljak.

During summer, when shepherds in the mountainous areas take their flocks to the higher meadows, you can ask permission to pitch your tent next to one of their traditional *katun* dwellings. Some agencies, especially around Durmitor and Kolašin, can organise stays in a *katun* itself.

Though it's a Slovenian-based website, www.avto kampi.si has a fairly thorough list of campsites in Montenegro.

Eco Villages

Traditional accommodation is offered in 'ethno' and 'eco' villages (*eko i etno sela*), particularly around Piva, and Durmitor and Prokletije National Parks. Quality can vary wildly, but generally accommodation is in rustic-style cabins, and meals come hot and hearty; *rakija* (fruit brandy) shots with the hosts are usually unavoidable. They're almost always run by families; if you're travelling with your brood, these are generally great for kids (think wide-open spaces, fresh air and plenty of livestock to pester).

Hostels

Hostels have made a relatively recent appearance on the scene, as they previously never fitted into tidy bureaucratic pigeonholes, being neither private accommodation nor a traditional hotel. Thankfully, that battle

has been fought and won, and some great places have sprung up – particularly in Kotor and Budva and recently in Podgorica. Some are little different from private rentals split into dorms. The better custom-built places have well-thought-out communal spaces and offer a roster of activities. Most have some sort of kitchen facilities; shared bathrooms are the norm.

Hotels

You'll find a large range of hotels of varying size and quality in the popular destinations. They usually have some form of restaurant attached and offer the option of half- or full-board (breakfast plus one or two meals). In Montenegro, a hotel spa centre is called a 'wellness centre'.

Generally, the further you travel from Budva, the cheaper the average price. Tourist-focused Žabljak and Kolašin are the most (relatively) expensive of the northern centres, but you'll find bargains in the other towns.

Private Accommodation

The cheapest options in any given town are almost always private rooms and apartment rentals. These can be arranged through travel agencies or, in season, you may be approached at the bus stop or see signs hanging outside the houses (they often read 'Sobe/Zimmer/Rooms'). Some local tourist offices publish handy guides to private accommodation. Rooms in local homes shouldn't be difficult to find, but some places will require minimum stays in high season (often a three-day minimum). Don't expect an en suite.

Apartments (apartmani) will always have their own bathroom and at least a kitchenette. Generally speaking, you'll get what you pay for. The cheaper options are usually a bit rougher and further from the attractions, but there shouldn't be a problem with cleanliness. For a range of luxurious apartments, some of which have swimming pools and cliff-top locations, try Explore Montenegro (www.exploremonte negro.com).

If you're armed with a bit of charm, an adventurous spirit, an unfussy attitude and a few words in the local lingo, it should be possible to turn up in remote villages and ask if anyone has any rooms to rent for the night. Some restaurants in out-of-the-way places also have rooms available that they don't otherwise advertise: just ask.

Children

Montenegrins absolutely adore babies and kids. For many parents this is half the battle won. Hotels, restaurants and cafes all warmly welcome children, and we've even seen the occasional young teenager boogying with their parents at beachside nightclubs.

With the relatively safe environment allowing them off the leash a little, older offspring should have a blast in Montenegro. You may find that they're kicking a ball around with the local scallywags in no time. The opposite is true for toddlers and small children, as a generally lower standard of safety regulations (missing railings, unfenced pools etc) means you'll have to keep a closer eye on them.

You'll struggle to get strollers along the cobbled lanes and stairways in the older towns and you'll often find yourself having to trundle them along dangerous roads due to parked cars blocking the footpaths. A baby carrier or sling takes up less luggage space and makes exploring easier. Still, bringing a pram is a good idea, if only so you can join the legions of other parents promenading with their sleeping babies on summer nights.

Any hurdles you may strike will be insignificant compared to the wonderfully family-friendly atmosphere, fresh air and gently lapping Mediterranean waters that Montenegro provides. Lonely Planet's Travel with Children offers further tips for hitting the road with the brood in tow.

Customs Regulations

➡ In a bid to stop tourists from neighbouring countries bringing all their holiday groceries with them, Montenegro restricts the quantity of food that can be brought into the country to a total of 1kg.

➡ Restrictions apply to entering with tobacco products (200 cigarettes or 50 cigars or 250g tobacco), alcohol (1L of wine and 1L of spirits) and perfume (250ml).

➡ Amounts greater than €2000 of cash or travellers cheques must be declared

SLEEPING PRICE RANGES

Prices are very seasonal, and we've listed prices for the shoulder season (June and September). Expect to pay more if you're travelling in the absolute peak months (July and August) and less in the off-season. In the ski resorts, the high season runs from January through to March, with the absolute peak around New Year. Discounts are often available for longer bookings.

All visitors are required to pay a small nightly tourist tax (usually less than €1 per person per night), which is sometimes included in the quoted rate but more often added to the bill at the end. This is almost always collected and paid by the accommodation provider; some private operators may leave it up to the guest to pay, but this is rare. The procedure varies from area to area and it can be nigh on impossible to find the right authority to pay it to. Theoretically you could be asked to provide white accommodation receipt cards (or copies of invoices from hotels) when you leave the country, but in practice this is almost never required.

The following price ranges refer to the cheapest option available for a double.

➡ € less than €45

➡ €€ €45 to €100

➡ €€€ more than €100

Climate

Podgorica

Kotor

Bijelo Polje

when leaving the country. If you're entering with a large sum and think you might have more than €2000 left when you leave, complete a currency declaration form on arrival or you may find your money confiscated on departure.

➡ Drug laws are similar to most other European countries. Possession or trafficking of drugs could result in a lengthy jail sentence.

➡ When you enter the country you need to receive an entry stamp in your passport. If you don't, you may be detained or fined when you seek to leave for entering the country illegally.

➡ The Montenegro Customs Bureau has more information (some in English) at www. upravacarina.gov.me.

Discount Cards

➡ The **Montenegro Card** (www.montenegrocard. com; €14) offers discounts on museums, restaurants, rental cars, activities, tours, shopping and more. Buy online or see website for vendors.

➡ The **International Student Identity Card** (ISIC; www.isic.org), which is issued to full-time students aged 12 years and over, entitles the bearer to discounts on train trips and some admission charges, shops, eateries, accommodation and other services in Montenegro. It's available online, from student unions, hostelling organisations and some travel agencies.

➡ The same organisation issues the **International Youth Travel Card** (IYTC; available to people who are between 12 and 26 years of age and not full-time students) and the **International Teacher Identity Card** (ITIC; available to teaching professionals), both of which give similar discounts to the ISIC.

Electricity

Type C
220V/50Hz

Type F
230V/50Hz

Embassies & Consulates

For a full list of foreign missions in Montenegro, see www.mvpei.gov.me. The following are all in Podgorica, unless otherwise stated:

Albanian Embassy (Map p102; ☑020-667 380; www.mfa.gov. al; Capital Plaza, Bul Džordža Vašingtona 98)

Bosnia & Hercegovinia Embassy (Map p102; ☑020-618 105; www.mvp.gov.ba; Atinska 58)

Croatian Embassy & Consulate Podgorica (☑020-269 760; www.mvep.hr; Vladimira Ćetkovića 2); **Kotor** (Map p46; ☑032-323 127; Trg od Oružja bb, Kotor)

French Embassy (Map p102; ☑020-655 348; www.amba-france-me.org; Atinska 35)

German Embassy (Map p102; ☑020-441 000; www.auswaer tiges-amt.de; Hercegovačka 10)

Serbian Embassy & Consulate Podgorica (Map p102; ☑020-667 305; www.podgorica.mfa. gov.rs; Ivana Crnojevića 10); **Herceg Novi** (Map p37; ☑031-350 320; www.hercegnovi.mfa. gov.rs; Trg Hercega Stjepana 15, Herceg Novi; ◷9.30am-1.30pm)

UK Embassy (Map p102; ☑020-618 010; www.gov.uk/ government/world/montene gro; Ulcinjska 8)

US Embassy (Map p102; ☑020-410 500; www.podgorica.us embassy.gov; Ljubljanska bb)

The following countries are represented from offices in nearby countries:

Australian Embassy (☑011-330 3400; www.serbia.embassy.gov. au; 7th fl, Vladimira Popovica 38-40, Novi Beograd, Serbia)

Canadian Embassy (☑011-306 3000; www.canadainterna tional.gc.ca; Kneza Miloša 75, Belgrade, Serbia)

Dutch Embassy (☑011-2023 900; www.serbia.nlembassy. org; Simina 29, Belgrade, Serbia)

EATING PRICE RANGES

The price indicators used in this book are based on the cost of the cheapest dish on the menu that could be considered a main meal, regardless of whether it is labelled as a main.

€ up to €5

€€ €5 to €8

€€€ over €9

Irish Embassy (☑1-301 4960; www.embassyofireland.hu; V Szabadság tér 7, Bank Center, 6th fl, Platina Tower, Budapest, Hungary; ◷10am-12.30pm & 2.30-4.30pm Mon-Fri; 🚇15, 115)

Etiquette

➡ **Greetings** Some Montenegrins (especially those of Serbian heritage) engage in a three-kiss hello.

➡ **Visiting** Take off your shoes when entering a home. Montenegrins are typical Slavs and are obsessed with draughts and cold extremities; they'll have slippers for you. Bring a small gift, like wine or bag of coffee.

➡ **Conversation** Politics, religion, history and ethnicity can be minefields; tread cautiously.

➡ **Religion** Walk backwards out of a shrine.

➡ **Personal space** Don't expect much; Montenegrins love to touch and huddle.

➡ **Dress** Be modest when visiting religious buildings. Topless sunbathing is usually reserved for nudist beaches.

➡ **Eating** If you're dining with locals, arrive hungry. This is a nation of feeders.

➡ **Drinking** Engaging in a toast without eye contact may result in calamity, as will pouring your own *rakija* (fruit brandy).

Health

Good, affordable health care is readily available in Montenegro and for minor illnesses, pharmacists can give valuable advice and sell over-the-counter medication. They can also advise when more specialised help is required and point you in the right direction. The standard of dental care is usually good, but it is sensible to have a dental check-up before a long trip.

Before You Go

A little planning before departure, particularly for pre-existing illnesses, will save trouble later. See your dentist before a long trip. Carry a spare pair of contact lenses and glasses, and take your optical prescription with you. Bring medications in their original labelled containers. A letter from your physician describing your medical conditions and medications, including generic names, is also a good idea. If you are carrying syringes, be sure to have a physician's letter with you documenting their necessity.

Recommended Vaccinations

The World Health Organization (WHO) recommends that all travellers should be covered for diphtheria, tetanus, measles, mumps, rubella, pertussis (whooping cough) and polio, regardless of their destination. You should also consider being vaccinated for hepatitis A, hepatitis B and tetanus. Since most vaccines don't produce immunity until at least two weeks after they're given, visit a physician at least six weeks before departure.

Tick-borne encephalitis is spread by tick bites and is thought to exist in forested areas of Montenegro. It is a serious infection of the brain and vaccination is advised for those in risk areas who are unable to avoid tick bites (such as campers and hikers).

The US Center for Disease Control recommends a rabies vaccination for long-term travellers and 'wildlife professionals, researchers, veterinarians, or adventure travelers visiting areas where bats, carnivores, and other mammals are commonly found'.

Sea Urchins

Watch out for sea urchins around rocky beaches; if you get some of their needles embedded in your skin, olive oil will help to loosen them. If they are not removed, they could become infected. As a precaution, wear rubber shoes while walking on the rocks and take care while bathing.

Snake Bites

To avoid getting bitten by snakes, do not walk barefoot or stick your hands into holes or cracks. Half of those bitten by venomous snakes are not actually injected with poison (envenomed). If bitten by a snake, do not panic. Immobilise the bitten limb with a splint (eg a stick) and apply a bandage over the site firmly, similar to a bandage over a sprain. Do not apply

a tourniquet, or cut or suck the bite. Get medical help as soon as possible so that antivenom can be administered if necessary.

Tap Water

As a general rule, tap water is drinkable in Montenegro but there can be problems. For instance, it's advisable not to drink the water in Herceg Novi in May as they close off and clean the pipes from the main reservoir (in Croatia) and revert to a local reservoir. Bottled water is cheap and readily available.

Insurance

A watertight travel insurance policy covering theft, loss and medical problems is recommended. While theft isn't a huge problem, rental cars are sometimes targeted by opportunists and Montenegro's roads aren't the world's safest. There are plenty of policies to choose from – compare the fine print and shop around.

If you're an EU citizen, you will be covered for most emergency medical care except for emergency repatriation home. Citizens from other countries should find out if there is a reciprocal arrangement for free medical care between their country and Montenegro. Strongly consider a policy that covers you for the worst possible scenario, such as an accident requiring an emergency flight home. Find out in advance if your insurance plan will make payments directly to providers or if it will reimburse you later for any overseas health

expenditures. The former option is generally preferable, especially if your finances are limited.

Some policies specifically exclude designated 'dangerous activities' such as scuba-diving, parasailing, paragliding, canyoning, white-water rafting, skiing and even hiking. If you plan on doing any of these things (a distinct possibility in Montenegro), make sure the policy you choose covers you fully and includes ambulances and emergency medical evacuation.

If you need to make a claim, ensure you obtain and keep all relevant documentation. This may involve a police report in case of theft and invoices for medical expenses incurred. Some policies ask you to call back (reverse charges) to a centre in your home country where an immediate assessment of your problem is made.

Worldwide travel insurance is available at www.lonelyplanet.com/bookings. You can buy, extend and claim online any time – even if you're already on the road.

Internet Access

Most accommodation providers (including a majority of private accommodations, unless you're really in the back of beyond) offer free wireless connections, although they may not always penetrate to every part of the building and can be limited to the reception area. Many bars and cafes also offer wireless. You'll find free wireless access in Tivat and Budva's Stari Grad, and at other tourist hot spots in bigger cities.

Some libraries and hotels offer internet access, but this practice appears to be on the way out with the proliferation of wi-fi. Internet cafes are similarly found in lesser numbers than before.

We've used the internet symbol (@) for

EMERGENCY & IMPORTANT NUMBERS

International access code	☎00
Country code	☎382
Police	☎122
Ambulance	☎124
Roadside assistance	☎9807

accommodations that have a computer linked to the internet for guests to use. Places that have a wireless connection are marked with the wireless symbol (🛜). Note that the symbols don't imply that the service is free, but in most cases it will be.

➡ There have been incidences of traffic police asking for money upfront for alleged violations. If this happens to you, ask for a full explanation of the situation from the officer and, if it's not forthcoming, ask to speak to your embassy.

Legal Matters

It may seem obvious, but while you are in Montenegro you're covered by Montenegrin law and these laws may differ from those in your home country.

➡ If you're arrested, you have the right to contact your country's embassy or consulate and arresting officers have a responsibility to help you to do so. They're also required to immediately notify you of the charges you're facing in a language you understand and to inform you that you're not required to give any statement. You have the right to a defence counsel of your own choosing during any interrogation.

➡ A lower court can choose to detain you for three months pending trial, while a higher court can extend this for a further three months. Minors may not be held for more than 60 days.

➡ The Montenegrin constitution enshrines a right to a fair and public trial with a defence, legal aid if required and a presumption of innocence.

➡ Montenegro has outlawed the death penalty, but if you're caught with drugs you may face a lengthy stint in a local jail.

➡ You are required to register with local police within 24 hours of arriving in Montenegro and whenever you change address. Accommodation providers usually do this for you (which is the reason you're asked to hand over your passport when you arrive at a hotel).

LGBTQI Travellers

Where's the party? The answer's nowhere. Although homosexuality was decriminalised in 1977 and discrimination outlawed in 2010, you won't find a single gay or lesbian venue in Montenegro. Don't be fooled by all the men walking arm in arm, or hand in hand in the Albanian areas. Attitudes to homosexuality remain hostile and life for gay people is extremely difficult, exacerbated by the fact that most people are expected to live at home until they're married.

In recent years there have been high-profile incidents of violence against gay activists, including the brutal beating in the centre of Podgorica in 2012 of three young men who were associated with an anti-homophobia video. In that same year, the government declared it would look into preparing a bill giving some form of legal recognition for same-sex couples, but nothing's happened since. In 2014, Podgorica's LGBTIQ social centre was attacked 26 times; years on, nobody has been arrested.

The country's first Pride parade was held in Budva in 2013; an Orthodox priest consecrated the town afterwards to 'stop the disease spreading'. Since then, Podgorica has held annual parades, though they're frequently disrupted by hooligans.

Many gay men resort to online connections or take their chances at a handful of cruisy beaches. These include Jaz Beach near Budva (far left-hand side) and below the ruins of Ratac near Bar. Lesbians will find it even harder to access the local community.

Check out Queer Montenegro (www.queermontenegro.org) for details on Pride, arts and cultural events and news updates.

Money

➡ Though they're not in the EU, Montenegro uses the euro (€) and we quote all prices in that currency, unless otherwise stated.

➡ You'll find banks with ATMs (bankomat) in all the main towns, most of which accept Visa, MasterCard, Maestro and Cirrus. ATMs tend to dish out big notes, which can be hard to break.

➡ Don't rely on restaurants, shops or smaller hotels accepting credit cards.

Opening Hours

Montenegrins have a flexible approach to opening times. Even if hours are posted on the door of an establishment, don't be surprised if they're not heeded. Many tourist-orientated businesses close between November and March.

Post offices 7am to 8pm Monday to Friday, sometimes Saturday. In smaller towns they may close mid-afternoon, or close at noon and reopen at 5pm.

Banks Generally from 8am to 5pm Monday to Friday, 8am to noon Saturday.

Shops 9am to 8pm. Sometimes they'll close for a few hours in the late afternoon.

Restaurants, cafes & bars 8am to midnight. If the joint is jumping, cafe-bars may stay open until 2am or 3am.

Post

Every town has a post office that locals use for paying their bills, so be prepared for horrendous queues. Parcels should be taken unsealed for inspection. You can receive mail, addressed poste restante, in all towns for a small charge. International postal services are slow.

Public Holidays

New Year's Day 1 and 2 January

Orthodox Christmas 6, 7 and 8 January

Orthodox Good Friday & Easter Monday date varies, usually April/May

Labour Day 1 May

Independence Day 21 May

Statehood Day 13 July

Safe Travel

➡ Montenegro's towns are generally safe places. You'll see children playing unsupervised on the streets and young women walking alone at night and hitchhiking (not that we necessarily recommend these things).

➡ The roads can be treacherous. They're generally in good condition but many are narrow and have sheer drops on one side. The main hazard is from other motorists, who have no qualms about overtaking on blind corners while talking on their mobile phones or stopping in the middle of the road without warning.

There's plenty of random tooting – don't let it faze you. It's best to keep your cool and stick to the speed limit: the traffic police (some of whom are wont to ask for bribes) are everywhere.

➡ Chances are you'll see some snakes if you're poking around ruins during summer. Montenegro has two types of venomous vipers but they'll try their best to keep out of your way. If bitten, you will have time to head to a medical centre for the antivenom, but you should head there immediately. Water snakes are harmless.

➡ Check with the police before photographing any official building they're guarding.

➡ Since Montenegro is in an active seismic zone, earthquakes strike from time to time. The last major one that caused loss of life was in 1979.

➡ Montenegro has a very active *mafija*, but it's exceedingly unlikely you'll be embroiled in any of their doings.

Smoking

Smoking on public transport and in bars, clubs and restaurants is apparently banned in Montenegro, but someone forgot to tell the Montenegrins. While you won't find passengers lighting up on a bus, the same

doesn't necessarily hold true for the driver. As for the rest: good luck. Cigarettes and coffee/booze go together like fish and soup in Montenegro, and if you get between a local and their after-dinner cigarette, you'd better have insurance.

A few eating establishments are starting to offer nonsmoking sections, and many hotels don't permit smoking in the rooms.

Telephone

➡ The international access prefix is 🖉00 or + from a mobile phone.

➡ The country code is 🖉382.

➡ Press the *i* button on public phones for dialling commands in English.

➡ Mobile numbers start with 🖉06.

➡ To make a domestic call, simply dial all the numbers (including the area code) given. If you're calling Montenegro from abroad, drop the first 0 of the number (area code or mobile telephone).

➡ The prefix 🖉80 indicates a toll-free number.

➡ You can make local and international phone calls at most larger post offices. Phone boxes are otherwise few and far between.

Mobile Phones

Local SIM cards are a good idea if you're planning a longer stay and can be used in most unlocked handsets. The main providers (T-Mobile, M:tel and Telenor) have storefronts in most towns. Many shopping centres have terminals where you can top-up your prepay account. Mobile calls are expensive in Montenegro but the main providers offer heavily discounted rates to calls within their network; it's not uncommon for businesses to advertise three different mobile numbers on different networks.

PRACTICALITIES

➡ **Print Media** *Vijesti* (The News), *Dan* (The Day), *Dnevne Novine* (Daily Newspaper) and *Pobjeda* (Victory) are all daily newspapers. *Monitor*, a weekly news magazine, joins local-language versions of international titles on the news-stands.

➡ **Radio & Television** RTCG (Radio TV Montenegro) is the state broadcaster, with two radio stations and three TV channels. In total there are 11 more-or-less national TV channels and six regional channels. There are dozens of independent radio stations broadcasting around the country.

➡ **Weights & Measures** The metric system is used.

Time

➡ Montenegro is in the Central Europe time zone (an hour ahead of GMT).

➡ Clocks go forward by an hour for daylight saving at the end of March and return to normal at the end of October.

➡ Outside the daylight-saving period, when it's midday in Montenegro it will be 3am in Los Angeles, 6am in New York, 11am in London, 9pm in Sydney and 11pm in Auckland.

➡ Montenegrins use the 24-hour clock, so hours are usually listed as '9–17' rather than '9am–5pm'.

Tourist Information

Official tourist offices (usually labelled *turistička organizacija*) are hit and miss. Some have wonderfully helpful English-speaking staff, regular opening hours and a good supply of free material, while others have none of the above. Thankfully the National Tourist Office (www.montenegro.travel) is more switched on and its website is a great resource for travellers. It doesn't have a public office but you can dial ☑080-001 300 at any time to receive tourist information from multilingual staff. The website has a listing of most of the country's regional tourist offices.

Travellers with Disabilities

The mobility-impaired will find Montenegro's many cobbled lanes and numerous stairways – especially in 'old towns' – extremely challenging. There are very few specific facilities for either travellers or residents with disabilities. Some of the top-end hotels have wheelchair-accessible rooms.

Visas

Visas are not required for citizens of most European countries, Turkey, Israel, Singapore, South Korea, Israel, Japan, Australia, New Zealand, Canada and the USA. In most cases this allows a stay of up to 90 days. If your country is not covered by a visa waiver, you will need a valid passport, verified letter of invitation, return ticket, proof of sufficient funds and proof of medical cover in order to obtain a visa. Go to www.mvpei.gov.me and follow the links to 'Overview of visa regimes for foreign citizens'; find your country on the drop-down map for visa regulations.

Volunteering

Montenegro isn't high up on international volunteering agencies' agendas, but there are ways you can get involved in local projects.

➡ **Responsible Travel** (www.responsibletravel.com) runs voluntourism projects in Montenegro; in 2016 they offered an expedition for volunteers to take part in a Balkan lynx-monitoring program in Prokletije National Park.

➡ **Green Home** (www.greenhome.co.me) is a Podgorica-based NGO dedicated to sustainable development, environmental protection and biodiversity conservation; contact it for volunteering opportunities in any of the national parks.

➡ Drop the good people at **Undiscovered Montenegro** (☑069-402 374; www.lakeskadar.com; ☺Apr-Nov) an email about volunteer work in the Lake Skadar region.

➡ While Montenegro doesn't have a national WWOOF (World Wide Opportunities on Organic Farms) organisation, there are still opportunities to volunteer in the country. See www.wwoofindependents.org for regularly updated lists of hosts and vacancies.

Women Travellers

Other than a cursory interest shown by men towards solo women travellers, travelling in Montenegro is hassle-free and easy. In Muslim areas, some women wear a headscarf but most adopt European fashions.

Work

Montenegro doesn't issue working visas, and working here is a complicated business that involves a forest's worth of paperwork and bucketloads of patience. A work permit, permission for permanent or temporary residence and a work contract are all required. The Employment Bureau of Montenegro (www.zzzcg.me, in Montenegrin) ostensibly can assist with the process. The www.gov.uk/guidance/living-in-montenegro website has more information.

Transport

GETTING THERE & AWAY

Whether you choose to fly, train, ferry or drive, it's not difficult to get to Montenegro these days. New routes – including those by low-cost carriers from the UK – are continually being added to the busy timetable at the country's two airports. It's also possible to make your way from neighbouring countries, especially Croatia. Dubrovnik's airport is very close to the border and the beautiful city makes an impressive starting point to a Montenegro holiday. Flights, tours and rail tickets can be booked online at www.lonelyplanet.com/bookings.

Entering the Country

Entering Montenegro doesn't pose any particular bureaucratic challenges. In fact, the country's dead keen to shuffle tourists in. Unfortunately, Croatia seems less happy to let them go, if the long waits at their side of the Adriatic highway checkpoint are any indication; if you need to be somewhere at a certain time, it pays to allow an hour. The main crossing from Serbia at Dobrakovo can also be slow at peak times.

Passport

Make sure that your passport has at least six months left on it. You'll need a visa if you're not from one of the many countries with a visa-waiver arrangement. There are no particular nationalities or stamps in your passport that will deny you entry. Make sure that your passport is stamped when you enter the country or else there may be difficulties when you leave.

Air

Airports & Airlines

➡ Montenegro's largest and most modern airport is immediately south of the capital **Podgorica** (TGD; ☎ 020-444 244; www.montenegroairports.com). The entire south of the country and everywhere as far north as Kolašin is within 100km of this airport. If you're wondering about the airport code, the TGD is a hangover from Podgorica's previous name, Titograd. Locals sometimes call it Golubovci airport as it's close to a village with that name. The airport's safety record is blemished only by a small plane skidding while landing in snowy conditions in 2005; there were no serious injuries.

➡ The second international airport at **Tivat** (TIV; ☎ 032-670 930; www.montenegroairports.com) is well positioned for holidaymakers heading to the Bay of Kotor or Budva and now welcomes close to a million passengers annually. Despite its mountainous surrounds and a runway that

CLIMATE CHANGE & TRAVEL

Every form of transport that relies on carbon-based fuel generates CO_2, the main cause of human-induced climate change. Modern travel is dependent on aeroplanes, which might use less fuel per kilometre per person than most cars but travel much greater distances. The altitude at which aircraft emit gases (including CO_2) and particles also contributes to their climate change impact. Many websites offer 'carbon calculators' that allow people to estimate the carbon emissions generated by their journey and, for those who wish to do so, to offset the impact of the greenhouse gases emitted with contributions to portfolios of climate-friendly initiatives throughout the world. Lonely Planet offsets the carbon footprint of all staff and author travel.

ends only 100m from the water, there has never been an accident here.

→ Montenegro's de facto third airport is actually in neighbouring Croatia. **Dubrovnik airport** (DBV, Zračna luka Dubrovnik; ☎020-773 100; www.airport-dubrovnik.hr) is a modern facility only 17km from the border and the closest airport to Herceg Novi. Commonly referred to locally as Čilipi airport, it's used by more than 1.3 million travellers annually.

→ The word for airport in Montenegrin is *aerodrom* (аеродром). This was also used in Croatia until independence, but in a fit of French-style linguistic nationalism the official Croatian term has been changed to a direct translation of the words for 'air' and 'port', *zračna luka* – a potential trap for English speakers.

→ Montenegro Airlines is the national carrier, running a small fleet of 102- to 116-seater planes. Apart from the skid at Podgorica airport mentioned previously, its safety record has been unsullied during its 10-plus years of operation. It has code-share agreements with Adria, Air France, Alitalia, Austrian Airlines and Russia's S7 Airlines.

Land

Montenegro may be a wee slip of a thing but it borders five other states: Croatia, Bosnia and Hercegovina (BiH), Serbia, Kosovo and Albania. You can easily enter Montenegro by land from any of its neighbours.

Bicycle

There are no problems bringing a bicycle into the country, though there are not many cyclists here so road-users are not cycle savvy – and remember that there's a *monte* (mountain) in the country's name for a reason.

If you want to bring your own bike, most airlines allow you to put a bicycle in the hold for a fee. You can either take it apart and pack all the pieces in a bike bag or box, or simply wheel it to the check-in desk, where it should be treated as a piece of check-in luggage. You may have to remove the pedals and turn the handlebars sideways so that it takes up less space in the aircraft's hold; check all this with the airline before you pay for your ticket. If your bicycle and other luggage exceed your weight allowance, ask about alternatives or you may find yourself being charged a small ransom for excess baggage.

Bus

There's a well-developed bus network linking Montenegro with the major cities of the former Yugoslavia and onwards to Western Europe and Turkey. At the border, guards will often enter the bus and collect passports, checking the photos as they go. Once they're happy with them they return them to the bus conductor who will return them as the driver speeds off. Make sure you get yours back and that it's been stamped.

Routes include the following:

→ **Belgrade (Serbia)** to Rožaje (€14, four daily), Pljevlja (€19, three daily), Podgorica (€25, frequent), Nikšić (€26, daily), Budva (€26, 15 daily), Petrovac (€24, five daily), Ulcinj (€29, two daily), Tivat (€28, five daily), Kotor (€30, seven daily) and Herceg Novi (€30, 10 daily). Allow 10 hours to Podgorica and 13 hours to Herceg Novi.

→ **Dubrovnik (Croatia)** to Herceg Novi (€10, seven daily), Kotor (€14, six daily), Petrovac (€20, daily) and Podgorica (€21, two daily). Allow two hours to Herceg Novi.

→ **Peć (Kosovo)** to Rožaje (€6.50, daily) and Plav

(€8.50, daily). Allow two hours to Rožaje; longer if there's snow.

→ **Priština (Kosovo)** to Rožaje (€11.50, daily), Podgorica (€18, daily) and Ulcinj (€16.50, six daily). Allow eight hours to Ulcinj.

→ **Sarajevo (Bosnia & Hercegovina; BiH)** to Pljevlja (€10, daily), Nikšić (€15, five daily), Podgorica (€20, four daily), Budva (€22, four daily), Herceg Novi (€24, two daily) and Ulcinj (€24.50, daily). Allow seven hours to Herceg Novi.

→ **Shkodra (Albania)** to Ulcinj (€6, 90 minutes, daily).

→ **Trebinje (BiH)** to Nikšić (€6.50, 1¾ hours, four daily).

Car & Motorcycle

Crossing into Montenegro with a private or hire car won't pose any problems as long as you have all of your papers in order. You must have vehicle registration/ownership documents and a locally valid insurance policy such as European Green Card vehicle insurance. Be sure to check your hire car insurance cover as some Western European companies will not cover you for travel in Montenegro.

From the major border crossings with Croatia, Serbia, Kosovo and Albania, you won't have to drive more than 25km to find a petrol station or assistance with mechanical repairs. From the Bosnian crossings, don't expect to find anything before Nikšić. You'll see the words *'auto šlep'* and an adjoining phone number spray-painted along all the roadways in the country; this is low-cost advertising for local towing services.

There have been incidences of attacks on cars

with Montenegrin plates in Croatia (particularly around Dubrovnik) and on cars with Croatian plates in Montenegro (particularly around the Bay of Kotor). These are usually limited to minor vandalism, such as cars being keyed while parked on the road.

Hitching

Although we don't recommend it, it's entirely possible to hitch in or out of Montenegro. As with any border crossing, be sure you have your passport and any relevant visas. Some drivers may ask for money, but it's not a common practice.

Train

Montenegro's main train line starts at Bar and heads north through the middle of Montenegro and into Serbia. At least two trains head between Bar and Belgrade daily (€21, 11 hours) with one continuing on to Novi Sad and Subotica. You'll find timetables on the website of **Montenegro Railways** (www.zcg-prevoz.me). From Belgrade it's possible to connect to destinations throughout Europe; see the website of **Serbian Railways** (www.serbianrailways.com) for timetables.

➡ Montenegro can be included as part of the **Eurail** (www.eurail.com) Select Pass, which offers varying days of rail travel over a two-month period in two, three or four neighbouring countries; for the purposes of this pass, Montenegro and Serbia are counted as one country, as are Croatia and Slovenia, meaning it's possible to get

four countries for the price of two. Adult prices range from €168 (five days, two countries) to €386 (10 days, four countries). There are youth discounts for those 25 years old and younger. Eurail's Global Pass offers five country passes, ranging from five to 15 days of hop-on hop-off travel over a one- to two-month period, plus continuous travel passes for 15 to 30 days. Only non-Europeans can use Eurail passes.

➡ **InterRail** (www.interrail.eu) passes can only be used by European residents of more than six months' standing. InterRail's Global Pass allows unlimited train travel in 30 countries (including Montenegro) during a set period. Some are valid over a continuous period, while others are more flexible. Prices depend on age and class; youth passes for those younger than 25 are cheaper than adult passes, and children under 11 years ride free. For some examples of prices, a Global Pass valid for five days of 2nd-class travel in a 15-day period costs €264/200 per adult/youth, or €626/479 for one continuous month. Terms, conditions and occasional surcharges may apply on certain trains.

➡ The Balkan Flexipass from **Rail Europe** (www.raileurope.com) covers rail travel in Montenegro, BiH, Serbia, Macedonia, Bulgaria, Greece, Romania and Turkey. A 2nd-class pass for five days' travel in one month is €134, or €280 for 15 days' travel in one month. Discounted passes are available for both

youth (under 26) and seniors (over 60).

➡ If you plan to travel extensively by train, it is worth getting hold of the European Rail Timetable (updated monthly), which gives a complete listing of train and ferry schedules and reservation information and indicates where supplements apply. Download a digital version (£11.99) or order the book (£15.99) online at www.europeanrailtimetable.eu.

Border Crossings

Getting in and out of Montenegro is generally a simple affair; just be sure to check your visa requirements (p16) before embarking on a trip.

➡ **Albania** There are two main crossings: Sukobin (between Shkodra and Ulcinj) and Hani i Hotit (between Shkodra and Podgorica). If you're paddling about on Lake Skadar, remember that the border runs through the lake and be careful not to cross it. Because of problems with trafficking (of cigarettes, drugs and women), the Montenegro police patrol the lake. The same caution should be applied while hiking in the Prokletije Mountains; you'll need a cross-border permit.

➡ **Bosnia & Hercegovina** There are two main crossings: Dolovi (between Trebinje and Nikšić) and Šćepan Polje. Other more remote crossings are marked on some maps but these may only be open to local traffic (if they are open at all) and we've heard of travellers being turned back at some crossings.

➡ **Croatia** Expect delays at the busy Debeli Brijeg checkpoint on the Adriatic highway (between Herceg Novi and Dubrovnik). You can avoid them by taking a detour down the Prevlaka Peninsula to the sleepy Kobila border post. It has been suggested to us that this crossing is only

FLIGHT-FREE TRAVEL

If you fancy a guilt-free, low-carbon journey from London to Montenegro, log on to www.seat61.com and click on 'Montenegro' on the side navigation. You'll find detailed instructions on how to get from London to Belgrade by train and then connect through to Montenegro, including departure times, fares and travel-pass information.

for locals, but we haven't experienced or heard of any problems crossing here. To reach it from the Croatian side, turn right off the highway a few kilometres before the main border crossing and pass through Pločice and Vitaljina. The road rejoins the highway on the Montenegro side just before Igalo.

→ **Kosovo** There's only one crossing, Kulina, on the road between Rožaje and Peć.

→ **Serbia** The busiest crossing is Dobrakovo (north of Bijelo Polje), followed by Dračenovac (northeast of Rožaje) and Rance (east of Pljevlja). The train crosses at Dobrakovo.

Sea

Montenegro Lines (www. montenegrolines.com) has boats from Bar to Bari, Italy, at least twice weekly from May to September (deck ticket €44 to €48, cabin €67 to €210, 10 hours); and from Bar to Ancona, Italy, at least weekly from July to August (deck €60, cabin €80 to €230, 16 hours). Cars cost €68 to €90, but are free for bookings for four cabin passengers.

GETTING AROUND

Air

Though there are two airports in Montenegro, there are no domestic flights available within the country.

Bicycle

Cyclists are a rare species even in the cities and there are no special bike lanes on the roads. Don't expect drivers to be considerate; wherever possible, try to get off the main roads. The wearing of helmets is not compulsory.

However, the outlook for cyclists isn't as grim as it sounds. The National Tourist Office has developed a series of wilderness mountain-biking trails, making a two-wheeled tour of Montenegro an excellent proposition. As most of the country is mountainous, you'll have to be exceedingly fit to attempt it.

The key to a successful bike trip is to travel light, and don't overdo it on the first few days. Even for the shortest and most basic trip, it's worth carrying the tools necessary for repairing a puncture. You might want to consider packing spare brake and gear cables, spanners, Allen keys, spare spokes and strong adhesive tape. At the risk of stating the obvious, these won't be much use unless you know what to do with them. Maintenance is also important: check over your bike thoroughly each morning and again at night when the day's touring is over. Take a good lock and always use it when you leave your bike unattended.

A seasoned cyclist can average about 80km a day, but this depends on the terrain and how much weight is being carried. Again, don't overdo it – there's no point burning yourself out during the initial stages.

The Montenegrin bike enthusiasts at www.pedalaj. me can help with trails, tours and accommodation ideas for those crossing the country by pedal power, as can **Montenegro Bed and Bike** (www.bedandbike.me).

Boat

There are no regular ferry services within Montenegro, but taxi boats are a common sight during summer. They can be hailed from the shore for a short trip along the coast or to one of the islands. They're harder to find outside the high season; look for them at the marinas. Some boats advertise set cruises,

but normally they operate on an ad hoc basis.

Bus

The local bus network is extensive and reliable. Buses are usually comfortable and air-conditioned; they're rarely full. It's usually not difficult to find information on services and prices from the bus station. Most have timetables prominently displayed, although they're not always up to date. As with many service-industry types in Montenegro, some station staff are more helpful than others. Where English isn't spoken, they'll usually write down the price and time of the bus for you.

It's a bit cheaper to buy your ticket on the bus rather than at the station, but a station-bought ticket theoretically guarantees you a seat. Reservations are only worthwhile for international buses, at holiday times, or where long-distance journeys are infrequent. Luggage carried below is charged at €1 per piece.

Smoking is forbidden on buses and this rule is generally enforced. The standard of driving is no better or worse than that of anyone else on the roads.

Car & Motorcycle

Independent travel by car or motorcycle is an ideal way to gad about and discover the country; some of the drives are breathtakingly beautiful. Traffic police are everywhere, so stick to speed limits and carry an International Driving Permit.

Allow more time than you'd expect for the distances involved as the terrain will slow you down. You'll rarely get up to 60km/h on the Bay of Kotor road, for instance. The standard of roads is generally fair with conditions worsening in rural areas, especially in winter and after bad weather. A particularly notorious road is the Podgorica–Belgrade highway as it passes through the Morača Canyon, which is often made dangerous by bad conditions and high traffic. It's a good idea to drive defensively and treat everyone else on the road as a lunatic – when they get behind the wheel, many of them are. That said, no matter how much they toot at you or overtake on blind corners, you should avoid confrontation.

The only toll in Montenegro is the Sozina tunnel between Lake Skadar and the sea (€3.50 per car).

Automobile Associations

The **Automobile Association of Montenegro** (Auto Moto Savez Crne Gore; www.amscg.org, ☑020-9807) offers roadside assistance, towing and repairs. The **UK Automobile Association** (www.theaa.com) has excellent information on its website, with specific driving advice for Montenegro.

Bring Your Own Vehicle

As long as you have registration/ownership papers with you and valid insurance cover, there should be no problem driving your car into Montenegro. If your vehicle has obvious signs of damage, the border guards should provide you with a certificate that must be produced upon leaving to prove that the damage didn't occur inside the country.

Driving Licences

It's recommended that you arrange an International Driving Permit from your home country before the trip. Although many rental companies will hire out a car based on your foreign driver's licence, there's no assurance that the traffic police will accept it and it doesn't pay to give them any excuse to fine you.

Fuel & Spare Parts

Filling up is no problem in any medium-sized town, but don't leave it until the last drop. There are few late-night petrol stations. Diesel, unleaded 95 and 98 octane are easy to find. Spare parts for major makes will be no problem in the cities, and mechanics are available everywhere for simple repairs.

Hire

It's not difficult to hire a car in the bigger towns. Budva, in particular, is overflowing with options. The major European car-hire companies have a presence in various centres including the airports, but the local alternatives are often cheaper. If you're flying into Dubrovnik, it will certainly be more convenient to arrange to collect your car at the airport, but this will need to be balanced against the (albeit minor) risk of vandalism against cars with Croatian plates in Montenegro.

Alamo (www.alamo.com) Pick up from Podgorica, Tivat or Dubrovnik airports.

Avis (www.avisworld.com) Pick up from Budva or Bar, or Podgorica, Tivat or Dubrovnik airports.

Europcar (www.europcar.com) Pick up from Podgorica, Tivat or Dubrovnik airports.

Hertz (www.hertz.me) Pick up from Podgorica or Budva, or Podgorica, Tivat or Dubrovnik airports.

In Montenegro (www.inmontenegro.com) Pick up from Herceg Novi, or Tivat, Podgorica or Dubrovnik airports.

Meridian Rentacar (www.meridian-rentacar.com) A reliable local option with offices in Budva, Podgorica and Bar, and Tivat and Podgorica airports; one-day hire starts from €30.

National (www.nationalcar.com) Pick up from Podgorica, or Tivat, Podgorica or Dubrovnik airports.

Sixt (www.sixt.com) Pick up from Herceg Novi, Tivat, Budva, Podgorica or Bar, or Podgorica, Tivat or Dubrovnik airports.

Insurance

Third-party insurance is compulsory and you'll need to be able to prove you have it in order to bring a car into Montenegro. You should get your insurer to issue a Green Card (which may cost extra), an internationally recognised proof of insurance, and check that it lists all the countries you intend to visit. You'll need this in the event of an accident outside the country where the vehicle is insured. The European Accident Statement (known as the 'Constat Amiable' in France) is available from your insurance company and is copied so that each party at an accident can record information for insurance purposes. The Association of British Insurers (www.abi.org.uk) has more details. Never sign accident statements you cannot understand or read – insist on a translation and sign that only if it's acceptable.

Some insurance packages (particularly those covering rental cars) do not include all European countries and Montenegro is often one of those excluded – make sure you check this before you rent your car. When you're renting a car, ensure you check all aspects of the insurance offered, including the excess (you may wish to pay extra to reduce it) and rules regarding where you may or may not drive it (on dirt roads, for example).

Parking

Local parking habits are quite carefree, so it's possible you can be blocked in by someone double-parking next to you. Sometimes parking that looks illegal (eg on footpaths) is actually permitted.

Road Rules

➜ As in the rest of continental Europe, people drive on the right-hand side of the road and overtake on the left. Keep right except when overtaking, and use your indicators for any change of lane and when pulling away from the kerb.

➡ School buses can't be overtaken when they stop for passengers to board or alight.

➡ Vehicles entering a roundabout have right of way.

➡ Standard international road signs are used.

➡ You are required by law to wear a seatbelt (including in the back seat if they're fitted), drive with dipped headlights on (even during the day) and wear a helmet on a motorbike.

➡ Children's car seats aren't compulsory but kids under 12 and intoxicated passengers are not allowed in the front seat.

➡ Using a mobile phone while driving is prohibited, although plenty of people do it anyway.

➡ Driving barefoot is a no-no.

➡ Penalties for drink-driving are severe and could result in jail time. The legal limit is 0.03% of alcohol in your bloodstream. Police can issue an on-the-spot fine but cannot collect payment.

➡ Standard speed limits are 50km/h in built-up areas, 80km/h outside built-up areas and 100km/h on certain roads. Often the limit will change several times on a single stretch of the road because of the mountainous conditions. Excessive speeding (30km over the limit) could lead to your driver's licence being temporarily confiscated.

➡ Cars must carry a set of replacement bulbs, a first-aid kit, a warning triangle and a reflective jacket.

➡ If you're involved in an accident resulting in major injury or material damage to your or another vehicle, you're legally obliged to report it to the police.

Hitching

Hitching is never entirely safe but it is a common practice in Montenegro. Wherever you are, there's always a risk when you catch a ride with strangers. It's safer to travel in pairs and to let someone know where you're planning to go. Once you've flagged down a vehicle, it's safer if you sit next to a door you can open. Ask the driver where they are going before you say where you are going. Trust your instincts if you feel uncomfortable about getting in, and get out at the first sign of trouble.

Local Transport

Most Montenegrin towns, even Podgorica, are small enough to be travelled by foot. Podgorica is the only city to have a useful local bus network, costing 80c per trip. Taxis are easily found in most towns. If they're not metered, be sure to agree on a fare in advance. Some Budva taxis have their meters set at extortionate rates, so ask to be let out if you suspect something's amiss.

Train

Montenegro Railways (Željeznica Crne Gore; www.zpcg.me) has services heading north from Bar and crossing the country before disappearing into Serbia; useful stops include Virpazar, Podgorica, Kolašin, Mojkovac and Bijelo Polje. A second line heads northwest from Podgorica to Danilovgrad and Nikšić.

The trains are old and can be hot in summer, but they're priced accordingly and the route through the mountains is spectacular. Apart from a derailment in 2006 and a crash in 2012, the trains are generally a good, safe option.

Language

Montenegrin belongs to the western group of the South Slavic language family. It is very similar to other languages in this group (Serbian, Croatian and Bosnian), and there are only slight variations in pronunciation and vocabulary between them.

Both Latin and Cyrillic alphabets are used in Montenegro. It's worth familiarising yourself with the latter in case you come across it on menus, timetables or street signs – see the box on the following page.

If you read our coloured pronunciation guides as if they were English, you'll be understood. The stressed syllables are indicated with italics – in most cases the stress falls on the first syllable in a word.

Some Montenegrin words have masculine and feminine forms, indicated after the relevant phrases in this chapter by 'm' and 'f'. Polite ('pol') and informal ('inf') alternatives are also included where necessary.

BASICS

Hello.	Zdravo.	zdra·vo
Goodbye.	Do viđenja.	do vi·je·nya
Yes.	Da.	da
No.	Ne.	ne
Please.	Molim.	mo·leem
Thank you.	Hvala.	hva·la

WANT MORE?

For in-depth language information and handy phrases, check out Lonely Planet's phrasebooks series. You'll find it at **shop.lonelyplanet.com**, or you can buy Lonely Planet's iPhone phrasebooks at the Apple App Store.

You're welcome.	Nema na čemu.	ne·ma na che·moo
Excuse me.	Oprostite.	o·pro·stee·te
Sorry.	Žao mi je.	zha·o mee ye

How are you?
Kako ste/si? (pol/inf)   ka·ko ste/see

Fine. And you?
Dobro.   do·bro
A vi/ti? (pol/inf)   a vee/tee

My name is ...
Zovem se ...   zo·vem se ...

What's your name?
Kako se zovete/   ka·ko se zo·ve·te/
zoveš? (pol/inf)   zo·vesh

Do you speak (English)?
Govorite/   go·vo·ree·te/
Govoriš   go·vo·reesh
li (engleski)? (pol/inf)   lee (en·gle·skee)

I (don't) understand.
(Ne) Razumijem.   (ne) ra·zoo·mee·yem

ACCOMMODATION

Do you have a room available?
Imate li slobodnih   ee·ma·te lee slo·bod·neeh
soba?   so·ba

Is breakfast included?
Da li je doručak   da lee ye do·roo·chak
uključen?   ook·lyoo·chen

How much is it (per night/per person)?
Koliko košta   ko·lee·ko kosh·ta
(za noć/po osobi)?   (za noch/po o·so·bee)

Do you have a ... room?	Imate li ... sobu?	ee·ma·te lee ... so·boo
single	jedno-krevetnu	yed·no-kre·vet·noo
double	dvo-krevetnu	dvo-kre·vet·noo

air-con	klima-uređaj	klee·ma·oo·re·jai
bathroom	kupatilo	koo·pa·tee·lo
bed	krevet	kre·vet
campsite	kamp	kamp
cot	dječji krevet	dyech·yee kre·vet
guesthouse	privatni smještaj	pree·vat·nee smyesh·tai
hotel	hotel	ho·tel
wi-fi	bežični internet	be·zheech·nee een·ter·net
window	prozor	pro·zor
youth hostel	omladinsko prenoćište	om·la·deen·sko pre·no·cheesh·te

DIRECTIONS

Where is ...?
Gdje je ...? — gdye ye ...

What's the address?
Koja je adresa? — ko·ya ye a·dre·sa

Can you show me (on the map)?
Možete li da mi pokažete (na mapi)? — mo·zhe·te lee da mee po·ka·zhe·te (na ma·pee)

at the corner	na uglu	na oo·gloo
at the traffic lights	na semaforu	na se·ma·fo·roo
behind	iza	ee·za
in front of	ispred	ees·pred
far (from)	daleko (od)	da·le·ko (od)
left	lijevo	lee·ye·vo
near	blizu	blee·zoo
next to	pored	po·red
opposite	nasuprot	na·soo·prot
right	desno	de·sno
straight ahead	pravo naprijed	pra·vo na·pree·yed

EATING & DRINKING

What would you recommend?
Šta biste preporučili? — shta bee·ste pre·po·roo·chee·lee

I'm a vegetarian.
Ja sam vegetarijanac/vegetarijanka. (m/f) — ya sam ve·ge·ta·ree·ya·nats/ve·ge·ta·ree·yan·ka

That was delicious!
To je bilo izvrsno! — to ye bee·lo eez·vr·sno

Please bring the menu/bill.
Molim vas donesite jelovnik/račun. — mo·leem vas do·ne·see·te ye·lov·neek/ra·choon

CYRILLIC ALPHABET

In 2009 two new letters – indicated in the following list with an asterisk (*) – were introduced to the Montenegrin alphabet.

А а	a	short as the 'u' in 'cut'; long as in 'father'
Б б	b	as in 'but'
В в	v	as in 'van'
Г г	g	as in 'go'
Д д	d	as in 'dog'
Ђ ђ	j	as in 'joke'
Е е	e	short as in 'bet'; long as in 'there'
Ж ж	zh	as the 's' in 'measure'
З з	z	as in 'zoo'
* З́ з́		soft zh
И и	i	short as in 'bit'; long as in 'marine'
Ј ј	y	as in 'young'
К к	k	as in 'kind'
Л л	l	as in 'lamp'
Љ љ	ly	as the 'lli' in 'million'
М м	m	as in 'mat'
Н н	n	as in 'not'
Њ њ	ny	as in 'canyon'
О о	o	short as in 'hot'; long as in 'for'
П п	p	as in 'pick'
Р р	r	as in 'rub' (but rolled)
С с	s	as in 'sing'
* С́ с́		soft sh
Т т	t	as in 'ten'
Ћ ћ	ch	as in 'check'
У у	u	short as in 'put'; long as in 'rule'
Ф ф	f	as in 'fan'
Х х	h	as in 'hot'
Ц ц	ts	as in 'cats'
Ч ч	ch	as in 'change'
Џ џ	j	as in 'judge'
Ш ш	sh	as in 'shop'

I'd like a table for ...	Htio/Htjela bih sto za ... (m/f)	htee·o/htye·la beeh sto za ...
(eight) o'clock	(osam) sati	(o·sam) sa·tee
(two) people	(dvoje) ljudi	(dvo·ye) lyoo·dee

I don't eat ...	Ne jedem ...	ne ye·dem ...
fish	ribu	ree·boo
meat	meso	me·so
nuts	orahe	o·ra·he

Signs

Izlaz	Exit
Muški	Men
Otvoreno	Open
Ulaz	Entrance
Zabranjeno	Prohibited
Toaleti/WC	Toilets
Zatvoreno	Closed
Ženski	Women

Key Words

bar	*bar*	bar
bottle	*boca*	bo·tsa
breakfast	*doručak*	do·roo·chak
cafe	*kafić*	ka·feech
cold	*hladno*	hlad·no
dinner	*večera*	ve·che·ra
fork	*viljuška*	vee·lyoosh·ka
glass	*čaša*	cha·sha
knife	*nož*	nozh
lunch	*ručak*	roo·chak
plate	*tanjir*	ta·nyeer
restaurant	*restoran*	re·sto·ran
spoon	*kašika*	ka·shee·ka
warm	*toplo*	top·lo

Meat & Fish

beef	*govedina*	go·ve·di·na
carp	*šaran*	sha·ran
chicken	*piletina*	pi·le·ti·na
cod	*bakalar*	ba·ka·lar
crabs	*račići*	ra·chi·chi
hake	*oslić*	o·slich
ham	*šunka*	shun·ka
lamb	*jagnjetina*	yag·nye·ti·na
lobster	*jastog*	ya·stog
mussels	*dagnje*	dag·nye
oysters	*školjke*	shkoly·ke
pork	*svinjetina*	svi·nye·ti·na
prawns	*škampi*	shkam·pi
salmon	*losos*	lo·sos
sausage	*kobasica*	ko·ba·si·tsa
squid	*lignje*	lig·nye
trout	*pastrmka*	pas·trm·ka
turkey	*ćuretina*	chu·re·ti·na
veal	*teletina*	te·le·ti·na

Fruit & Vegetables

apple	*jabuka*	ya·bu·ka
apricot	*kajsija*	kai·si·ya
banana	*banana*	ba·na·na
beans	*pasulj*	pa·suly
beetroot	*cvekla*	tsve·kla
cabbage	*kupus*	ku·pus
capsicum	*paprika*	pa·pri·ka
carrot	*šargarepa*	shar·ga·re·pa
cauliflower	*karfiol*	kar·fi·ol
cherry	*višnja*	vish·nya
cucumber	*krastavac*	kra·sta·vats
fig	*smokva*	smok·va
grapes	*grožđe*	grozh·je
lemon	*limun*	li·mun
lettuce	*zelena salata*	ze·le·na sa·la·ta
melon	*dinja*	di·nya
mushrooms	*pečurke*	pe·chur·ke
olives	*masline*	mas·li·ne
onion	*crni luk*	tsr·ni luk
orange	*pomorandža*	po·mo·ran·ja
peach	*breskva*	bres·kva
pear	*kruška*	kru·shka
peas	*grašak*	gra·shak
plum	*šljiva*	shlyi·va
potato	*krompir*	krom·pir
spinach	*spanać*	spa·nach
strawberry	*jagoda*	ya·go·da
tomato	*paradajz*	pa·ra·daiz
watermelon	*lubenica*	lu·be·ni·tsa

Other

bread	*hljeb*	hlyeb
cheese	*sir*	seer
egg	*jaje*	ya·ye
honey	*med*	med
pepper	*biber*	bee·ber
rice	*pirinač*	pee·ree·nach
salt	*so*	so
sugar	*šećer*	she·cher

Drinks

beer	*pivo*	pee·vo
coffee	*kafa*	ka·fa
(fruit) juice	*(voćni) sok*	(voch·nee) sok
milk	*mljeko*	mlye·ko

tea	čaj	chai
(mineral) water	(mineralna) voda	(mee·ne·ral·na) vo·da
(red/white) wine	(crno/bijelo) vino	(tsr·no/bye·lo) vee·no

bank	banka	ban·ka
market	pijaca	pee·ya·tsa
post office	pošta	posh·ta
tourist office	turistički biro	too·ree·steech·kee bee·ro

EMERGENCIES

Help!
Upomoć!   oo·po·moch

Leave me alone!
Ostavite me na miru!   o·sta·vee·te me na mee·roo

I'm lost.
Izgubio/   eez·goo·bee·o/
Izgubila sam se. (m/f)   eez·goo·bee·la sam se

Call a doctor!
Zovite ljekara!   zo·vee·te lye·ka·ra

Call the police!
Zovite policiju!   zo·vee·te po·lee·tsee·yoo

I'm ill.
Ja sam bolestan/   ya sam bo·le·stan/
bolesna. (m/f)   bo·le·sna

I'm allergic to ...
Ja sam alergičan/   ya sam a·ler·gee·chan/
alergična na ... (m/f)   a·ler·geech·na na ...

Where are the toilets?
Gdje su toaleti?   gdye soo to·a·le·tee

SHOPPING & SERVICES

I'd like to buy ...
Želim da kupim ...   zhe·leem da koo·peem ...

I'm just looking.
Samo razgledam.   sa·mo raz·gle·dam

May I look at it?
Mogu li da pogledam?   mo·goo lee da po·gle·dam

How much is it?
Koliko košta?   ko·lee·ko kosh·ta

That's too expensive.
To je preskupo.   to ye pre·skoo·po

Do you have something cheaper?
Imate li nešto   ee·ma·te lee nesh·to
jeftinije?   yef·tee·nee·ye

There's a mistake in the bill.
Neka je greška na   ne·ka ye gresh·ka na
računu.   ra·choo·noo

Question Words

How?	Kako?	ka·ko
What?	Šta?	shta
When?	Kada?	ka·da
Where?	Gdje?	gdye
Who?	Ko?	ko
Why?	Zašto?	za·shto

TIME & DATES

What time is it?
Koliko je sati?   ko·lee·ko ye sa·tee

It's (10) o'clock.
(Deset) je sati.   (de·set) ye sa·tee

Half past (10).
(Deset) i po.   (de·set) ee po

morning	jutro	yoo·tro
afternoon	poslijepodne	po·slee·ye·pod·ne
evening	veče	ve·che
yesterday	juče	yoo·che
today	danas	da·nas
tomorrow	sjutra	syoo·tra

Monday	ponedjeljak	po·ne·dye·lyak
Tuesday	utorak	oo·to·rak
Wednesday	srijeda	sree·ye·da
Thursday	četvrtak	chet·vr·tak
Friday	petak	pe·tak
Saturday	subota	soo·bo·ta
Sunday	nedjelja	ne·dye·lya

January	januar	ya·noo·ar
February	februar	feb·roo·ar
March	mart	mart
April	april	ap·reel
May	maj	mai
June	jun	yoon
July	jul	yool
August	avgust	av·goost
September	septembar	sep·tem·bar
October	oktobar	ok·to·bar
November	novembar	no·vem·bar
December	decembar	de·tsem·bar

TRANSPORT

Public Transport

boat	brod	brod
bus	autobus	a·oo·to·boos
plane	avion	a·vee·on
train	voz	voz

Numbers

1	jedan	ye·dan
2	dva	dva
3	tri	tree
4	četiri	che·tee·ree
5	pet	pet
6	šest	shest
7	sedam	se·dam
8	osam	o·sam
9	devet	de·vet
10	deset	de·set
20	dvadeset	dva·de·set
30	trideset	tree·de·set
40	četrdeset	che·tr·de·set
50	pedeset	pe·de·set
60	šezdeset	shez·de·set
70	sedamdeset	se·dam·de·set
80	osamdeset	o·sam·de·set
90	devedeset	de·ve·de·set
100	sto	sto
1000	hiljadu	hee·lya·doo

I want to go to (Dubrovnik).
Htio/Htjela bih   htee·o/htye·la beeh
da idem u   da ee·dem oo
(Dubrovnik). (m/f) (doo·brov·neek)

Does it stop at (Budva)?
Staje li u (Budvi)?   sta·ye lee oo (bood·vee)

What time does it leave?
U koliko sati kreće?   oo ko·lee·ko sa·tee kre·che

What time does it get to (Podgorica)?
U koliko sati stiže   oo ko·lee·ko sa·tee stee·zhe
u (Podgoricu)?   oo (pod·go·ree·tsoo)

Could you tell me when we get to (Cetinje)?
Možete li mi reći   mo·zhe·te lee mee re·chee
kada stignemo do   ka·da steeg·ne·mo do
(Cetinja)?   (tse·tee·nya)

I'd like to get off at (Kotor).
Želim da izađem   zhe·leem da ee·za·jem
u (Kotoru).   oo (ko·to·roo)

A ... ticket.	Jednu ... kartu.	yed·noo ... kar·too
1st-class	prvo- razrednu	pr·vo- raz·red·noo
2nd-class	drugo- razrednu	droo·go- raz·red·noo
one-way	jedno smjernu-	yed·no· smyer·noo
return	povratnu	po·vrat·noo
first	prvi	pr·vee
last	poslednji	pos·led·nyee

aisle seat	sjedište do prolaza	sye·deesh·te do pro·la·za
platform	peron	pe·ron
ticket office	blagajna	bla·gai·na
timetable	red vožnje	red vozh·nye
station	stanica	sta·nee·tsa
window seat	sjedište do prozora	sye·deesh·te do pro·zo·ra

Driving & Cycling

I'd like to hire a ...	Htio/Htjela bih da iznajmim ... (m/f)	htee·o/htye·la beeh da eez·nai·meem ...
4WD	džip	jeep
bicycle	bicikl	bee·tsee·kl
car	auto	a·oo·to
motorcycle	motocikl	mo·to·tsee·kl
bicycle pump	pumpa za bicikl	poom·pa za bee·tsee·kl
child seat	sjedište za dijete	sye·deesh·te za dee·ye·te
diesel	dizel gorivo	dee·zel go·ree·vo
helmet	kaciga	ka·tsee·ga
mechanic	auto- mehaničar	a·oo·to· me·ha·nee·char
petrol	benzin	ben·zeen
service station	benziska stanica	ben·zeen·ska sta·nee·tsa

Is this the road to (Herceg Novi)?
Je li ovo put za   ye lee o·vo poot za
(Herceg Novi)?   (her·tseg no·vee)

(How long) Can I park here?
(Koliko dugo)   (ko·lee·ko doo·go)
Mogu ovdje da   mo·goo ov·dye da
parkiram?   par·kee·ram

The car/motorbike has broken down (at Bar).
Automobil/   a·oo·to·mo·beel/
Motocikl se   mo·to·tsee·kl se
pokvario (u Baru).   pok·va·ree·o (oo ba·roo)

I need a mechanic.
Treba mi   tre·ba mee
automehaničar.   a·oo·to·me·ha·nee·char

I have a flat tyre.
Imam probušenu   ee·mam pro·boo·she·noo
gumu.   goo·moo

I've run out of petrol.
Nestalo mi je   ne·sta·lo mee ye
benzina.   ben·zee·na

I've lost the keys.
Izgubio/   eez·goo·bee·o/
Izgubila   eez·goo·bee·la
sam ključeve. (m/f) sam klyoo·che·ve

GLOSSARY

aerodrom – airport
autocamp – camping ground for tents and caravans
Avars – Eastern European people who waged war against Byzantium from the 6th to 9th centuries

bb – in an address the letters 'bb' following a street name (eg Jadranski Put bb) stand for *bez broja* (without number), indicating that the building has no street number
Bokelj – inhabitant of Boka Kotorska (Bay of Kotor)
Bosniak – Slavic Muslim, not necessarily from Bosnia
burek – heavy pastry stuffed with meat or cheese

čaršija – old market area
Cattaro – Venetian name for Kotor
ćevapčići – small spicy beef or pork sausages
čojstvo i junaštvo – literally 'humanity and bravery' (ie the concept of chivalry present in Montenegrin culture)
crkva – church
Crna Gora – Montenegrin name for Montenegro (literally 'black mountain')

Dom kulture – cultural centre
Dom zdravlja – medical centre
donji (m), donja (f) – lower
Duklja – early Serbian state considered a precursor of Montenegro
džamija –mosque

galerija – gallery
garderoba – left-luggage office
Glagolitic – ancient Slavic alphabet (precursor of the Cyrillic alphabet) created by Greek missionaries Cyril and Methodius
gora – mountain
gornji (m), gornja (f) – upper
gorske oči – literally 'mountain eyes'; name for glacial lakes in mountainous regions

grad – city
guslar – singer/composer of epic poetry accompanied by the *gusle*
gusle – one-stringed folk instrument

hammam – Turkish bathhouse
Hitna pomoć – emergency clinic

Illyrians – ancient inhabitants of the Adriatic coast, defeated by the Romans in the 2nd century BC
ispod sača – (meat) roasted under a metal lid covered with hot coals

jezero – lake

karst – highly porous limestone and dolomitic rock
katun – traditional shepherds' mountain hut
klapa – a traditional form of unaccompanied singing from Dalmatia
klima – air conditioning
kolo – lively Slavic round dance in which men and women alternate in the circle
konoba – the traditional term for a small, intimate dining spot, often located in a cellar; now applies to a wide variety of restaurants; usually a simple, family-run establishment
kula – a blocky tower-like house built for defence

mali (m), mala (f) – little
manastir – monastery
most – bridge
muzej – museum

novi (m), nova (f) – new

obala – waterfront
oro – traditional Montenegrin circle dance
ostrvo – island

palačinke – pancakes
Partisans – communist-led WWII resistance fighters
pivo – beer
plaža – beach
polje – field
pršut – smoke-dried ham
put – path; road; trail

rakija – fruit brandy
ražnjići – small chunks of pork grilled on a skewer
restoran – restaurant
rijeka – river
rruga – Albanian word for 'street' (used in Ulcinj street names)

šetalište – walkway
sladoled – ice cream
sobe (pl) – rooms (available for hire)
stara maslina – literally 'old olive', a famous 2000-year-old tree in Bar
stari (m), stara (f) – old
Stari Grad – Old Town
stećci – mysterious carved stone monuments from the Middle Ages found throughout northern Montenegro
sveti (m), sveta (f) – saint

trg – square
turbofolk – version of Serbian music, a mix of folk and pop

ulica – street

veliki (m), velika (f) – large
vladika – bishop-prince
vrh – peak; summit

Zakonik – legal code (historic term)
Zdravstvena stanica – medical centre or emergency clinic
Zeta – early Serbian state considered a precursor of Montenegro
zimmer – German word for 'rooms' (available for hire)

Behind the Scenes

SEND US YOUR FEEDBACK

We love to hear from travellers – your comments keep us on our toes and help make our books better. Our well-travelled team reads every word on what you loved or loathed about this book. Although we cannot reply individually to your submissions, we always guarantee that your feedback goes straight to the appropriate authors, in time for the next edition. Each person who sends us information is thanked in the next edition – the most useful submissions are rewarded with a selection of digital PDF chapters.

Visit **lonelyplanet.com/contact** to submit your updates and suggestions or to ask for help. Our award-winning website also features inspirational travel stories, news and discussions.

Note: We may edit, reproduce and incorporate your comments in Lonely Planet products such as guidebooks, websites and digital products, so let us know if you don't want your comments reproduced or your name acknowledged. For a copy of our privacy policy visit lonelyplanet.com/privacy.

OUR READERS

Many thanks to the travellers who used the last edition and wrote to us with helpful hints, useful advice and interesting anecdotes: Anders Sjögren, Andrew Knight, Annah Nelson-Feeney, Antoine Fouquet, Bob Dunkley, Borja de Muller, Brian Hairsine, Carol Gelfer, Christopher McDonald, Daniel Davies, Dave Tootell, Des Read, Gavin Parnaby, Greg Kondrak, Jaiminee Pancholi, Jake Sullivan, Joe Sullivan, John Malone, Kate McMahon, Lorraine Francis, Marina Paul, Mark Ostryn, Viktoria Urbanek.

WRITER THANKS

Tamara Sheward

Mnogo hvala na (many thanks to) Drago, Andja, Miša, Rajan, Lola, Dutch and the rest of the Lučići, the Lješević crew, Srdjan, Gordana and Aleksa, Zoran and uncountable more. On the LP front, heartfelt high-fives to Brana Vladisavljević, Peter Dragicevich and the beleaguered geniuses on the SPP help

team. Greatest thanks and love always to Dušan and Masha: you are the *kajmak* to my bread, the squid to my risotto, the *urnebes* to my *pljeskavica*.

Peter Dragicevich

Researching in Montenegro and Croatia is always a joy but even more so with company – so many thanks to Robert Carpenter and Catherine Cole for joining me on the road. Once again I'm indebted to Vojko and Marija Dragičević for their wonderful hospitality.

ACKNOWLEDGEMENTS

Climate map data adapted from Peel MC, Finlayson BL & McMahon TA (2007) 'Updated World Map of the Köppen-Geiger Climate Classification', Hydrology and Earth System Sciences, 11, 163344.

Cover photograph: View of Kotor's Stari Grad (Old Town) and the Bay of Kotor, Doug Pearson/AWL ©

THIS BOOK

This 3rd edition of Lonely Planet's *Montenegro* guidebook was researched and written by Tamara Sheward. Peter Dragicevich wrote the Dubrovnik (Croatia) chapter. The previous edition was written by Peter Dragicevich and Vesna Maric. This guidebook was produced by the following:

Destination Editor Brana Vladisavljevic

Product Editor Joel Cotterell

Senior Cartographer Anthony Phelan

Book Designer Wibowo Rusli

Assisting Editors Samantha Forge, Carly Hall, Victoria Harrison, Helen Koehne, Fionnuala Twomey

Assisting Book Designers Nicholas Colicchia, Katherine Marsh

Cover Researcher Naomi Parker

Thanks to Carolyn Boicos, Sasha Drew, Andi Jones, Claire Naylor, Karyn Noble, Kirsten Rawlings, Tony Wheeler

Index

Map Legend

Sights

- Beach
- Bird Sanctuary
- Buddhist
- Castle/Palace
- Christian
- Confucian
- Hindu
- Islamic
- Jain
- Jewish
- Monument
- Museum/Gallery/Historic Building
- Ruin
- Shinto
- Sikh
- Taoist
- Winery/Vineyard
- Zoo/Wildlife Sanctuary
- Other Sight

Activities, Courses & Tours

- Bodysurfing
- Diving
- Canoeing/Kayaking
- Course/Tour
- Sento Hot Baths/Onsen
- Skiing
- Snorkelling
- Surfing
- Swimming/Pool
- Walking
- Windsurfing
- Other Activity

Sleeping

- Sleeping
- Camping

Eating

- Eating

Drinking & Nightlife

- Drinking & Nightlife
- Cafe

Entertainment

- Entertainment

Shopping

- Shopping

Information

- Bank
- Embassy/Consulate
- Hospital/Medical
- Internet
- Police
- Post Office
- Telephone
- Toilet
- Tourist Information
- Other Information

Geographic

- Beach
- Gate
- Hut/Shelter
- Lighthouse
- Lookout
- Mountain/Volcano
- Oasis
- Park
- Pass
- Picnic Area
- Waterfall

Population

- Capital (National)
- Capital (State/Province)
- City/Large Town
- Town/Village

Transport

- Airport
- Border crossing
- Bus
- Cable car/Funicular
- Cycling
- Ferry
- Metro station
- Monorail
- Parking
- Petrol station
- Subway station
- Taxi
- Train station/Railway
- Tram
- Underground station
- Other Transport

Note: Not all symbols displayed above appear on the maps in this book

Routes

- Tollway
- Freeway
- Primary
- Secondary
- Tertiary
- Lane
- Unsealed road
- Road under construction
- Plaza/Mall
- Steps
- Tunnel
- Pedestrian overpass
- Walking Tour
- Walking Tour detour
- Path/Walking Trail

Boundaries

- International
- State/Province
- Disputed
- Regional/Suburb
- Marine Park
- Cliff
- Wall

Hydrography

- River, Creek
- Intermittent River
- Canal
- Water
- Dry/Salt/Intermittent Lake
- Reef

Areas

- Airport/Runway
- Beach/Desert
- Cemetery (Christian)
- Cemetery (Other)
- Glacier
- Mudflat
- Park/Forest
- Sight (Building)
- Sportsground
- Swamp/Mangrove

OUR STORY

A beat-up old car, a few dollars in the pocket and a sense of adventure. In 1972 that's all Tony and Maureen Wheeler needed for the trip of a lifetime – across Europe and Asia overland to Australia. It took several months, and at the end – broke but inspired – they sat at their kitchen table writing and stapling together their first travel guide, *Across Asia on the Cheap*. Within a week they'd sold 1500 copies. Lonely Planet was born.

Today, Lonely Planet has offices in Franklin, London, Melbourne, Oakland, Dublin, Beijing and Delhi, with more than 600 staff and writers. We share Tony's belief that 'a great guidebook should do three things: inform, educate and amuse'.

OUR WRITERS

Tamara Sheward

All Montenegro chapters, Plan Your Trip, Understand, Survival Guide After years of freelance travel writing, rock'n'roll journalism and insalubrious authordom, Tamara leapt at the chance to join the Lonely Planet ranks in 2009. Since then, she's worked on guides to an incongruous jumble of countries including Montenegro, Australia, Serbia, Russia, the Samoas, Bulgaria and Fiji. She's written a miscellany of travel articles for the BBC, *The Independent*, *Sydney Morning Herald* et al; she's also fronted the camera as a documentary presenter for Lonely Planet TV, Nat Geo and Al-Jazeera. Tamara's based in far northern Australia, but you're more likely to find her roaming elsewhere, tattered notebook in one hand, the world's best-travelled toddler in the other.

Peter Dragicevich

Dubrovnik (Croatia) After a successful career in niche newspaper and magazine publishing, both in his native New Zealand and in Australia, Peter finally gave in to Kiwi wanderlust, giving up staff jobs to chase his diverse roots around much of Europe. Over the last decade he's written literally dozens of guidebooks for Lonely Planet on an oddly disparate collection of countries, all of which he's come to love. He once again calls Auckland, New Zealand his home – although his current nomadic existence means he's hardly ever there.

Published by Lonely Planet Global Limited
CRN 554153
3rd edition – June 2017
ISBN 978 1 78657 529 6
© Lonely Planet 2017   Photographs © as indicated 2017
10 9 8 7 6 5 4 3 2 1
Printed in China